BACKCHAT

by

Andy Back

NB the green tint used for the cover art has been carefully selected
to reflect various contexts and refer to popular culture:
minty freshness; herbal; semi-skimmed; cheese and onion;
ecological sustainability; Napier/Bentley/BRM racing cars;
er, Starbucks; Heineken; BP; Land Rover; Subway; WhatsApp…

ICI paint mixing formula 284-8120 Hex: #004225; HSV: 153.2°, 98.5%,25.9% RGB: 13, 24, 23; Pantone: 60, 35, 85, 40

By the same author

Non-fiction:
Children's Ministry Guide to Dealing with Disruptive Children
Children's Ministry Guide to Building a Team
Children's Ministry Guide to Working with 9-13s
Dynamic Youth Leadership
101 Dynamic Ideas for your Youth Group

Paraphrase
Acts of God
Dan the Man

Bible 'commentary'
The Lost Son

Fiction
substitute [novel]
They Didn't Meet Jesus [short stories]

SozoPrint
Birmingham, UK

ISBN: 978-1-3999-2478-8

Designed and published by SozoPrint
Unit 650, 20 Corn Mill Close, Bartley Green, Birmingham B32 3BH
Produced for the publishers by Ingramspark
Printed in Great Britain

by Andy Back

Acknowledgements

Some of these articles began life in *Y-Zone Red,* the young teens magazine that is part of the *Children's Ministry Teaching Programme*. I'm grateful to Sue Price, Executive Director of Kingsway Publications' Children's Ministry for allowing them to be borrowed and extensively revised for this book.

Yuletide for Raluces owes inspiration and more to CS Lewis' satirical essay *Xmas and Christmas: A Lost Chapter from Herodotus* (1954). Meanwhile, *Privet Lives* reflects the great joy with which I appreciate Jerome K Jerome's sublime comic novel *Three Men in a Boat* (1889, Arrowsmith).

Thanks to the wise and thoughtful assistance provided by Katy Hollway, checking early drafts and being sufficiently bold to suggest changes, improvements and fresh ideas; much required. Errors or clumsy nonsense remaining are entirely my own.

Deep gratitude also to the provocative hefty-lump-of-grit-in-the-oyster irritation provided by marketing guru Adrian Willard, whose belief has been as long-standing as it is unshakeable.

For

Rachel Martin

a friend and fellow-worker I respect and admire;
a repository of considered theology,
who hears the calling of God, gets on with the task,
recognises his voice through familiarity,
and brings enormous joy and blessing
to many at Churchcentral, Birmingham
- including the youth group **emerge**

Contents

Introduction

When I was a young lad – I joined up in 1966 – I attended a boy's Bible Class called *Crusaders*. They've long-since changed the name of the organisation to *Urban Saints*.

I enjoyed the Bible lessons and the singing of *Youth Praise* classics such *Jesus is the Saviour whom I Love to Know*, which was a 12-bar blues with John 3:16 as the chorus; *Looking Unto Jesus* and *If Any Man will Follow*.

We'd get together on a Friday evening for interesting sports and inventive activities. I vividly remember one spectacular competition in which we were divided into teams and each was supplied with sledgehammers and an upright piano; the winners were the first team to reduce their piano to pieces small enough to pass through a suspended car tyre. Young boys, extreme violence, flying splinters, seven-pound sledgehammers swinging wildly, high-tension piano wires twanging and snapping without warning; it was destructive, noisy, dangerous. Excellent fun in every way!

And thanks to local leaders, our Sunday afternoon Bible Class meetings featured a scientific illustration, usually with a tenuous Bible application. One I shall never forget: I was sitting in the front row while a leader fired up a petrol-driven chainsaw and demonstrated how to cut logs. Unfortunately, he forgot that the teeth of the saw flings chippings both forward and back. This matters not, out in the forest. But what if there is an audience just a metre or two away? Huge chippings flew directly into our eyes, which were already watering from the thick blue fumes of the chainsaw engine filling the room. Doubtless this sight-threatening performance illustrated some important spiritual principle, but sadly memory fails me on this matter.

Oh yes, these were days of fun and adventure. Activities were counted a success if all the participants survived. It was nothing special for challenges to end with someone rushing to hospital, probably riding pillion and helmetless on a speeding motorbike, with their severed left arm in a carrier bag. Oh, so commonplace. Crusaders activities were, I am certain, entirely responsible for the creation of the *Health and Safety Executive* in 1974.

I always looked forward to the Anniversary, because this meeting featured *Chairman's Remarks*, an opportunity for the appointed individual to make a speech on a topic of his own choosing.

Sometimes, (if the Chairman had done his homework) this would be a review of activities and achievements over the previous year. But my imagination was fired by the unrestrained blank canvas that was presented to the Chairman to say whatever he liked. He probably wasn't at liberty to preach, but anything short of that was within the remit. I thought this was a brilliantly exciting freedom.

It never occurred to me that the watertight way to ensure that the Chairman's Remarks didn't go off topic or express radical opinion was to be careful when selecting the candidate for the job. That's why we never had anyone abuse the platform and do something that would have been considered sacrilegious, like juggling or referring to a recent movie or reading a passage from the Living Bible (which, after all, was a paraphrase, not a True Translation). I would have liked to be given the opportunity… but such delights were reserved for men in suits.

Then, suddenly, later in life, I found myself responsible for the yawningly blank and dangerously exciting white space on the last page of a magazine. I had been cast in the same role as the Chairman, given the opportunity to ramble without having to stay too close to a topic.

I was being given a large amount of rope by the publisher and I'm grateful for that. In return, I worked hard to maximise the dynamism, variation and unexpectedness, knowing I had the safety net of a sensible editorial team to draw me back from the brink of disaster, when the need arose. Which it did. But not that often.

I did a reasonable job of keeping the variety going and I don't recall ever being prevented from submitting my copy. It was probably knowing that the editorial team were empowered to 'blue pencil' my efforts that ensured I was risky and adventurous, but always stayed the right side of the line that should not be crossed.

So, here are some of those articles, reproduced, edited, reduced to fit or extended to impress; along with fresh ones. I've chosen to recount stories within themes, to develop my points. I recognise that this can be frustrating for those who prefer to see the chronological order, so I have included a Timeline to show the activity of God over many decades.

Nowadays, these might be called *blogs* – personal, brief, opinionated. One important way in which they differ from that electronic form of self-indulgence is that (broadly speaking) they are, unlike so many examples of the blog genre, on the whole, correctly spelled.

1 Try not to slaughter your guests

Elijah vs the prophets of Baal 1 Kings 18:20-40

Honestly, he wasn't comparing himself with Elijah on Mount Carmel, but this was the closest Ben would get.

He was in a friend's back garden, trying to get her barbecue started. Yes, he had made a rash offer.

Ben reckoned the situation like this: Lynette was an attractive young woman; he was hoping she might be interested in him; this was a golden opportunity to spend the whole afternoon in her company, some of it alone together. But if she proved impervious to his animal magnetism, he could console himself with hamburgers and such-like.

Lynette and Ben had known each other for a while. She was, so he hoped, just beginning to wise up and realize that it would be in her best interests to soften and warm towards him. This was a process he'd observed in a number of women, before and since. His self-styled legendary charisma and allure (not to mention what he considered impressive looks and admitted was a slightly disconcerting spirituality) gave some girls reason to hesitate at first, but they usually came around in the end. He hoped they would eventually recognize that he was a fine, charming person well worth getting to know.

As it happens, many of them also decided that having spent so long in the warming-up part of the process, that they would cut their losses and go off him a lot more quickly, to save time and trouble.

But that's another story; one that may never be told. In the case of Lynette, she was sound in wind and limb, keen of intellect, elegant of couture and had what can readily be called a meaningful relationship with God, which were all attributes Ben admired and coveted. She also had the most delightful green eyes, shoulder-length naturally wavy blonde hair and quite superb culinary skills. Quite a lot going for her, in fact.

Anyway, when he turned up, Ben was welcomed, offered a coffee, provided with one and shown out into the back garden, where his ritual kipperisation by the traditional hot-smoking method would take place.

Lynette had provided what she called a barbecue kit: a bag of charcoal briquettes; and a cardboard box containing a few pieces of wood from a broken chair, some old newspapers, a box of matches and a can of lighter fluid bought specifically for the purpose.

Ben set to with a cheery whistle, emptying the sticks into the bowl of the barbeque and then began screwing up sheets of Daily Mail (*fit for burning,* he thought) into loose balls, chucking them in too. He ripped open the bag of briquettes and shoved a few on top of the sticks. *How difficult could this be?* he thought, ignorant – and that's not too strong a word, friends – of the ordeal with which he was now confronted. He rummaged for the matches and the can of lighter fuel. *I shall be efficient, helpful and spectacular,* he thought to myself. *She's bound to be impressed. She'll be putty in my hands; oh, yes, in my hands…*

He waxed exuberant with the flammable liquid. This is a dangerous activity and should normally only be undertaken by fully trained and responsible adults, but in this case, it was the untrained, irresponsible post-teenage Ben squeezing the can rather too hard, liberally soaking the newspaper. [*Editor's Note: don't try this at home.*]

With flamboyant ritual but without appropriate caution, the match was struck and flung; a sheet of flame engulfed the scene. Yes, the inflammables had done their thing. Result. He turned away, punching the air in triumph at this major success and anticipated the pleasant conversation he was about to have with the beauteous Lynette. She was in the kitchen, preparing the soft rolls, wielding a bread knife with dexterity and vigour when Ben entered, thoroughly intoxicated with my success. Er, I mean, his success, of course.

Anyway, leaning casually against the doorframe, Ben tried what he called Conversational Gambit #4, *Happy Association*. 'So, when was the last time you had a barbecue?'

'Yesterday,' she replied, looking over his shoulder towards the garden, 'but we got the fire going much more efficiently than you seem to be doing. Do you need more paper? There's a lot of smoke, isn't there? There was hardly any yesterday, when Steve was helping me.'

H'mm. Steve. This was a bit of a blow.

Rugged, tanned, toned; annoying, able, irritating; less spiritual than Lynette deserved (in Ben's view); self-absorbed, handsome (Ben conceded) and a bit too proud of his convertible; considerably trendier hair; plus evidently better at barbecue-construction, as if that's the be-all-and-end-all of manliness. But it was clearly close to the top of Lynette's list of *Boxes a Bloke Ought To Be Ticking.*

And she'd looked somewhat wistful when she said his name, rolling it around on her breath, letting the syllable spend a moment on her ruby-reds… This wasn't the way Ben had been hoping today would go, although admittedly he had the advantage over Steve right now, since Steve wasn't here and Ben was.

So, Steve could take a flying leap at himself and his trendy hair. Ben needed to make sure Steve didn't get another mention, somehow. He turned around to see if anything was not as it should be with the barbecue.

He was thinking to himself *I'll show her I can do this just as well or better than Captain Muscles* but the reality deserved no such bragging rights. On closer inspection, he was able to discern what had happened: the fuel-soaked paper had burned furiously but briefly, produced a lot of impressive flames and many tiny bits of ash and that was it. The charcoal remained completely affected: dark; cold; mocking him. Could it be that the way those bits of coal were positioned they were trying to spell an 'S'? Probably not, but it was jolly annoying anyway. So, I had to start again. No, er, obviously, I mean Ben.

So, he took the stone-cold charcoal and the entirely unburned sticks out of the bowl and this time used a lot more paper, twisting it into dense packages – *similar to Steve*, Ben thought, unkindly. He realized now that the trick is not only to ignite the paper, but to make it blaze for long enough to set the wood alight, so that the wood in turn raises the ambient temperature in the coals to get them to co-operate in the conflagration required and thereafter cook the food.

So, he prepared the paper and the wood and finally the coals with more precision. He tried again, without the lashings of lighter fuel he'd liberally squirted before, mainly because he'd used nearly the whole can.

When all was ready for the second attempt, he lit the paper and watched with considerable dismay while the paper smoked generously once again, but hardly burned at all, before going out in the gentle breeze.

He was frustrated and disappointed, true, although the tears that ran down his cheeks were caused not by some over-wrought emotional response, but by acrid smoke.

There was clearly a happy medium required here: the first attempt had been spectacular but ineffective; the second, frankly, feeble. Right. Armed with this research information, he wiped his eyes. Unfortunately, his hands were still a little dirty from handling the charcoal briquettes, so the effect on his face was panda-esque and amusing, which he later discovered. He went back to where Lynette was constructing vast bowls of salad by means of slicing and dicing and mixing and fixing.

'Er, do you have any more paper at all? Oh, and we could probably do with a drop more lighter fuel, too,' he said, breezily.

She managed to ignore his ridiculous appearance. 'It was a full can I gave you...'

'Uh, there doesn't seem to be any left, for some reason. Do you have another can?'

She succeeded in finding additional supplies; she was not only attractive and generous, but resourceful, too!

Not wanting to get involved in any further discussion about where the full can of fuel had gone, Ben returned to the garden and tried again. The second can was also nearly empty, which explains why Lynette had gone out to buy a fresh can in the first place, so, he knew this time it was going to have to work.

His preparation of the paper could not have been more painstaking: each page was accurately folded and twisted to create dense fire lighting materials, guaranteed to burn for a while and not just blaze spectacularly like his previous efforts. He delicately splashed a small amount of lighter fluid on the paper and, with a prayer (starting to sound marginally like Elijah here, perhaps?) struck his next match and hoped for the best, fingers crossed (oh, maybe not so patriarchal, after all).

Ah ha! The paper caught beautifully and burned briefly; the wood lying on top began to warm up from the heat of the combustion doing its stuff. So far, so good.

He knew he was behind schedule, perhaps, but then people are quite relaxed at barbecues, aren't they? What's the hurry? It's nice hanging about outside, breathing smoke and watching the aproned alfresco cook giving it large with the tongs and other utensils among the sausages and economy burgers.

Confident that this time he had been successful, Ben reassumed his casual (some might say jaunty) angle against the kitchen door and continued the Grand Wooing with Conversational Gambit #7, *Complimenting the Physical*. 'That's a very nice blouse you're wearing, Lynette.' He reckoned himself to be on top of his game, as you can tell.

'Nice of you to say so, but I think you should be keeping your eye on the fire,' she replied. 'It's started to fade a bit, you know.' She was smiling, but more out of politeness than pleasure. Perhaps Ben was starting to wear a bit thin on her. She might even have been wondering *Where is Steve when he's needed?*

Ben could see that the flames from the paper had subsided and yet by no stretch of the imagination could it be said that wood was burning; indeed, the coals were barely warm.

The doorbell rang, signalling the arrival of the first of the guests. The barbecue was not alight, let alone cooking the food. Meanwhile the queue for hot lunch was already forming before his eyes. It would not be long before hunger turned them into an angry mob, so Ben rushed back to his duties.

Lynette showed her visitors through to the gazebo at the end of the garden, where the drinks and nibbles were available. On her way back to the kitchen, she glanced at the unimpressively cool coals and sighed, probably because she was tired of watching Ben waste his time and effort. Her guests were in place, but the food was going to be some time yet.

Ben allowed himself a brief moment to hope she would stay and help. *She might even take the fire lighting utensils from my hands or gently barge me aside with a waggle of her shapely hips or even – dare I allow the words to form? – put a hand on my shoulder, go up on tip-toe to kiss me on the cheek in thanks for what I had thus far achieved, but ask me to go and mingle with the guests while she got on with completing the job of lighting the coals…*

But no.

'What you need is airflow,' she said, enigmatically and disappointingly, going back indoors.

Ben's characteristic joie de vivre began to wither. He had grown weary of putting emotional energy into getting nowhere fast with either of his warming-up initiatives. 'It's all very well making remarks,' he said, mostly to himself, 'but what I need to do is to raise the temperature of the wood, the coals and subsequently, the sausages; and ultimately, mine hostess. Comments about wind? Not so much.'

A moment or two later the Blonde One reappeared with a hair dryer and an extension cable. 'Use this,' she said, with the merest hint of a smile; although, on reflection, it may have been a wry or even sardonic grimace. There is no way it was indigestion.

'I'm trying to light the barbecue, Lynette, not style my barnet!' Ben quipped, quite wittily, he thought.

She sighed; her patience was close to breaking point. 'Use the dryer to intensify the flames and blow them through the wood and the coals.

It'll help them to catch light properly and to direct the smoke away from your eyes, you…'

'Oh, I see.'

Some paper was still burning, so with the hairdryer, he directed a flow of air through the wood and across the coals, which glowed first red and then white, the colour required for perfect barbecuing.

A few minutes later, when the burgers and chicken drumsticks and sausages and chops (pork & lamb) were placed on the rack, the coals were very hot, but not flaming or smoky. The food was quickly cooked to perfection and was soon ready to serve to the gathered throng. Ben was beaming with satisfaction, feeling particularly pleased with himself.

He discovered later that Lynette had observed his many mistakes and made up for the time he was wasting. She had mega-multi-tasked and continued to welcome guests and supply them with refreshing beverages in addition to preparing the folding tables, tablecloths, bread, crudités, crisps, plates, cutlery, slices of tomato, shredded iceberg lettuce, four types of gherkin, tomato/mild chilli/extra-hot chilli sauces, three mustards, four dips, guacamole, mayonnaise, corn chips and salsa. Simultaneously had put the chops, steaks and drumsticks on the grill in the kitchen and cooked them through, ready for the barbecue effect to come into play for the perfect finish.

This way her guests managed to avoid salmonella poisoning (via underdone chicken) or overdosing on bitter carbon due to cremation of emulsified offal tubing.

Ben's abiding memory of the event itself was a haze of meaty aromas; the anticipated general amusement of the guests at the sight of a young man in a frilly apron; much brandishing of the fish slice; mild panda-mockery; and several Native-American-style war-dances when he burned his fingers on the vast heat radiating from those glowing coals.

He prided himself on perfecting the apparently casual flinging of the tea towel over one shoulder. He even awarded himself *Chivalrous Gentleman of the Month,* having retained a particularly skilfully cooked lamb chop for Lynette.

Unfortunately, some latecomer snaffled it up when he wasn't looking.

No, it wasn't Steve, but that might have made it a better story, so if you like, you can imagine that it was.

Ben was more successful in reserving for himself a piece of steak he'd spotted in the back of the fridge. He cooked it with great care and attention after everyone else had been fed. Oh, it was delicious: delicately rare and perfectly juicy, served in a soft bap with cheese, lettuce, tomato, mayo and a splash of chilli sauce.

The chief success of the occasion was that everyone survived the ordeal of the risky meat. Many of the guests were kind enough to say they'd had a good time.

Once it was all over, Ben and Lynette cleared up (how had he ever volunteered with no certainty of squeezy thanks?) Reviewing his attitude, it seems that Ben's chief incentive for helping this woman throw a party was inappropriately directed towards romantic rewards. That doesn't sound particularly righteous, does it? But then we all occasionally do things for the wrong reasons (or at least with muddled motivation). Don't we? Perhaps it's just me. I mean Ben.

Anyway, all that aside, they were filling refuse sacks, washing up, dismantling the gazebo and trying to get it back into the inadequately-sized bag supplied, putting away trestle tables and making the still-hot coals safe. Meanwhile still-smokin'-hot Lynette commented on how helpful Ben had been and flashed a smile at him over the ketchup-smeared Formica.

His heart melted and suddenly he wished he'd been able to reserve that lamb chop for her. *Ah,* he thought to myself, *perhaps I can gain a handful of brownie points by telling her that I'd tried to do so. After all, it's the thought that counts, right?*

'I was disappointed with just one thing, you know, Lyn,' he said, using a familiar abbreviation of her name to ensure she knew he was talking to her heart (Conversational Gambit #14 *Connecting Emotionally*). She was wielding a dishcloth, sweeping little bits of crisps, tortillas, bun crumbs, coleslaw and sweetcorn relish into her hand, in the way that some girls are trained by their mothers to do.

'What was that, Steve?'

The world stood still for a moment.

Steve? Steve? She called me Steve! I go weak! Ben thought. Various coagulating lumps of haemoglobin within Ben's cardio-vascular system started to form themselves into centimetre-high letters, spelling out MUM'S GONE TO ICELAND. His cheeks flushed; his tummy did an impression of *The Flying Fredericos*, the circus trapeze troupe famous for their triple-rotating, twisting hands-free reversed Fosbury double-release undersling with pike, tuck and quadruple lutz. Except the impression was inadequately completed and my tummy (still attempting to deal with partly-digested rare steak, remember) missed one of the necessary catches and ended up in the slack, momentum-absorbing safety net of disappointment, denial and deferred hope.

'I mean Ben…' she said, with the grace to say it quietly.

It seemed pointless now to try to impress her with the feeble story of the lamb chop. But he tried anyway.

Unfortunately, so much wind had been removed from his sails that he told the story (and storytelling is what he thought he was rather good at, too) in a way that lacked any spark of charm or mellowness.

'Oh, I don't know who that could have been,' the Blonde One chattered, continuing to wipe and sweep and clear and clean and bag and rinse and tidy. 'But I wasn't really that hungry, you know. I thought I'd eat later. There's a lovely little steak in the back of the fridge I've rather cunningly reserved for my supper, so that's something I'm looking forward to…'

Ben forgave himself a tiny smile picturing her expression when she had a rummage in the fridge and discovered it was gone. *Perhaps she's not the girl for me,* he thought to himself. *She's far too wrapped up in her own personal preferences (selfish steak, semi-spirituality, stupid Steve).*

So, what lessons can we learn from this incident?

1 Select potential girlfriends more wisely.

2 Serve with a better attitude.

3 Don't bother with Conversational Gambits; they don't work.

4 Keep your eye on lamb chops.

5 Don't steal from other people's fridges.

Lynette showed mercy to her guests but sadly didn't go on to show much forgiveness or tenderness towards Ben. On his more wistful days, he might admit that was probably the hand of the Lord at work, keeping him from further rejection.

~

Oh yes, I was meaning to make Elijah the focus of this. You know, the chap who took up the challenge to demonstrate that the One True God was superior to the false gods of the prophets of Baal by calling down fire from heaven on an unlikely barbecue.

There are several important differences between Ben and Elijah.

1 Ben's not an Old Testament prophet.

2 Elijah might have found a different use for the hairdryer (if he'd managed to locate a power socket) in the traditional task of drying his

hair. Oh, and his beard, too. Yes, I had to look it up to double-check, but it was his sidekick Elisha who was famously lacking in the long, flowing locks department.

3 Ben didn't think to call down fire from heaven.

4 Ben used lighter fuel; Elijah used water and faith in God's power.

5 Lynette's guests were resourced with a lot less beef than Elijah (he had a whole bull but the guests merely had Findus Quarterpounders, Happy Shopper Veggieburgers, a lamb chop, some chicken drumsticks and four pork tenderloin medallions, plus that delicious little bit of porterhouse, which I really enjoyed).

6 None of the barbecue guests (we assume) were worshippers of Baal, nor were they responding to a challenge to their false gods.

7 Elijah was eager for the sacrifice to be burned to a crisp, although what Ben had in mind was for the end result to be considerably more edible than that.

8 Ben's primary goal was not quite similarly God-honouring.

9 Just to be clear, Ben ate the steak, not me. I don't know how that confusion crept in.

10 Elijah looked more like a heavy metal fan than Ben.

So, there isn't really a lot of connection at all. The Bible says that Elijah was a man just like us. Weak and fallible, like us and sometimes emotionally unstable and cowardly. Yet when he listened to God and obeyed the commands he was given, he defeated the priests of Baal, showing that the One True God was powerful and answered by fire. Eventually, Elijah ran faster than a chariot, managed accurately to prophesy the end of the drought he had also prophesied and gave the wicked monarchs a hard time.

He never won the heart of a woman called Lynette.

But then neither did Steve, thank the Lord.

2 Noise, grace, chips & spears

David & Jonathan 1 Samuel 19:9–17

Friendship is a marvellous part of life.

I know, because I have many very special friends. Yes, some of them are on Facebook, but lots of them were very dear to me long before the electronic social networking phenomenon slightly devalued the term. My friends add fun, laughter, depth and so much more to everyday experiences. I can't list all my many friends, but here are a couple of insights into just a few of them.

First, then, there's HD.

He has for several decades been a source of continual merriment with his unpredictable approach to life, which accounts for his nickname *Human Dynamo*, hence the initials HD, geddit?

He lives near the seafront in Brighton on the south coast, became a member of the same church at about the same time as I did and owns one of the beach huts that stand on the promenade. In there he keeps nine plastic chairs – four green, three white and two off-white – plus three tables, two windbreaks (one plain, one striped), and a sunshade that sometimes has to serve in the role of umbrella. Plus a radio with no battery, a small selection of cups and mugs, half a dozen empty diet lemonade bottles, several broken thermos flasks, two towels, a selection of drip trays, a few beer mats and coasters, a pile of old slightly damp newspapers, many sachets of sugar, an airtight plastic container full of teabags, a small jar of Smartprice instant decaff coffee granules, seventeen assorted packs of cards, most of a jigsaw and less of a travel scrabble set, a supermarket carrier bag full of supermarket carrier bags and a fully inflated dinghy complete with oars, in case anyone wants to paddle out to sea. It's all packed in brilliantly.

On one occasion, when I went there to meet him after work, he'd already set up a table, with four chairs and the striped windbreak. I sat down and we chatted briefly, waiting for the other guests to arrive. HD had provided the setting, I was there to ensure everyone was fully entertained and our other guests (a younger Christian couple from the church) had agreed to provide a picnic. Quality distribution of labour, right?

After a brief wait in the sunshine, Kate and her husband Sean bowled along the promenade, armed to the teeth with comestibles.

Oh! Not just sarnies and crisps, which I had anticipated, but a vast bowl of steaming hot pasta with a lovely, fishy, mushroom cream sauce, plus another dish full of crunchy salad, with crusty bread, a bottle of red wine and two puddings (frozen cake and melted trifle). They had even remembered to bring plastic plates/bowls/cups and cutlery, plus butter, mayonnaise, a corkscrew and serviettes. HD and I choose our friends rather wisely.

Kate had clearly pulled out all the stops – generous and thoughtful! We set everything up and tucked in with great enthusiasm, relish, mayonnaise and lots of laughter. The cake was a bit crunchy; the trifle was slightly sloppy; but they tasted great!

Always keen to educate me in the ways of modern music and social phenomena, Kate then proceeded to work hard to persuade me to attend a free open-air music performance which was due to happen further along the beach-front later that evening.

Apparently, it would feature an artiste called Fatboy Slim. I'd not heard of him, nor of the event, which turned out to be the *Big Beach Boutique*, Brighton, 6th July 2001.

To be perfectly honest, there seemed little to recommend it. Apparently, a bloke in his late 30s (old enough to know better) would stand behind a large PA system and play records. Not big, not clever. Sounded like a major yawn: the sort of thing I'd grown out of many years before Kate was born, but for some unaccountable reason there was a large crowd expected. She got her way, of course, (she has such a winning smile) and when the picnic was all finished, we packed up the plates, stowed them in the beach hut along with everything else and made our way towards the throng gathering for the gig.

I've already mentioned that it sounded like it would be dreary and uninteresting. I was so wrong. It was considerably worse than that.

I found the entire gathering deeply appalling, with the Slimlad doing his thing with his hat and Zoë Ball (HD was ridiculously pleased to have spotted her) and his decks and his dreadful taste in so-called music, designed to induce a migraine.

Many thousands of irresponsible young people spread broken glass all over the beach in the process of becoming vastly intoxicated over the course of the evening, thanks to bottled beer and what might be termed incendiary pharmaceuticals. By the end of the event, even taking a breath was risky on account of the dangerous, sweet cloud which enhanced the light show.

Yes, I should have resisted Kate's powers of persuasion. I thought at least Sean was trustworthy and that it might turn out to be better than they suggested. But the opposite was true. See, this is what friendship is all about. You trust someone and they let you down, dreadfully.

No, no! Seriously, our friendship is strong enough for me to be honest and tell them that taking me to the concert was at best ill-judged, although at worst cruel and possibly an arrestable offence. I still care for my friends, despite their lack of discernment or the shocking fables they told to get me to go with them. I guess I'd reflect on lessons learned, differences in taste and assume the best of their intention, which was to introduce me to a more youthful form of music and performance. They learned this was not achievable.

Sean and Kate now have two sons and have been devoting their lives to serving the people at the church where all three of us got involved (perhaps it is no coincidence that Birmingham is pretty much the furthest from the seaside it is possible to get, in the UK). They tell the truth much more often. Their musical taste still leaves a great deal to be desired, but their sons have an appropriately positive opinion of me. Kate's picnic menus, however, have become less ambitious, revolving around shop-bought scotch eggs. A treat, I agree, but lower league.

In the meanwhile, HD has sold his beach hut and now owns two taxis. One he uses every day, while the other is parked around the back of his home. He has somehow managed to persuade someone else to make the payments on the loan he took out to buy the car and to pay the parking fees, too. It's the world's first and only Static Cab.

HD makes me smile.

I don't want you to get the wrong impression of HD. For several years he's been the building manager of the block of flats in which he lives, administering all kinds of maintenance work on the Grade II listed property; he's worked hard to establish excellent relationships with local councillors and politicians for the sake of the locale; and he's recently been elected to be the Chair of the resident's association, which means he'll be able to shape the way the community cares for the location and for each other.

Quite a dude. And other people think that, too.

~

Then there are the Lambraynes, who live in Abergavenny, for some reason. Enough said. I got to know Jeff through an evangelism event and we've been friends for decades. HD and I were the Best Men at Jeff & Nancy's wedding (chapter 28 refers) and are informally godfathers to their children. I suggested they should call HD *Don* and me *Corleone*. But it didn't catch on.

The family very kindly provide hospitality for me and HD when we visit from time to time. HD sleeps on the floor in Lambrayne's office and I take the sofa cushions in the conservatory. The first couple of times, when we went to stay in the warmer months, this worked well.

However, we then visited in the winter, when the single-glazed conservatory was very chilly indeed. So, my restless attempts to snooze were resulting in little more than sporadic dozing and shifting the sofa-cushions about on the polished surface; and then the cat came in.

Now, I shouldn't speak ill of this creature, since he died not long afterwards (nothing to do with me, honest), but he was the most peculiar animal that ever roamed those valleys.

He was called Jesus, which seems so very wrong. He was roughly fifteen years old, which made him about 493 in cat years. Arthritis, poor sight and non-specific-yet-global cat-rot had destructively ravaged his physical well-being. Jesus (I must say that this blind, limping elderly feline didn't remind me of the risen, victorious Lord of glory one little bit) was accustomed to coming into the house at night via the catflap, walking across the conservatory and through into the kitchen area, where a litter tray and a bowl of Whiskas Supermeat were waiting.

Trouble is, I was lying right in his path. If Lambrayne had remembered to warn me, I'd have positioned myself elsewhere; the truth is, it was never mentioned, yet I suspect he knew what would happen.

So, I was woken from light, fitful sleep by a blind, smelly cat mewling in confusion at his established pathway so confusingly blocked. Of course, in the darkness, neither of us were able to see anything and I would guess I was the more alarmed.

And this explains why I was already awake when the amusing little practical joke Lambrayne had planned for me went into operation. He'd put a transistor radio in the bottom of the children's toybox, on a timer, set to turn itself on, quite loudly, at 3.42am. This would be bad enough in the ordinary context, but it was not quite tuned in properly to a low-rent Welsh-language pop station. *Radio Lllllllllll* is what it sounded like.

The irritating sound of crypto-Celtic electro-rap interrupted by a dead-of-night Llocal Radio DJ *look you boyo it's forty-two minutes past the hour, isn't it, so now by 'ere I'll spin a tidy toe-tapper-platter by sheepshearin' duet Myfanwy Jones & Blodwyn Evans* could be neither ignored nor tolerated.

It took me several annoyed minutes to find that radio. Meanwhile my affection towards my host waned slightly, I have to admit. Perhaps in the interests of maintaining high standards of politeness and calm, I should draw a veil over the confrontation we had during breakfast. I tried so hard to be the mildly amused guest, grateful for the hospitality and the whimsical quirks of Chez Lambrayne.

But it is possible that I may have lacked grace. Perhaps there may have been shouting and thumps on the table; I admit such reactions were possible.

Lambrayne and his family visited my home not long afterwards and I arranged for them no nasty surprises, no poorly animals, no theological conundra and no sub-zero conservatory. Indeed, (though I say it myself) I was the very personification of niceness, engaging each of the family in witty and sparkling conversation.

Also, I agreed to play a fiendish card game at which the children were evidently world champions; I, a total novice, was still confused about the rules when, after three rounds, they beat me 25,400,009 to 17. Yet still I didn't get cross. Outwardly.

~

Another friend, Olly, never used to cook anything at all. He lived in a small but pleasant terraced house with dodgy laminate flooring and his kitchen didn't have a stove. It had a sink full of dirty crocks, a microwave oven for heating ready-meals and a bin constantly overflowing with carrier bags, cardboard and polystyrene containers, pizza boxes, packaging from cuppa-soups and pot-based noodles, plastic cartons from *Lotus Blossom CarryOut Pagoda*, foil trays from *Taj Mahal Tandoori & Balti Kitchen*, greasy, used bargain buckets and, of course, a huge assortment of chip papers.

Olly's a great chap with a kind heart and a good sense of humour – but I learned to beware of invites to dinner from him. Warmed-up *Happy Shopper Frozen Bangers & Mash with Gravy for two* – no thanks! Going out for a doner kebab would be a much better plan.

He eventually moved away from his take-away-carton museum. He went to South America, married a beautiful Brazilian woman and works to help provide schools and medical facilities for children who live near the Amazon River. Sadly, I've not had the chance to ask him, but I suspect he hasn't had a chinese take-away for more than a decade.

~

The advantage of friendship is that you care enough for one another to put up with weaknesses and peculiar behaviour.

Friendship transcends bad concert choices, weird pets and lack of culinary expertise, choosing rather to focus upon the positive qualities of hospitality, generosity, charitable attitudes, distinctiveness and constant merriment.

Space and self-respect do not permit me to give examples of how deep friendship overcomes ropey judgement and harsh pranks; extremely potent aromas of triple-strength brie cheese in confined spaces for extended periods of time; using the first draft of my novel for kindling; vague appointment times which result in all-day waiting; a vegan breakfast (oh, don't ask); woefully inaccurate estimations of walking distances; shockingly ill-considered choices of places to eat; and having to be civil with a range of insubstantial women and girls temporarily associated with various blokes of my acquaintance.

Or the members of the Bible Study group with whom I shared my heart, who expressed their gratitude for my faithful service by presenting me with a Bible they had purchased and inscribed, on the front page, with a verse of particular significance. I was appropriately touched by this thoughtfulness and immediately attempted to turn to the reference, to read it in context. At this point I discovered they had given me a dud Bible which had been remaindered by the Christian Bookshop (they paid £1 for it) since most of the Psalms, all of Proverbs and some of Ecclesiastes were missing, yet most of Job and the other half of the Psalms were included twice – some form of printing or binding error. The reference they had mentioned in their heartfelt inscription was, of course, completely missing. They laughed themselves silly at this.

These, folks, are the kinds of friends I have cultivated over many years. Is it me? Is it?

~

Take a Biblical example – say, David and Jonathan, for instance.

When King Saul (Jon's father) attempted to murder David, the friendship between David and Jonathan was severely tested. But it proved strong enough for Jonathan to help David make his escape from Saul, even though Johnny-boy might have been expected to take the side of his father instead.

Think about your friends. Not just your 'best friend' if you have one, but what about other people that you know quite well? What would you do for them? Have there ever been times when they have inconvenienced themselves for your sake? Have they given up time to assist you when you were in need? How can you tell that they are true friends? Do you tell each other things you might not mention elsewhere? Do you share hopes, fears, longings, secrets? Do you laugh and laugh for no reason? Do you sometimes even dare to cry together?

Do you put up with their poor taste in music or football team or even make the ultimate sacrifice and go to KFC when the need you're trying to fulfil is a MacAttack?

Does his father chuck spears at you? Do you just 'hang' without having to say anything very much? Do you arm-wrestle or share make-up or spend time taking selfies of each other pulling faces?

Greater love has no one than this;
that he lays down his life for his friends. John 15:13

Cautionary note: the verse quoted here does not imply that you should ever allow anyone's father to throw spears at you, under even the most justifiable of circumstances.

The verse has more to do with the selfless love Jesus showed us when he was crucified in our place.

3 The waiting game

Abraham receives his promise Genesis 12:1-4; 21:2-5

Wormholes in the fabric of the space-time continuum are the stuff of science fiction, generally, but it seems that time actually does warp and flex when it flows into the doctors' waiting rooms, those strange palaces of disinfectant and bad-tempered receptionists. Perhaps I have just had some negative experiences, but I find that when I have an appointment at the surgery (not very often), I do my best to be there on time, since I'm polite and responsible. I have a life and don't want to keep other people hanging around and would like to be treated in the same way.

Why do they call it a *surgery*, when they don't have an operating theatre and perform nothing more invasive than inserting a thermometer or the occasional hypodermic needle? While I was wondering, I found out that an operating theatre is called a *theatre* because operations were once a popular spectator sport, with bleacher-style seating for the bloodthirsty onlookers. Medicine has a chequered history, indeed.*

Anyway, I rush about and make sure I'm hurrying up the path to the doctors' with a couple of minutes to spare.

Now, before I become enraged and start moaning about how doctors' surgeries used to be, I ought to pause and make it clear that these days, many medical centres are located in modern, even purpose-built blocks, with disabled access, wide doorways, air conditioning and lifts fitted with recorded warnings like *doors closing; lift going up; second floor; doors opening* or whatever else is obviously happening.

Set in a clean, functional building, the clinic I occasionally attend has a computerised touch screen on which each patient registers their arrival, whereupon the system confirms the appointment and provides real-time information about how many minutes behind schedule they are currently running. Meanwhile, multiple infections are covertly passed between patients, ensuring repeat business for the doctors.

However, it's difficult to get the receptionists to maintain telephone etiquette (answering my call might be a good start) or eye contact, except when you quietly ask for a urine specimen container. Upon such a request, they hand you the bottle and expansively point out where the

*please note, my criticism and extended bleating is about harsh treatment dished out to me by specific doctors' receptionists (not identified) and not in any way an attack upon the NHS, an organisation I applaud (sometimes literally) and for which I am so grateful

toilet is, to make sure absolutely everyone else in the crowded waiting room knows exactly what you're about to be doing. Awks.

Anyway, this essay is supposed to be about how things were in the past. So, please picture the scene.

Like I was saying, I bowl up the path and climb three steps to the dark, imposing oak door of a large semi-detached house and into a hallway with colourful floor tiles, white walls, an ornate ceiling rose and Victorian architrave. I proceed through an internal door and follow a sign marked RECEPTION, where fierce women sit at a counter behind reinforced glass panels. Perhaps they anticipate armed gangs of ruffians demanding at gunpoint that the safe be ransacked.

Once at the receptionist's window, I wait. This is always a daunting prospect, especially if you're not feeling well, which is, after all, probably the main reason you're visiting the doctor in the first place. I ask myself: should I interrupt the essential paper-shuffling she's doing?

Is she aware I'm here? If I don't speak soon, she will justifiably assume I've come in to shelter from the cold outside or I'm here to meet someone or whatever. Unless I can get her to notice me in the next few moments, my opportunity will be gone and I'll feel like a fool and have to draw attention to myself… The situation fosters insecurity.

Then, the phone rings. Suddenly, I have a reason to wait politely until she is ready to deal with me. This is better. I can observe her technique on the phone to inform me of her customer relations style.

She grabs the phone without looking. Funny that; it rings never less than 68 times when I call the surgery, unless it simply provides an engaged tone. 'Doctor's appointments.' She sings the expression in a way that conveys not only vast boredom but also effortless distain for the caller, who has interrupted something far more important, combined with joyful relief that the irritating ringing has mercifully ceased. She searches for a pen, finds one and then puts it down immediately, since she needs to jab fingers at the computer keyboard. 'Doctor Lecter doesn't do Thursdays…' she barks. Then, with a light chuckle, 'no, no, no, Friday's out of the question.' No hint of which days he is available, or of alternative physicians who might be on duty to help the suffering patient. 'Name?'

Now this is an interesting moment in the encounter. I've been here enough times to know that this receptionist isn't strong on smiles or eye contact and I suddenly fear that she might actually be speaking to me, even though she's still got the telephone receiver to her ear and is still looking at her computer screen. I pause, uncertain, watching her face for a flicker of movement, in case she means me. The unexpected happens. She looks up and appears to notice me for the first time. I step forward half a pace and assume she must be trying to multi-task – to process me and at the same time wait for the caller to guess the roster of GPs in this practice.

'An...' I start, but she raises a hand with the universal signal for *halt* (actually, her gesture was *HALT, you loser*) and I close my mouth. It seems she might have been considering dealing with me and with the telephone caller at the same time, but then abandoned this idea. It seems she was distracted from dealing with the caller by me and then distracted from me by the caller. It takes a special skill borne of long practice to be able to achieve this with one glance and one hand gesture.

'Next Wednesday at eight forty-three or the following Monday at eleven-seventeen. Right, Monday week at eleven-seventeen. Your name? Gloria Blenkinsopp ... to see the nurse ... boil lanced... date of birth? Thirteen eleven seventy-eight. Goodbye.'

It strikes me slightly inappropriate to have information about your pus-filled abscess announced to the world. If you happened to know Mrs B, it could be rather awkward next time you see her sitting down carefully, because you'd know why. And you might have thought she was a bit younger than that. Anyway, this is now my opportunity to try to get the receptionist's attention again. Or is she going to make an entry on the database? It seems not, but then...

'Name?' This time there is no doubt. She means me and her tone reveals that she's weighed me in the balances and I've been found wanting, lacking even any worthiness to have my presence registered on the computer system. So, I state my name, state it again when asked to repeat it because she wasn't listening properly before and I mention the time I was supposed to have been seen. Trouble is, the extended wait during which the receptionist dealt with the caller may have pushed me past the time for the appointment, so now I'm rude and late on top of being a drooling simpleton. See what I mean about insecurity?

Unsurprisingly, I am directed with a vague wave of the hand to one of the waiting rooms and I join the hacking, wheezing, snuffling throng and wait for a long, long time. This room is unattractively laid out with a ragbag assortment of plastic chairs arranged around the walls, with a low table in the middle of the floor groaning under the weight of eighty-three inexplicably dog-eared magazines of undoubted vintage and disputable interest. More than half of them are copies of Meccano Monthly and the rest either lack a cover or are hopelessly out of date: a *TV Quick* from last year; a copy of *Smash Hits* from 1991; and *Hallo's Special Princess Elizabeth & Phil the Greek Get Engaged Edition, with a cut-out-'n'-keep Photo section.*

There's a sort of mini cheese plant jungle growth in one corner, with leaves gently crisping where they touch the radiator.

The walls are littered with an array of severe warnings in the form of unpleasant posters. A tar-riddled lung enhances the appearance of the fireplace. A super-giant magnification of a head louse oversees the book table. A photo of a sad-looking teenager regretting her pregnancy (but consoling herself with a cigarette, I notice) has been pinned above the plastic box of children's toys.

EMERGECY APPOINTMENTS ALLECATED IN STRICT ORDER OF IMPORTANCE, NOT NECCCESSARILY ACCORDING BY ORDER OF REQUESTING

Photos of other sick people of various descriptions with diseases too horrifying to contemplate (skin eruptions, vast goitres, alarmingly bloodshot eyes, extreme mental instability) stare down hopelessly from the opposite wall. And all of these gross conditions are caused, it seems, by not eating your five a day with wholemeal bread, failure to get regular exercise (undefined) and by being late for appointments, which inconveniences the doctors.

Or at least that's how it seems from the other signs around the room. These are A4 sheets with poorly laid-out, disgracefully ungrammatical and badly-spelled block capitals and many are impossible to comprehend.

IF YOU HAVE TO CANCELL AN APOINTMENT, ALLOW THREE DAYS NOTCE

Yes, I know I'm starting to sound like the *Eats Shoots & Leaves* woman, but sometimes, it really matters.

After all, communication is about expressing yourself and engaging with your audience, not just hoping the people who need to know what you consider to be important will work out what you were intending to say. With so many of these hurriedly-composed notices, it seems the only thing effectively communicated is the transparent irritation of the receptionist, who seems to have failed to take into account the *by definition* poorliness of everyone who has to see, read and try to understand the terse, ill-considered instructions. Customer service is a distant dream, eons away.

WAITING TIME'S
MAYBE LONGER
THAN EXPECTED,
THIS IS'NT
RECEPTIONISTS
FAULT

These are either complaints about the difficult circumstances in which these receptionists have to work, or unnecessarily complex messages attempting to brow-beat sick people into following protocols and administrative procedures apparently established by unrepentant Prisoner-of-War Camp Commandants.

Sitting there, trying not to inhale germs, reading these notices sets me thinking. Waiting time's (sic) may indeed not be their fault. The problem may well be that *time itself* operates in a different way in the doctor's clinic. Look, it was 4.58pm when I arrived for my 5pm appointment. It was 5.01pm when I spoke to the receptionist. And yet, somehow, twenty minutes later, it's still only 5.08pm. Perhaps I'm bored, or maybe time is stretching out in a way unique to this building. Another ten minutes pass and it's eventually ... 5.12pm.

Two things are happening here. Not only is time running a few minutes slow, but also, the confusion this causes is so severe that no one except me has noticed that the scheduled moment for my appointment has come and is long gone.

The truth is, that no matter what time the clock in the clinic may say or what the Greenwich Time Signal might suggest, the time for me to see the doctor has passed. So, should I still be here? In the rest of the adult world, when the time allocated for a meeting has passed, the meeting finishes unless someone in authority agrees it can over-run. In this case, it has not yet started, but the right to be having a meeting with my GP now belongs to another patient, since the time for their

REPEAT PRECRIPTIONS
CAN BE COLLECTED ON
THE 2ND DAY IF POSTED
BEFORE 10.00 A.M.

their appointment has arrived and they can stake their claim. You see, my doctor should be on to the next bloke after the woman after me by now and it's clear that the wheezer and the mum with the odd-looking baby are yet to go in before me, in addition to the anorak-wrapped person of indeterminate gender and the chap with blotches sitting huddled by the gas fire.

turn you
mobilephone of

I begin to wonder what might be wrong with the person who is seeing the doctor right now – perhaps they have just a cold or a nasty suppurating wound of some description, but quite possibly some seriously infectious contagion with the potential to wipe out half the county... Whatever's wrong with them, they're taking more than their fair share of doctor's time.

Over the next two hours the clock only advances forty-five minutes. Now, perhaps I'm making more of this than I should, but the long wait between my arrival and actually getting to see the doctor is always, always longer than it should be, no matter how long it actually is, or how long the receptionist and the doctor guessed it needed to be (when the appointment was first made), even if that's not strictly according to order of requesting (sic).

WHEN YOU WANT
A SHAPERONE, SHE
CAN BE ARRAGNED
BY NURSES

And then, abruptly, several minutes after I'd given up hope, the receptionist barks at me. 'Room Two.'

Please note: I arrived in good time, have been delayed exclusively by the administrative failure of the staff and suddenly I'm being made to feel pressure to hurry up, since now I'm apparently the one keeping the doctor waiting. This feels more than a tad unjust.

Anyway, I've been sat down for so long that my head swims when I stand, unused to being at altitude. I nervously step over shopping bags, small children and other peoples' feet and wander tentatively down the unlit, narrow, forbidding passageway's bare boards.

The smell becomes familiar and I vaguely remember how to find the consulting room from being here a year or two earlier. First, manoeuvre along the corridor, through a series of unlikely-looking archways and past another waiting room and then it's a sort of jog-left-then-right-and-right-again. Here you should avoid making contact with some electricity meters with a lethal array of dangling cables (this fearsome panel smells of super-heated dust. It hums darkly, so that the air is filled with powerful static, making your hair stand up briefly). Then you turn back on yourself where the creaking floor drops away sharply towards the sluice room and you half-fall, half-trip up three stairs and stumble towards a dark, thick door, cracked ever-so slightly yet intensely uninvitingly ajar.

There is a sign: Consulting Suite 7a (but we all know this is Room 2, somehow). Within sits the Ultimate Grand Wizard Of Unctuous Potions & Medicinal Brews, The Supreme Wonder-Working Master Of The Brusque Word Of Advice & Brief Appraisal, During Which Assumptions Are Made, Pill-Prescriptions Printed And *While I'm Here, Doctor* Introductions Of Secondary Afflictions Are Inadmissible.*

His tiny half-spectacles somehow obscure more of his face than seems possible and his green corduroy jacket (with leather elbow-patches and cuffs) has a familiarity about it that makes me feel like I'm at the same time in a geography lesson and being visited by a rarely-seen uncle. He has evidently been mentoring the receptionist in Customer Relations, since his ability to talk to me and simultaneously look at several papers on his desk, each of which is more important than any other, is deeply unsettling and demonstrates the technique at a higher level.

By this time, I have not only utterly forgotten why I booked the appointment, but I don't think I could make even a fair stab at providing my name or guessing how many arms I have.

The actual time spent in the doctor's room is mercifully brief.

'What seems to be the matter?'

'Nothing, ta, I've been waiting so long I got better.'

'Well, eat brown bread, have your five a day, get plenty of exercise, won't you?' He scribbles something indecipherable onto a small pink sheet, tears the note from the pad, screws it up and flicks it into the overflowing bin. With a grunt, the Doc indicates that the consultation is over, and that he is surprised I'm still there.

And so, I rush out of his consulting room, down the corridor, up the three stairs and around the corner by the meters and eventually out of

*again, no criticism of the medical profession as a whole is intended

the building via a glass-panelled door featuring yet another notice: this one is somehow simultaneously rude, mysterious and confusing.

Once outside, I gratefully draw lungfuls of fresh air into my body and try to re-orientate myself.

AUTOMATIC DOOR — TO
OPEN, GRASP HANDEL,
TWIST
ANTE-CLOCKWISE & PULL
(CAN BE STIFF
DO NOT USE IN EMEGRENCYS
DO NOT WEDGE OPEN
FIRE EXIT IF OTHER DOOR
LOCKED

I find that not only has the sky grown dark and the local chemist has closed, so I can't ask them to dispense my prescription anyway, but also vast mountain ranges have been eroded away to nothing and a new race of beings rules the scorched earth, evolved from mutated mallards.

Time has indeed passed.

Perhaps I exaggerate. But you know what I mean. Time and reality function differently in such places.

~

I think perhaps that if I'd been Abraham, (woah, crunching gear-change, but I do have a point to make) I'd have been tapping my foot, too. The promises of God eventually came to pass and his wife did finally (about 24 years later) become pregnant and she gave birth to a son. And the fulfilment of the original visionary promise was greatly delayed: it didn't happen until long, long after Abraham had died.

Making descendants more numerous than the sand on the seashore is a lengthy process, you know!

But poor old Abraham found waiting very taxing, despite not having to sit endlessly with contagious and noisy folk in a depressing and anti-intellectual environment. The father of many nations got off to a couple of false starts, behaved rather badly and then very nearly killed his son due to a misunderstanding. The business with Hagar and Ishmael and disobedience to God was ultimately brought about by lack of patience.

This would be a good way of reducing the length of the queues in the doctor's waiting room – a lack of patients!

4 Wither leviathans?

Bible reading

There's a number of ways we can all use to keep our Bible reading fresh, interesting, regular and meaningful.

Sometimes I might use Bible reading notes, which help me follow a set of readings systematically, and contain thought-provoking comments and prayer suggestions along the way.

Another method (suitable for occasions when I have a bit more time at my disposal) is to read long passages all at once to try to get the big picture. This might even mean tackling a whole book in one sitting. This can be especially helpful for a historical book with a strong narrative such as, for example: Exodus; 1 Samuel; Jonah; Acts of the Apostles.

There are times when I look carefully at a single verse and think about each word, examining why it's there, what it means and any symbolic value it might have. I also consider how the verse can make a difference to me – perhaps there's a command to obey or an example to follow or avoid (this is called 'application').

Studying like this can be considered a form of meditation, where a reader or student of the Word can find far deeper meaning than is possible (or likely) on a quick scan through the passage. It can be very spiritually enriching; but it's not much use to me if I want to make sure I see the grand scheme of the majestic sweep of the story of salvation. A lot depends on what I am attempting to achieve.

The letters of Paul and the writings of the Minor Prophets are rich and valuable for this sort of thoughtful study, but I can still benefit from a quick overview of the content and then go back to look at each passage in detail.

However, when I'm looking at a poetry book such like Psalms or Proverbs, I usually find it more helpful to read slowly and carefully. There's not much storyline but considerably more hidden meaning in the words and the structure. And when I've finished reading, I often feel inspired to conclude with a time of worship, thanking God the Father for sending his Son, in the power of the Holy Spirit.

All of these approaches to the Word of God are valid and helpful. You may find it worthwhile to try out some of these, just for a change, especially if you usually stick to one proven method, and even more so if you've grown weary, run out of steam or become bogged down, losing interest. In these circumstances trying a new approach might reignite your interest and get you back into the good habit of regular time in the Word of God.

Evangelist Smith Wigglesworth (1869-1947) only learned to read in later life. It was noted that he preferred never to read anything but the Bible. His comment, in his gruff Yorkshire accent, was 'When I read t'newspaper, 'appen I end up dirtier than before. When I read t'Bible, I end up cleaner than before. I want to be clean!'

I hear you ask 'Well, just supposing I was wanting to read the Bible, what can I do to make sure I get the most out of it, then?' Good question, my friend.

You may have noticed that many people are recommending that we use a modern translation of the Bible. Popular ones include the *Good News Bible* (published in 1976), the NIV (*New International Version*, published in 1978), and the ESV (*English Standard Bible*, published in 2001). Perhaps not what we usually consider *modern*, but sufficiently recent to avoid accusations of *ancient* levelled at, for example, the *Revised Standard Version* (1952), *Young's Literal Translation* (1862) and the classic *Authorised Version* (1611).

The recent publications mentioned make it easier to grapple with the deeper meaning, since they bypass the problems of interpreting the old-style language. 'Lo, dost not thou reckon thusly, methinks, thrice forsaking the rock badger; yea, even unto the next generation, unless thine tongue cleaveth to the roof of thy mouth.' See what I mean?

Why so many translations? Perhaps it's because some have a rather academic focus, working hard to bring depth and meaning to every word (for example, the *New American Standard Bible*, 1971); yet others give a stronger emphasis to storytelling and freshness – such as *The Living Bible* (1971), *The Message* (2002) and *Passion Translation* (NT only) (2017).

But be aware that some modern translations do not pretend to be the most appropriate for study; the text may have been simplified or re-ordered in such a way which makes it easier to read. Some are even written for or by a specific type of person. This is from the *Cockney Lord Luvvaduck Noo Testament & Sarms, Stanstereason* version.

S'obvious, innit, Gawd loved the 'ole world such big time
that he gave 'is one and only Currant Bun, di'n't 'e,
so that the likes of anyone 'oo swears wiv 'is 'and on a stack of Bibles

*that they reckons this is on the money, they will not be left aht taters**,
but have life that goes on and on and on and on,
and you can slap my thigh and call me toothpaste if it's not so,
and it's yer top dollar style, not just endless, gettit? John 3:16

Reading the Bible can sometimes feel dry or heavy, and in places it really is genuinely difficult to understand. It's a great idea to put a good deal of effort into applying our minds to the word of God, of course, yet it's not a cause for embarrassment to admit that some bits are beyond us. Many passages are complex or so packed with symbolism that we can't fathom them out unless we have insight into each of the hidden meanings. For example, can anyone explain why the Psalmist feels like he is 'a wineskin in the smoke' (Psalm 119:83)?

It's worth the hard work because the Bible is a gift from God to be the Maker's Handbook on living, for human beings.

All scripture is God-breathed and is useful for
teaching, rebuking, correcting and training
in righteousness, so that the man of God may be
equipped for every good work. 2 Timothy 3:16-17

But then there are other truths in the Bible that can only be understood spiritually. It's not simply a matter of hard work or knowledge or scholarship; they require the activity of the Holy Spirit to bring revelation. But we sometimes forget to ask for help.

So, if a particular passage seems hard to fathom, ask God to shed some light on the topic or explain it to you and he'll be only too pleased to reveal the truth, without tutting or thinking you're being spectacularly dense. He doesn't treat us like that; he's the best teacher ever, always willing to assist and never critical or judgmental.

If any of you lacks wisdom, he should ask God,
who gives generously to all, without finding fault,
and it will be given to him. James 1:5

There may be times when we've simply stopped trying to understand and God isn't thrilled about that, but his love for us motivates him to encourage us to try again. He'll always help us get through a season when the Bible seems dull, helping us into fresh encounters.

---

* cockney rhyming slang: (po)taters in the mould, cold – left out in the cold, perishing

Another reason for hitting a dry patch in your reading may be a question of practicalities. Change the time or location for your daily session, or to use a different translation. Perhaps you could read the Psalms from *The Message*, or 2 Kings in the *Living Bible*. Or what about checking out Colossians from JB Philips' lively translation?

Alternatively, you may prefer to get hold of a commentary on a particular book and slowly work your way through it. Or use one of the many excellent Bible reading notes resources available.

There are some particularly poor Bible jokes.

When did the apostles play cricket?

Peter stood up before the eleven and was bold (bowled).

When did Daniel play tennis?

He served in the courts of Nebuchadnezzar.

Where did the Children of Israel get their sausages & ice cream?

From Walls of Jericho.

What proves Noah was a good financial director?

He floated his stock when the rest of the world was going into liquidation. Enough!

There was once a man who was very eager to receive guidance from the Lord and he reckoned that the best way was to look at Bible verses, but he was unsystematic. *The Lord inspired it all,* he thought, *so whatever I read will be directly from God.* He opened his Bible at random and pointed to a verse. He happened to find Matthew 27:5 'So Judas went and hanged himself.' *That can't be right,* he thought and tried again. This time he found Luke 10:37 'Go and do the same.' Slightly concerned at this guidance, he looked for more, this time turning way back into the Old Testament. His finger stopped at Genesis 27:20. 'How did you find it so quickly, my son?' 'The LORD your God gave me success.' Not only did the Bible appear to be directing him to do away with himself, it sounded a note of urgency, too! Alarmed, he gave up this hit-and-miss method, which was based on several serious misunderstandings.

Sadly, there have been Christians who have leaned way too much on their own interpretation of the Bible than they have on the unchanging, loving, powerful, eternal God who inspired it.

Beware of falling into the error of giving the Bible more honour than we should. The holy trinity isn't Father, Son and Holy Scriptures. Remember, we should make God himself our highest authority, because he desires that we have a relationship with him, through the Holy Spirit, on account of Christ's death on the cross.

Some of the mistakes people have made include over-emphasising one verse beyond others that provide a balancing view; or taking narrative and turning it into a command.

One example, which you may think is far-fetched, is a practice which regularly leads to people bursting through the doors at the A&E department of their local hospital. These are the Christians who spend time in their meetings deliberately handling poisonous snakes, in order to demonstrate the power of God, or even to display an outward sign of their faith for salvation. The verses they cite say:

> *And these signs will accompany those who believe…*
> *they will pick up snakes with their hands; and when they*
> *drink poison it will not hurt them at all.* Mark 16:17,18

I'd say this promise of protection is not best interpreted as a suggestion for what to do after the second hymn on a Sunday morning, although it might liven things up a bit! There's an incident in Acts 28:1-6 when Paul was adding kindling to a bonfire and a poisonous snake crawled out of the sticks and bit him; he calmly shook the snake from his hand (into the fire!) and continued helping. The people around watched to see if he would swell up or fall down but he did neither; they were so impressed they thought Paul was super-human, when actually, he was no more than God's man for the task.

Churches where snake-handling is practiced (mostly in the US) have reported more than ninety deaths from rattlesnake bites since the practice began in 1910. Who knows how many others were not reported, especially as the practice is illegal in most states? And how many hundreds of frantic dashes for anti-venom injections? The pain of a bite from a small rattlesnake is described thus: 'It's like having your hand on fire, and every time your heart beats, you take a hammer and put the fire out – and you do that for several weeks. The best way to learn about snakebites is through experience. Someone else's.'

Surely the Bible is reminding us that God will protect us miraculously when disaster strikes and is not suggesting we should deliberately put ourselves in harm's way as a kind of test or in some attempt to add a sense of adventure to matins.

Consider this: when the Devil was tempting Jesus in the wilderness (Luke 4:1-12) the evil one accurately quoted from Psalm 91 'he will command his angels concerning you… you will not strike your foot against a stone'. Yet Jesus didn't throw himself confidently off the temple roof. Instead, he stated the command 'Do not put the LORD your God to the test' (quoting Deuteronomy 6:16, which refers to an incident of angry defiance). However, God does invite us to test him when it comes to generous giving – but that's another story; an issue more concerning financial risk and less to do with daredevil stunt work. Check out Malachi 3:10.

Taking isolated Bible verses and building not only theology but specific practices upon them is unwise. Some have ended up being exclusive, reverting to religious rites from Judaism, or trying to calculate exactly when to expect Christ's return.

Probably, these errors began in a sincere effort to be obedient to the Word, but unhelpful emphases were being developed and false doctrines took over. Wisdom reflects on hearing 'the whole counsel of God' (i.e. ask if other verses support your interpretation) and on ensuring that the person and work of Jesus Christ takes precedence over other issues.

A wise preacher I heard taught that if you discover, during your studies, a new practice or a new doctrine, read on, because you almost certainly haven't. I know that sounds rather dismissive, but I think his point was to emphasise that the Bible is a commentary on itself, helping us check that we're not drifting off the point.

Finally, here are some questions about the Bible to ask yourself.

- When did I last read any of it?
- Did I understand it?
- Has God spoken to me through the Bible?
- Do I give first priority to the person and work of Jesus Christ?
- Is the Bible more important to me than other books?
- Is it my final authority?
- Do I ask the Holy Spirit for his help to interpret it?
- What colour is the cover?
- Where on earth did I leave it?

5 Yuletide for Raluces

with apologies to CS Lewis

Once upon a quite recent time on an island not far away, there are two nations living in one country; in almost every way they are identical and thus are just one people. But in one important respect they are very different indeed. The nation called *Raluces* has a much bigger population than the other, which is known by the name *Lufthiaf*.

For the first half of each year, both nations enjoy relative peace and prosperity, family love and general harmony. Commercial outlets provide food, clothes, electrical goods, hobby and specialist interest products, home furnishings, art, books, music, travel agency and pharmaceuticals. There are also restaurants, pubs and hotels.

But during their summer holidays, the Raluces begin preparations for their major festival, known by the name *Xmas*. Most of the shops are filled with tinsel, lights and special off-catalogue expensive items, called 'gifts', many of which are badly manufactured and all of which are unwanted.

The appointed time draws closer and the Raluces harvest a combination of wood and rag to make paper products called 'cards', which they send in the post to their friends and relatives; each person sends many cards and each person receives many.

The laws concerning cards are strict: it is a matter of honour to have a longer card list than anyone else you know; each person must send a card to every other person on their list; but if any member of the Raluces nation receives a card from someone to whom he has not sent a card, he must quickly send one or face ritual humiliation and disrespect.

Then comes the season for the giving of gifts; if one is received, the value of that gift must quickly be calculated and one of similar or greater value returned. However, if the gift received is of less value than those exchanged the previous year, this is noted and revenged.

The Raluces are contrary – they are a religious people and they take the celebration of Xmas seriously, claiming it's 'for the children'. They tell a simple and sanitised tale of a baby, a mother and the cleanest stable filled with animals, straw, a choir and pleasant aromas. The narrative ends with visits from working-class yokels mixing with three kings. The meaning of the tale is obscured; any power it may once have had is diluted with unrelated images of robins, puddings, fir-trees, snowmen and holly. The moral (apparently) is that we should give, out of guilt, to charity and turn for consolation to nostalgic entertainment.

Children are told about a bearded foreign stranger who will break into their homes in the dead of the night (as promoted by a fizzy-drink manufacturer) to consume pies and alcohol. This fills them not, as one might imagine, with dread, but with hope, for he also is supposed to leave presents for them. This includes the traditional citrus fruit at the toe of a sock, which is a great comfort.

When the special day approaches, Raluces invite all their relatives to join them and there is great feasting and drunken excess. The gods of gluttony and intoxication are worshipped from dawn until dusk and way beyond, with Xmas-unique food with names like WhiteMeat, Cranber Esorz, No-One-Likes-Prouts, Goo-Sphatroasties, and Xmas Pudding-Wi-Coy-Nzin and Bran-Deebuht-Ah. The five Chief Priests – *NatWest, Lloyd, Aitchessbeecee, Barclay,* and *ArBeEss* – burn incense all day and all night to provide for the celebration.

The high priests, known by strange names like *Tesco, Emaness, Gamblies* and *Oddbins*, ensure that the Raluces nation have all they need for the time of celebration. *Asda, BHS, ToysRUs, Thresher* and other associates serve alongside them with seasonal competitiveness and selected special offers. At this time, acolytes called Plasticard, Never-Never and Payday Loan dance and clap their hands with merriment despite embracing blinkered irresponsibility.

Once the celebrations end, some Raluces make humble penance for their indulgence, although for many it has the appearance of simple regret. Some emphasise their foolishness by worshipping the graven idol Hairothedog and others abase themselves, meekly kneeling at the bowl-throne of *Alka-Seltzer*. A few make sacrifices, perhaps dedicating themselves to Januarydiet or even Fitness-ClubMembership.

The Lufthiaf, on the other hand, do not bow down and worship those false idols, although they take some advantage of the provision of the high priests, since their special feast-day is at exactly the same time of year as Xmas. They also invite their families to gather and they also eat and drink and celebrate all day. But their festivities are entirely less fleshly. They give honour to a god who, say some, seems to be less powerful than the gods of gluttony and drunkenness, or is at least worshipped in a different way.

Their god, apparently, does not have a name, just a capital letter; he is called God. Lufthiaf also have a tale about a baby and his mother and downbeat lodgings, but they lack belief in the much more exciting legends. They fail to place importance or emphasis upon the weather, birds with feathers of vermillion hue, prickly evergreens and climbing Hedera, or a ghostly character called Jacob Marley. Instead, they sing of other characters called Gloria, Noel and Joy Totheworld.

They are undoubtedly aware of the small boy in a dressing gown who flies away with a cartoon snowman to meet the foreign stranger who breaks into Raluces homes to hide satsumas in hosiery during the night, but they consider this a harmless fable about generosity.

Their so-called 'far-fetched' stories are of symbolic gifts which are not child-friendly; of pregnant women and over-booked hotels; of astronomical signs and God taking the vulnerable form of a baby, brought into impoverished circumstances. In their celebrating they remember the poor, visit the sick, provide for the elderly and invite friends to sing, wearing festive woollen garments.

Once, a prominent Lufthiaf man was asked 'Since your festival is so different from the jollifications of the Raluces, why do you risk having them muddled by celebrating on the same day?'

'Ah, now that's a good question,' replied the Lufthiaf man. 'True to tell, we have always held our festivities on that day, since way back in the mists of time. The Raluces were fewer in number then. But they have grown vastly and our multitudes have reduced; they have hijacked our feast-day and made it Xmas (a name which means little to them: probably they reckon it a day for kisses, for mysteries, for buried treasure… perhaps even for things going wrong).

'We even considered cancelling our festival, or combining it with our other special day, which we call Easter (the Raluces have made this into Retsae, the Chocolate Egg/Hot Bunny spring holiday). But on reflection, we felt it best to continue.'

'What do you call the day we Raluces call Xmas?'

'We call it Christmas.'

'May I ask why you use a name so similar?'

'Because we know the God whom we worship: his name is Christ.'

Do your Yuletides resemble those of the Raluces (seculaR) tradition, or a God-honouring celebration of Lufthiaf (faithfuL) folk?

6 Naan can compare

currying favour

When some dear friends had a child, I became aware of a rota so that others from the church family could offer to provide meals for them. This took pressure off mundane chores like shopping and cooking, helping the new parents to focus on the child and each other, at least for the first couple of weeks. I managed to muscle in – the rota was only circulated among other parents, since it was (inaccurately) assumed they were more likely to know how helpful this might be.

I suppose the list comprised mostly people who could cook or had time to cook, so they were used to knocking our dinners for their family. And not the people my friends usually hung out with, went to restaurants with or shared takeaways with.

Having seen who was on the rota, I realised that my dear friends would very likely be inundated with extremely well-meaning dishes such as lasagne, cottage pie, tuna bake and moussaka. They'd be grateful that they didn't have make a meal for themselves, but I suspected they'd be craving something a little tastier. I wasn't going to cook for them, but I knew a man who can and I was prepared to finance the treat. So, I wrote this menu and waited on my rostered evening.

FANCY A FREE CURRY?

USE THE DELIVERY SERVICE

PROVIDED BY BIRMINGHAM'S ANTI-LASAGNE LEAGUE

Available only on Friday 12th November 2010

Please call between 6pm & 6.30pm for delivery by 7.15pm

Delhi Belli Andhi Tandoori

0121 405 7194

All meals cooked freshly to order and delivered to your door within a reasonable time by our highly-trained and friendly staff.

Free popadums with every order

Chicken

Our hens are hand-reared in air-filled barns and fed from time to time. They spent their short but plump lives roaming freely along the 3½″ dowelling carefully styled for their use. Any eggs that are laid are used for hatching. All dishes made with breast meat at no extra cost to the chicken.

Beef

All our cows are worshipped morning and night and fitted with special woollen udder-cosies for the harsh winter months.

Lamb

Young spring lambs are permitted to gambol as far as they desire to do so for the first few months of their lives. Then they are lovingly gathered in, using only gentle caresses of a cattle prod, transported by luxury coach to AberTwah, a pretty resort in Wales, where they are slightly killed in the most pleasant ways. Their carcasses are carefully marinaded in rich, spiced unctions and returned to our kitchens for inclusion in your meal. You may be assured that no lamb curry is ever served from our kitchens with lamb flesh more than seventeen hours dead, which means the flavour, texture and mouth-feel of the meat is at the very peak of perfection.

Our motto: *'For the Balti that almost says Baa-aa-alti'*

Prawns

Our prawns are pink, small and delicate, while our King Prawns are of Royal Blood by Divine Right. The Lord Himself hath ordained it; dare you risk eating them? Please note: any injuries caused by thunderbolts are not covered by most house contents insurance policies.

Garlic

Only vegetarian, gluten-free garlic cloves are grown here, hand-picked, gently broken from the bulb, skinned and lightly sliced or humanely crushed to provide enhancement of flavour to the food on your plate.

Tomato

Only approved full-flavour plum tomatoes; none of those 7p tins of tasteless red water with sloppy lumps from well-known sub-standard supermarkets.

Coriander

Peshawari, dhansak, Coca-Cola, parsley, rosemary, I'll have an advocaat, make mine a Malibu, wi' a chaser Lagavulin. And a popadum. Have you got a Suzuki? Bring it in a Mitsubishi or on a Yamaha. Speaking in tongues a speciality of the house.

Peppers & Chillies

We're fans of the Scoville scale, rating Jalapeño Peppers 3000units Bird's Eye Chillies 50,000units Scotch Bonnets 150,000units and Ghost Peppers 1,300,000units.

A broad selection of dishes for your enjoyment or courageous indulgence

Tandoori

Cooked to perfection; dark red in colour combined with an appropriate charring. Pleasure confidently assured. Naan bread accompaniment is traditional.

Tikka

Meat firmly roasted on the most tenderly-inserted of spits.

Balti

Steel, with two handles, sturdy in construction. Food: over-rated.

Bhuna

Tender, aromatic, warm and very profitable for us. Recommended.

Korma

Vanishingly mild, for the feeble.

Biryani

Chicken with rice & spice; 'when a korma is too fiery for you'.

Shashlique

Our variation of the traditional skewered meat and peppers tandooré-style-continentale.

Madras

Hot & sour; disguises beyond-best-before meat rather well.

Vindaloo

Napkins provided to soak up sweat. Upsettingly powerful: awarded three Rolls in the *BurnsUTwice (Paper from the Fridge) Fiery-Food To Make You Cry* Championships.

Phall

Painphully, ludicrously **hot** and scovilletastically **spicy**. Utterly unphorgettable. Free, if you're able to finish it. Prohibited for persons with a dodgy tikka.

Other main course dishes available; please enquire.
Mild Curry • Jalfrezi • Nawab • Dopiaza • Sagwala
Dhansak • Korai • Kulchari • Pasanda • Pathia • Rogan Gosht, etc.

Side dishes

Make it up as you go along. Most things are permissible, even if they are neither pleasant nor recommended.

Select from: Ladies' fingers • Old man's beard • Tarka dhal • Egg-plant • Brinjal • Aubergine • Baby panda tongue in warm brine (with devilled banana garnish) • Spatchcocked elephant tusk steamed in rose water • Ugli fruit duff boiled in Ghandi's loincloth • Young Punjabi orphan's toenail • Bengal tiger eye on a skewer • Frogspawn knickerbocker glory with hundreds and thousands • Sautéd koala claw with dill & molasses • Raven & baby carrot compote in onion gravy • Habanero & Jalapiño paté with extra ghost chilli • Panther sweat jelly • Fillet mignon wellington…

Rice dishes

Egg fried rice • Pilau rice • Plain boiled rice • Mushroom fried rice • Rice with peas • Rice with coriander • Rice with spinach • Coconut rice • Chef's special fried rice • Chicken fried rice • Lamb fried rice • Rice with extra rice • Rice cakes • Boil in the bag rice

Bread etc

Plain naan • Peshawari naan • Cheese naan • Garlic naan • Double garlic naan • Keema naan • Chilli cheese naan • Naan of the above • Chronicles of Naania • Chapati • Dosa • Puri • Paratha

English menu

Plain omelette with chips • Fried button mushroom omelette with chips • Ham omelette with chips • Spam fritter with chips • Avocadoburger with asparagus and chips • Baconbananaburger with cheesy chips • Turkey twizzlers with chips and beans • Chicken nuggets with onion rings • Battered sausage in a bun

Drinks

One cool bottle (or can) of fizzy Lager is provided *free of charge* with every main dish ordered. Diet Coke, Pepsi Max, Mountain Dew, Fanta, 7up, Sprite, Irn Bru, Fresca, Dandelion & Burdock, R Whites Lemonade also available

Afters

A slab of Cadbury's chocolate is provided *free of charge* with every order. State preference: Bubbly • Caramel • Crunchie • Mint • Bournville • Turkish Delight • NEW Double Choc or pure, straight CDM just as the good Lord originally intended.

Say *thank you but begone*
(just for a night) to dull, healthy & strict-control portions
and lather into hot spices and the genuine tastebudburn
of the mysterious Orient

Korma & Praise the Living God

**If the dish you require is not listed,
then please go without.
Be aware that a smack in the mouth often offends,
and you don't have to be helpful to work like mad,
or something. Service is FREE**

7 Time for a conversation

talking to God and listening, too

I discovered a number of important things about praying a few years ago when I faced a horrible set of circumstances and I felt the strong desire to talk about it. I was in need of someone who would understand how I felt, who wouldn't stop being my friend or get bored (even though I was very focused on one topic during this period), who wouldn't judge me for being in an agitated state and who cared for me enough to let me rave and rant – at least until I had expressed myself.

I had to get things off my chest. It was so significant to me, so painful, so undermining to my self-esteem and wellbeing. Having to try to explain myself to another person didn't work, because I realised all too quickly that they were likely to be forming an opinion or getting ready with 'a helpful answer' or 'wise advice' long before I'd finished telling them about how sad and defeated I felt.

I wasn't seeking pity or criticism or sympathy or some clever solution or sage suggestion. I didn't want my friends to have a reason to have their opinion of me lowered, and pride kept me from telling them everything I was feeling, since some of it was rebellious or emotional or angry and perhaps immature and certainly rooted in insecurity. Can you tell that my stability had been dealt a serious blow?

But I knew that God was certainly big enough and tough enough to cope with me, and that really, only he would be able to provide any comfort. A number of close friends did their best, but their ability to help was limited and I feared they might fail me or run out of steam. Some of my best friends understood very little of what I was feeling, but they were willing to stand with me, knowing I needed to vent my anger, sadness and disappointment, without trying to soothe me or correct me. They had enough faith in me to play the long game, knowing that if I had the opportunity to express how I felt, then the worst may pass.

Fortunately, no-one was stupid enough to peddle the lie 'time heals all wounds'. I fear I might have attempted to show them how wrong they were by inflicting a permanent wound on them.

God never resorts to shallow or vapid platitudes or easy solutions. He understood, thoroughly empathised, honoured the reality of the sadness and rejection I was experiencing and was angry about and my heavenly Father chose to draw near with perfect love and sincerity. He also has the sensitivity and the authority to tell me 'enough!' when there was danger of me overdoing it.

The depth of passion did recede after a time. Similar to all significant bereavement, the loss and sadness remain, ready to spring up with those grieving feelings, but they stop being all-day-every-day and subside in regularity, if not intensity.

One very wise remark a pastorally gifted friend made to me was to acknowledge 'if we can just carry on like nothing has happened, it suggests even our deepest relationships are impoverished'. I held on to that, knowing the feelings I was experiencing sprang from a deep place within me and so couldn't be expected to be shrugged off. It was okay to be upset. There would come a time to move on, but there was no need to rush or belittle my feelings or pretend to myself that I felt fine or to everyone else that there had never been a problem.

To be surrounded by such caring, wonderful friends did me the power of good and they helped me more than I can say. I returned to my Bible very quickly and to a much more polite form of address to my heavenly father.

But in the meanwhile, praying with this level of honesty and emotion was a new experience for me and something of a dangerous experiment, too. You see, I grew up learning by observation that prayer was a sort of ritual where you used old-fashioned language to talk to God, who only really started to hear you after you'd been going for a few minutes and only then if your theology was watertight and your phrases well-chosen: 'Oh, our most gracious and eternal heavenly Father and our God, who hath sent thy only begotten son, our Lord Jesus Christ, to live providing an example and to lay down his life in our place; whose blood hath been shed for us upon the cross and who hath been raised again to newness of life by the mighty power of thy Holy Spirit, we do most fervently beseech thee, incline thou thine holy ear to thy humble servant and listen unto mine heart's cry…' etc.

No-one specifically taught me to pray like this, you understand, but it's what I heard in church week after week, so it kind of stuck.

And I'd been at a few prayer meetings where it seemed the emphasis was more on showing-off your flowery, impressive prayer-language to one another than on talking to a loving, generous, personal God.

As a child, I was told in all seriousness (and with the best of intentions) that to use the Authorised Version style of language when speaking to

God demonstrated to him that you held him in high honour and had taken the trouble to learn how to speak to him. The result was, I thought, that God was supposed to be chuffed that you'd bothered to talk to him using ancient grammar and verb-endings long since abandoned by regular, sensible English-speaking folks. Obediently, I was prepared to learn how to speak like this, so I enquired about the proper times and places to use *thee, thou, wilt, verily, doth* and *hath* but it seemed that the rules were long-forgotten. 'Just do your best,' I was told. God is impressed when we try hard, I reckoned. Thus, prayer became not only a foreign language, but also an attempt to please God.

Sadly, I was still a very long way from understanding anything about God and his attitude towards me…

Anyway, among those who had praying experience, they could hardly wait for each other to finish so that they could contribute their two-pennyworth.

It made my head spin the way some ancient saint might pray for the missionaries in Africa (nothing specific, just 'uplifting them before thee') and then someone else would remind God that we needed good weather for the Sunday School Outing and then another person thanked the Lord for their mother's bunions not aching so much this week, only to be followed by an enthusiastic prayer for revival.

'We cry unto thee, O merciful God, rend the very 'eavens (look you) and pour down a flood of r-r-r-r-reeevi-i-i-i-val upon this wicked and perverse land of ours, isn't it!' – you had to be there to hear it said properly, in ringing Welsh tones with all the accompanying theatrical arm gestures.

This seemed like a shopping list of requests (demands?) and didn't make much room for asking politely, let alone worshipful acknowledgement of God's kindness. Everyone had made their plans and was now, finally, it seemed, asking God to rubber-stamp them with a blessing of sunshine or pain-free feet or mass conversions.

And there was usually a bit of a competition to think of things that the almighty, eternal, omniscient Creator might have somehow forgotten.

One person might pray for next Sunday's church meeting (obviously), another may chip in asking assistance for the preacher (worthy but predictable, although I always reckoned the people who could do with perseverance and long-suffering was the congregation) and then a third pray-er happily trumps everyone with a request for large crowds and loud singing.

I've also been in prayer meetings where silence reigned and nobody prayed at all. Someone once called this 'quietly praying to yourself' but I always thought that was a bit sacrilegious; surely prayers are directed towards God? I think the reality was that we were either waiting for someone to speak, or praying for the leader to end the prayer time! It was all rather painful and benefitted nobody. However, times of quietly waiting on God and sharing what he says are of eternal value.

Spectacles are usually removed for prayer (NB I know the Bible says something about hats, but I'm not sure facial furniture gets a mention), to allow the pray-er to 'hold the pose'. For this, there are two stages.

Beginners simply pinch the bridge of their nose with thumb and forefinger, with the rest of the fingers splayed out or as if taking tea in bone china cups with an elderly aunt. This is righteous enough. But mature Christians progress to spanning the full width of their eyebrows. One's measure of holiness was proportional to the distance between thumb and forefinger, then?

There was an even more spiritual prayer pose (let's call it *phase three*), often used by those known to be 'full-on charismatics'. This term referred to anyone who knew more than a dozen of the new 'choruses' by number, which gave them a significant advantage when we were singing, since so many worship times (in the days before worship leaders) were structured according to the rules of Praise Bingo – a style of vox pop song selection, shouting out the song numbers in popular chorus books). As I was saying, Phase Three was the 'washing your face' move, which involves removal of the specs (natch) and then clamping both palms onto the cheeks, with the fingers gently massaging the forehead. The pose fell into disuse after the release of the film *Alien* (1979), because it was reminiscent of the creature that leapt out of the egg-thing onto John Hurt's face, only to emerge a little later from his ribcage during dinner.

The only time I saw the pose briefly revived was when a dear friend used a single-handed version of it to produce impressively loud hand farts from his eye socket, which was both entertaining and rather disconcerting. You might have guessed this hugely gifted chap has gone on to church leadership.

I seem to have become distracted...

These are also the kinds of prayer meeting that end when you lift your head and look around to check if everyone else is still 'eyes down' or if they too are checking the pupil-visibility factor. It's inappropriate to make actual eye-contact with someone during this important checking time, since that would show them that you've noticed they've stopped praying, which is an implied criticism.

I have to admit that I have sometimes been a little naughty (almost impossible to imagine, I agree, but hear my confession). One prayer time was far from over when I gained eye contact with a particular friend who also happened to have his eyes open way too early. I tilted my head at him and looked down in a way to make him think I was indicating that his flies were open. He couldn't resist the temptation to check. Of course, everything was firmly zipped and he realised I had hoodwinked him and then we both got the giggles and it all was really rather immature and silly.

Even more foolish (and perhaps I should say that I'm embarrassed to be admitting this one, since it was not only disrespectful to a prayer meeting, but also to some continental friends) is the Portuguese story. Here's what happened.

It was an evangelism afternoon at an international evangelism conference in a British seaside resort. We had been teamed up to approach holidaymakers and complete a survey/questionnaire, with the goal of having a conversation about Jesus. English-speakers would take the lead when asking the questions, and delegates from all over Europe would tag along and join in when and/or if they were able, which was a brave thing for them to do.

I was assigned to be with some other English-speakers and with a group from Portugal. Now, none of us English-speakers spoke any Portuguese – *Eusébio? Benfica!* was about my limit* – so it was shocking and shaming that these folk from so far away spoke such excellent English. At least, it was certainly sufficient for them to communicate with us.

Perhaps they would have struggled in an evangelistic discussion (and they certainly felt nervous about that), but otherwise they did pretty well. So, having had a reasonable conversation about all of this, we turned to a prayer time.

---

* Eusébio da Silva Ferreira played football for Benfica and Portugal, winning the Golden Boot for scoring nine goals in the 1966 World Cup. Benfica famously lost 4-1 to Manchester United after extra time in the final of the 1968 European Cup.
Other Portuguese words I knew, but wasn't aware they were Portuguese: *albatross, albino, banana, baroque, breeze, buffalo, caramel, cashew, cobra, coconut, commando, cougar, embarrass, fetish, indigo, jaguar, junk, labrador, lacquer, marimba, marmalade, molasses, monsoon, mosquito, potato, savvy, tank, tapioca, teak, verandah, vindaloo, zebra.*

I was thinking more about the encounters we would have on the streets than about the language issues.

Anyway, I and one or two other English-speakers prayed and then the leader of the Portuguese group took his opportunity. His command of English, like I say, was excellent, but his confidence to lead in prayer wasn't quite up to the mark, so he prayed in Portuguese. It was the obvious thing to do, since all the other Portuguese-speakers would be able to follow along. He began pouring his heart out to God, getting faster, louder and more intense; his fellow-countrymen were clearly loving it, eagerly agreeing with his requests.

Now, the truth is, I was so self-centred and parochial that I gave in to feeling excluded. Please remember, this was a long time ago; I was young and foolish. These days, I am neither. Although I am foolish.

Unfortunately, I made my key mistake at that moment. I opened my eyes and frowned slightly at the Portuguese bloke, who was still going at full pelt, punching the air, determined to batter on the doors of heaven until he had got through on whatever he was praying about.

I caught the eye of another of the English-speakers. She was similarly lost and bewildered by this situation. We exchanged a glance, a brief smile and then looked away.

I decided to try to make the best of it and feign spirituality. I tuned in to the other Portuguese-speakers' agreements with the prayer, since they followed a similar tonal pattern to ours – grunts, uh-huh, *sim* (Portuguese for 'yes'), m'mm. It was the same selection of barnyard noises heard in prayer meetings the world over.

So, I started to join in, seeming like I knew what was being prayed. In truth, part of me was overcoming the sense of boredom/exclusion, because there were also elements of *I'm trying to concentrate here* and making some attempt at being encouraging to the bloke who was praying, by expressing trust in him.

I was pretty confident that he'd be asking God for things I'd agree with, such as good weather, worthwhile conversations, Holy Spirit presence, excellent communication, expressions of concern for people, showing them the love of Jesus, being able to challenge them and speak truth and being friendly and winsome, perhaps having time for an ice cream, definitely be home in time for dinner – nothing wrong there, surely?

My grunting and *yes, mmm, sim* noises grew more intense and then I made my second tactical blunder. I accidentally opened my eyes again and saw that several of the English speakers were staring at me, some in disbelief and others with wide grins. Of course, we all started giggling, silently snorting and chuckling while Cabelero, PorFavour and their mate Obrigado continued pleading for souls.

It was not a particularly grown-up way to behave.

Perhaps pay-back time (some might call it) came a few years later when I found myself in Denmark on a brief tour of speaking engagements. In general, most Danes speak fantastically good English. I was booked to address a number of groups of Danish pastors, which was a great honour for me and quickly discovered they were fluent in English. In Danish schools, English is taught at a high standard from an early age, so I was able to speak and preach willy-nilly. For the very few who needed my pearls turned into Danish, this was also provided by a woman who was skilled at simultaneous translation.

Cue the moment when I used my brilliant gag about Noah being a good Jewish boy, yet he called his son *Ham*. Those who understood English laughed at the sparkling wit, but not the small number who were listening to the translator – theirs was a confused silence… followed by a laugh, after a rather long pause. Afterwards, I asked the translator about this and she explained that the Danish word for Noah's son *ham* doesn't sound a bit like the Danish word for cured pork, or indeed any kosher food at all. Puns, she said, giving me a hard stare, almost never work in translation.

This explained the confused silence, but not the later chuckle. I asked her why her audience responded that way. She sheepishly explained she had covered for me by making some remark about 'stupid English joke', and that had gained her the late laugh at my expense. I was sufficiently ashamed of my foolishness that I even resisted the temptation to tell her to stop building her part up. My embarrassment at making a schoolboy error double underlined (do you see what I did there?) my determination to avoid such incongruities.

My language skills were still utterly pathetic. Yes, like most people, I could praise God when the fizzy drinks arrive, wherever in the world they happened to be – *Hallelujah, Coca-Cola!* – but that was my limit. I did try to learn to say a few things in Danish during the course of my trip, but after my first attempt, I was quietly taken aside and told that the words I had uttered had a Swedish accent, which was likely to cause considerable offense, especially in Copenhagen, so that was very nearly the last time I tried.

Nevertheless, I was determined to participate when I was in a gathering of theology students in Kolding. It's conceivable that my motives were slightly awry, since one of these high-powered post-grad students was spectacularly lovely, and I felt particularly drawn towards her... But I was also genuinely grateful to God for the opportunity I had been given to speak to them since they were strategically significant characters within their denomination.

We stood in a circle to pray together and off they went, full speed and top volume, in Danish, crying out to Almægtig (God, obviously). By this time, I was familiar with the Danish habit of adding to the farmyard noises of agreement with an *I strongly concur* sharp intake of breath. I did my best to concentrate, but the prayers were unintelligible and all I could do was hope there had been some impartation of what I had spoken about. Listening to each of them pray with conviction, I felt a strong desire to participate. So, I wracked my brain for some way of doing so and I realised I could probably muster 'Lord, Thank you, Amen' in Danish. Oh yes, I was fluent indeed!

I chose my moment and went for it. '*Herr, mange tak, Amen,*' I said, with not a lot of confidence, but a genuine sincerity. It was the right words, strung together. I couldn't be sure if my grammar was right, or even if I'd used the correct forms of address. I was certain my pronunciation was more Benny Andersson (the bloke from *Abba*, fiercely Swedish) than Hans Christian Andersen (famously Danish).

But I'd made the effort and knew that God had heard me, interpreted my intention and was satisfied. He was a loving Father in Heaven, delighted at his much-loved son.

Of course, it broke up the prayer time with ribald laughter and sympathetic noises. To this day, no-one has explained what I did wrong, but I'm guessing my tone, pronunciation and vocabulary selection in that context was sadly rather clumsy. Ho hum. I still maintain that God knows my heart was right.

The good outcome was that the pretty girl student took more than a little pity on me, with comforting words of reassurance. The group went for dinner afterwards, which was highly delightful in addition to being relaxingly easy on the eye. Even better, all conversations were in English. I like to imagine she still thinks warmly of me from time to time, and of my theologically solid downtown Gothenburg twang ...

But enough of foreign languages and distractingly attractive Bible College students; back to the prayer meeting.

Closing in prayer is always tricky. Sometimes, the leader will attempt a summary prayer and may even end with the 'grace' together:

> *May the grace of the Lord Jesus Christ, the love of God,*
> *and the fellowship of the Holy Spirit be with us all,*
> *now and forevermore. Amen* 2 Corinthians 13:14, amended

This always makes me feel hungry. But there are some folk who don't even pick up that remarkably obvious signal, starting up all over again after we've done the doxology. Once this has happened, I suppose you might try to revisit 'the grace', but there's a danger that the person who failed to read the signal will feel criticised (quite rightly) and you don't want to do that in a prayer-time. Disappointing, especially when you took the trouble to plan ahead.

Sometimes it's possible to engineer obvious end-moments before you start, by discussing a list of prayer requests and then proceeding through the list. Once we've ticked them all off, we're done. Simples. But more often, it's a running-out-of-steam silence that signals the end. It's not peaceful meditation, or waiting on God, or listening to his voice, like they say in the prayer seminars. This is just fizzling out; nothingness. When that empty, resounding, nervous and awkward prayer-free silence has become too uncomfortable to bear any longer, someone (preferably a person whose leadership gift is recognized) should shift their bottom on the chair or clear their throat or say 'amen' in an authoritative way. Then everyone can surface with a flawless conscience. Spectacles are replaced on faces, because the lenses are engraved with the letters AM on one lens and EN on the other.

At this point, the meeting usually becomes reasonably animated once more, suggesting we were embarrassed to be praying together, but it's alright again now we're just chatting.

~

Then came this season I mentioned earlier, when I needed to tell God how I felt, due to the horrible context in which I found myself.

It wasn't self-pity; this was a genuinely painful collection of circumstances and emotional reactions that needed to be expressed to the only one who could do anything about it; my Father in heaven. Could it be that I was discovering the Biblical practice of *lament*?

I spent quite a lot of time that summer and autumn just walking on the beach late at night talking to God. Sometimes I would shout, often through tears, fairly frequently throwing stones. Anyone observing me must have thought I was one of those sad, weird people who wander around ranting! They would surely have been right.

But I found it so helpful to unburden my heart before God; praying words, rather than just praying silently in my head. Speaking aloud helped me concentrate, made me ensure I was being genuine and it was also good to be able to shout or cry or whisper tenderly or whatever.

I deeply needed to know that God took my prayers seriously and I certainly felt that I got through to him. The spiritual reality?

You keep track of all my sorrows.
You have collected all my tears in a bottle.
You have recorded each one in your book. Psalm 56:8 NLT

God keeps a count of the hairs on my head – an-ever decreasing statistic, admittedly, but despite this I'm still not bothered about the exact number. God's compassion for me when I'm out-of-sorts extends so far that he preserves the saltwater droplets my eyes generate and saves them. This is unfailing love!

I can't be precise about the answers to my prayers, since I didn't ask for detailed specific things, like good weather or evangelistically-blessed missionaries. But the object of all that exercise was to express myself to my heavenly Father and know that he had heard the honest cry of my heart. My circumstances were unchanged (horrible, like before), but they were more bearable, knowing the Lord was walking protectively and comfortingly alongside me through the valley of the shadow (Psalm 23:4).

Now when I pray, I try to avoid using old-fashioned words or clichéd phrases. And I've stopped trying to out-guess God or make suggestions about how to achieve something, which presumes he'd not thought of it. I express how I feel about life and tell God what I'd like to happen. When I'm at my best, I use phrases from the Lord's prayer about God's will and his kingdom reigning on earth, plus the repentant bits about trespasses and the lunch request. I know he's sovereign and that he alone has the power.

So, I pray, and leave the results to God.

I'm sometimes pleased, occasionally flabbergasted and always conscious of his hand at work. And often surprised at how worthwhile prayer meetings turn out to be.

8 The wrong guy?

CV for Moses *Exodus 2:11 – 4:17*

On the face of it, Moses was a poor choice for leader of the Israelites. I mean, check out his CV.

First of all, he was, to all intents and purposes, a member of the ruling classes, an enemy of the Israelites and a symbol of all that was unjust and cruel about life in that part of the world at that time. He had been brought up benefitting from the opulent wealth and splendour of the Egyptian royal court, like a grandson of the Pharaoh. All the other Israelites were in appalling, backbreaking slavery to Egyptian masters. It must have wound them up big time to see Moses' manicured fingernails and neatly-trimmed beard, while they had to make bricks from straw and mud, and later manage with just mud. Did he not realize the antagonism this must have been storing up against him? Had he no leadership sensitivities at all?

Secondly, look at his choice of a wife. He'd been one of a handful of male children to survive the purge (consider Exodus 1:22 and then look at Matthew 2:16). So, years later, the population was a little imbalanced: there were a lot of Israeli women with just a handful of potential husbands. It would have been highly appropriate for Moses to choose an Israelite girl or maybe more than one, since that was an acceptable custom in these parts at that time. But no, he married a foreigner named Zipporah, from the neighbouring land of Midian! Moses gives another opportunity for his people to criticize him by this choice that apparently disregarded the needs of his nation.

Once again, he seems to be maximizing his chances of being disliked, disrespected or downright hated by his countrymen. Future greatness does not appear to be on the cards, Mo.

And then there are his significant personality problems. His temper boiled over big-time when he saw an Egyptian taskmaster beating a slave and Moses lashed out, unthinking. He hoped he'd got away with murder, but when he was found out, he wasn't man enough to face his guilt. He ran away, becoming a fugitive from justice, with a shady past and left a shallow grave from which his crime could at any time rear up and hijack his political career.

And he was a poor choice for a public speaker, since he had a stutter. 'M… m… m… men of I… I… Is… Is… rael…' Brilliant.

Later, when he was being commissioned by Almighty God, he refused to do what God was asking. Disrespectful or what? He questioned God's promises.

I was told once that the phrase *No, Lord* is a contradiction in terms, because if God is Lord, then you don't say no to him. Saying no to someone suggests that you do not hold that person in authority over you. I'm not certain this 'rule' should be followed in every circumstance, but the principal is sound when the authority figure is perfect, holy and loving. After all, we were slaves to sin and now we're slaves to righteousness, to God himself. We should be ready and willing to obey him and do his will, not to turn around and say *I shan't do what you ask* – like a temperamental child defying a parent.

Moses stamped his foot on the sand and refused to obey.

In summary, then, Mo was not exactly the sort of bloke you want to lead the nation:

- brought up by the enemy (he was even mistaken for an Egyptian)
- lacking the political nous to marry one (or more?) of the many thousand nubile Israelite babes of his own age
- had no control of his temper, was violent and a murderer
- was under threat from his past
- was weak-willed, lily-livered chicken, running away from guilt
- and was hardly able to speak, except to turn round to Almighty God with the bush blazing merrily before him and say 'n… n… n…no'!

What on earth did God think he was playing at when he appointed Moses to be leader of the people of Israel?

However, we must be careful, because God sees past the surface; the Lord looks on the heart (see 1 Samuel 16:7).

Sometimes, God selects his warriors from those who seem the least likely, almost despite their faults. Consider Gideon, who initially hid from his enemy (Judges 6:11). Or David, who started out too small and weak to be able to stand once he'd been dressed for battle (1 Samuel 17:38,39). What about Saul of Tarsus? He was a self-righteous, intellectually arrogant, violent Pharisee seeking out believers in Jesus in order to execute them (Acts 8:3; 9:1).

Each of these unpromising chaps was central to the glorious plan God had for his people.

Gideon led a small but brave army in sensational victories. David famously defeated Goliath and went on to 'kill his tens of thousands'. Saul became Paul and preached grace and peace throughout Asia

Minor, establishing the early church in the power of the risen Christ, and standing up before monarchs and the might of Rome.

Each of these pivotal Bible characters underwent massive changes to become servants of God.

None of them were chosen because they were special, but each one was made special because they were chosen.

At other times, God's plan is so magnificent, so world-changing, that he organises circumstances over a number of generations to provide experiences and attributes in the men he is selecting.

In the case of Moses, God had clearly been planning his appointment to leadership for several generations.

Years before, Joseph irritated his brothers into selling him to slave traders; he survived imprisonment, making influential friends on the way; he interpreted Pharaoh's dream; he was raised to high office to save Egypt from famine; his people took up residence and multiplied there. Enough time passed for the rulers of Egypt to forget how beneficial Joseph's presence had been; all they saw was the vast number of Israelites and feared they might become too powerful, so they enslaved them. Eventually, they decreed that male Hebrew children should be killed at birth. Then came the bulrushes story and that's where we came in.

My point is that this was several generations of preparation, establishing the nations of Egypt and Israel before Moses could even appear, let alone develop his character ready to be God's chosen leader.

What God saw in Moses was a man who was passionate about his people. This showed itself immaturely in hot temper and violence, but later in his determination to see the nation released from slavery, which motivated him to continually return to stubborn Pharaoh to demand 'let my people go'.

Remember, this wasn't a lovely family meeting of a beloved adopted son twisting his old Pa around his finger; this was the leader of the slave-peoples defiantly insisting that they be set free, with nasty plagues turning up every time the despot King asserted what he thought was his authority.

And what God saw in Moses was a man who could identify with both Egyptians and Israelites. Who else could have gone into Pharaoh's court to bargain for his people? A slave? A mere shepherd? Chief mud-brickmaker to the royal household? No, God had established Moses to be Pharaoh's close relative.

Furthermore, what God saw in Moses was a man who had learned to be patient, prepared to ask repeatedly for his people's freedom. He was trained to look after the flock all day: a job which requires patience and determination – yes, occasional shows of strength towards hostile enemies, but mostly good pasture-spotting skills and the ability to stay awake when counting sheep.

And most of all, God saw a man willing to serve his people, and to be the sort of leader who knows how to serve. Pharaoh continuously imposed his will when he repeatedly said 'I shall not let your people go' and so the population of Egypt suffered ten plagues.

But Moses served his nation and served them some more and kept on serving despite the difficulties until God delivered them from their slavedriving enemies.

Are you a likely lad, or a girl most likely to succeed? Are you being prepared by God for some task he has for you? Maybe you are aware of weaknesses – a bit of a temper, or something in the past of which you're ashamed? Possibly you have a speech impediment or feel you're part of a minority. Or perhaps you've dabbled with unhelpful internet sites or you have a tendency to tell lies...

Remember, God looks into the deepest places and sees what's at the core of your being (bad and good). He can change the heart of the least promising character, just like Moses; God turned weaknesses into advantages.

Okay, so the chances are that you won't need to lead your nation out of slavery, with vast walls of water piled up on both sides, leaving you free to step forward across dry sand, muscles rippling and hair blowing in the wind, like Charlton Heston.

But on the other hand, perhaps you will, like Moses, rise above your weaknesses or the circumstances in which you find yourself, and obey God, serving him with a whole heart, fulfilling the plan he has for you.

I pray that you will.

Will you dare to pray that you will?

9 Riding the epact cycle

Easter

Easter's a funny sort of time of the year, isn't it? No, funny peculiar, I mean.

For a start, you never know when it's going to be. With Christmas, you can plan ahead: you know it'll be at the end of December (25th, every year, without fail, unless it's a leap year when it's – no, it's the same). Oh, except in Australia when it's hot and sunny and you have your turkey, stuffing and cranberry jelly sandwiches cold on the beach... no, that's the same date, too.

But Easter changes. It could be early (22nd March) or late (25th April), which is a range of more than six weeks. It can fall on any one of 35 dates. It's decided, you see, according to one or more of these factors: the phases of the moon; the Quintodeciman position; the Gregorian calendar; the dominical letter; metonical calculation; the golden number and the epact cycle. I kid you not.

All the above have to be taken into account. It would be so much simpler if we just settled on 10th April, for example. That would be straightforward, unmistakable, dependable and would need no special... but hang on, what if the 10th wasn't a Sunday? H'mm, okay.

Let's consider, then, the second Sunday in April. I realise it would be a different date each year, but it could only vary by six days. This way we can be certain Good Friday is indeed a Friday and it wouldn't be too hard to work out the date on which it falls.

We usually manage perfectly well identifying May Day (first Monday in May, even if this is the weekend after a late Easter) and the May Bank Holiday (last Monday in May).

However, just to be awkward, there is talk of moving May Day to October, which would even out Bank Holiday regularity a bit, but would be slightly confusing (someone should give thought to what name the new holiday gets, since *May Day* is clearly unhelpful and *October Day* doesn't rhyme).

By the way, the Easter issue is relatively simple, compared to the rules governing when Muslims start and finish observing Ramadan.

Their lunar-month-long period of strict daytime fasting and religious observance marches forward pretty relentlessly by eleven days each year (i.e. there is a gap of about forty-six weeks between the end of one and the start of the next), so that although it began in mid-May in 2018, it's coinciding with Easter in 2021. It will overlap Christmas in 2031-32 and 2063-65, just like it did in 1998 and previously in 1965, when daytime fasting began on Christmas Eve. That must be very awkward, especially in ethnically diverse households.

Anyway, to get back to Easter, it seems some church denominations actually are currently discussing the possibility of fixing Easter to the second Sunday in April, but so far it's merely a conversation. Some prefer the third Sunday in April and others are considering the Sunday after the second Saturday in April (presumably so that the festival retains its mysterious vibe). Watch this space.

Historically, of course, Easter lines up with the Old Testament festival of Passover, which was celebrated each year in the spring. At this time the Israelites remembered the night when God's angel passed over Egypt, killing the firstborn of each family, unless the house had been protected through the shedding of blood from a pure spotless lamb. This final plague also gave the Israelites the chance at last to leave. They escaped through the Red Sea and into the wilderness beyond (see Exodus 12:3-51). It was a night of terror for those who did not belong to God's people, but one of wonderful salvation for those who did.

God encouraged the Israelites to establish a regular reminder of this amazing miracle of redemption; we do well to have a similar discipline and remember how God sent his Son to shed his blood – an innocent, sinless lamb, dying so that we might live.

It may be helpful to add at this juncture that the Hebrew year started at Passover (springtime), usually in late March or early April, although their months broadly corresponded with what may appear to be astrological divisions. The month of Nissan comes at a similar time to Aries (I hope you're following this and not worrying about makes of car or male sheep) and Tishri falls during Libra. Of course, if the month of Adar ended before the barley was ripe, then Adar2 would begin and would be a leap month. Obviously.

For additional unfussiness, the number of the year related to the length of the rule of the king in power, no matter when that rule began. So, if someone ascended to the throne on the last day of the year (which might be 30th Adar, 30th of Adar2 or 30th of Elul), the next day was the start of his second year; but keep in mind that during the time of the books of 1 Kings and 2 Kings, the dates of the kings of one kingdom is given in terms of the year of reign of the king of the other kingdom, which may or may not clarify anything. Once all that is taken into account, of course, you can make your calculations accordingly.

On reflection, this system was probably more relevant to an agrarian community and made sense once you'd got used to it. I suspect people learned not to make plans until the issues were settled.

Anyway, we can be glad that the calendar is a lot more predictable for us in the West these days, but we have to admit that Easter's constantly changing date business makes it complicated for everyone.

Some years, the so-called Spring term at school is unbearably extended and drawn out, seeming never to end, all through the horrible weather which follows Christmas, ceaselessly going on and on without conclusion, making everyone bad-tempered and desperately aching for the holidays to arrive; during other years, it's a whole month longer, if you can believe it.

It's particularly rough if your birthday coincides with any of the possible Easter dates. Sometimes, your birthday falls on a holiday. But other years, it's slap in the middle of term-time. You can never guess and it's even more disappointing than the simple but harsh reality of knowing it'll almost always be on a school day, which is what most of us have had to face.

Observing Easter begins for some people way back on pancake day and then continues throughout Lent, with six extensive weeks of abstaining from rich food, sugary treats, luxury items, etc.

And Easter itself is a sort of stop-start thing too. Good Friday is a day that has deep significance: terrible betrayal, cruelty and abandonment, along with sadness and injustice combined in a powerful drama of purpose, nobility and wonderful love.

Easter Saturday, spiritually speaking, is a bit of a lull.

Then comes Easter Sunday with the splendour of the resurrection and the confirmation of Christ's identity and glory hallelujah when the celebrations begin. The angels announce that Christ is risen, the disciples run to the tomb and there's the shenanigans with the look-alike gardener. Thus, Christianity gets under way.

Unfortunately, this all fizzles out into Bank Holiday Monday, which seems completely unrelated, with a sale at B&Q, Homebase and Wickes (other out-of-town DIY warehouses are available). And so often, it rains.

Just like Christmas, Easter has become a confusing collection of hard-to-interpret symbols and rampant commercialism. Hundreds of tons of chocolate, rabbits, chicks, hot cross buns; plus bonnet parades, football fixtures, egg hunting; these are a long way from the reality of the first Easter in the same way that snowmen, tinsel, extra-gloomy editions of your favourite soap opera, robins and tins of Quality Street are distant from Christmas.

When I refer to tins, I mean of course a term implying the metal construction of (usually) cylindrical containers formerly made from aluminum, latterly from steel. Tins require use of a can-opener, except those containing colourfully-wrapped chocolates, shoe polish or petticoat tails, which were supplied in tins with replaceable lids of slightly larger circumferences than the rest of the tin. Also, gloss paint tins, cans of fancy speciality tea leaves and catering size tins of coffee granules have what's called a *double friction* lid of smaller circumference and are opened with a screwdriver or similar lever. Oil cans are very different, since they have a spout and a pump-trigger; and a can of drink (which once required a tin-opener having a curved triangular business-end with which the drinker punctured two holes – one to drink from and the other acting as a vent) now usually has a stay-on pull tab, although one particular brand of Australian lager is supplied in cans called *tinnies* or *toobs*. In the specific case of wrapped chocolates, all the brands currently supply them in plastic tubs.

This additional detail has been brought to you free of extra charge.

Anyway, returning to my theme, both the stable and the cross speak of rejection and humility; the star of Bethlehem and the three hours' darkness demonstrate God's intimate involvement with the circumstances; there was at least one Mary at each event, too.

Side note: it occurred to me the other day that with the names of the twelve tribes of Israel and the names of the twelve disciples, there a Levi in both lists. That is all.

And another thing about Easter is that it's physically bad for you. Hot cross buns are made using (among other things) fat and sugar, not to mention the lashings of melted butter or cheese or Nutella we have on ours. Chocolate eggs are packed with sugar and fat in addition to being disgracefully overpriced; so are those delicious crème eggs (how do you eat yours?) and the lovely little ones with the crunchy shells (like sugared almonds) you get in cornflake or popcorn nests; and so are the giant slabs of CDM.

Don't be fooled by the Swiss brands. Yes, it's true, you tend to eat less of it since they are thinner, more powerful slabs of dark chocolate with extra carob, packing a fine punch in the mouth and it's manufactured using a smaller proportion of sugar and/or cocoa butter, but it's still firmly in the indulgent luxury bracket.

When my parents suddenly realised the amount of unhealthy food we kids were scoffing at Easter, they decided to ban chocolate in our house at that time of year. They gave me a big bag of peanuts instead, in mistaken belief that this was (a) better for me and (b) equally symbolic of new life, resurrection, forgiveness and hope.

Some say a kilo of salt and grease is healthier than a kilo of sugar and grease. But it's a close call…

Neither made me quietly consider the scourging, crucifixion and death of Jesus or his resurrection to newness of life. The egg image is slightly too far removed from the cross image, in my view. It's not like Biblical symbols, which are of great value since they genuinely remind us of the truth they represent. Although it has to be said that a five-year-old friend recently explained the hollowness of Easter eggs by suggesting this was symbolic of the empty tomb; I was impressed.

Bread and wine, for example, give us cause to reflect on the last supper and the significance of Christ's sacrifice for us (see p158 for much more on this.) The image of fire representing the Holy Spirit can provide opportunities for reflection on God giving light and warmth, providing guidance and protection (the pillar of fire by night through the wilderness) or God being the power source for Elijah on Mount Carmel or for the apostle's gifts of boldness and courage when the Holy Spirit descended on them like tongues of fire…

Peanuts, on the other hand, have no Biblical significance.

What does a peanut signify? *Peanuts,* the Charlie Brown cartoon; Georgia is the peanut state, on account of producing so many. However, the peanut is a Chinese symbol meaning 'give birth' or 'lots of babies'. So, peanuts just might, I suppose become an Easter symbol, since they mean 'new life' in a way that eggs represent new life. But ultimately they would be just another distraction and I am utterly certain that my parents knew nothing of Chinese symbology (and would be horrified to think they were embracing meaningfulness from what they'd consider a false religion) when they switched from chocolate (sugary grease) to peanuts (salty grease).

A peanut isn't even a nut, technically; it's a pea. So, the name *peanut* is half right, but not the half we all thought. I don't know why that matters, though.

On the other hand, Easter is very good for you. It's the day we celebrate glorious, wonderful, excellent and amazing news.

Jesus has taken our place (Mark 10:45).

Jesus, who knew no sin, has become sin for us (2 Corinthians 5:21).

Jesus has suffered the wrath of God, so that we can be declared forgiven (Luke 23:34).

Jesus has experienced separation from God, so that we might never have to know what that is like (Mark 15:34).

Jesus is indeed who he claimed to be (Matthew 16:16).

Jesus has power over death (Acts 2:32).

Jesus is reigning forever, able to forgive and willing to welcome any who come to him (Revelation 21:6; John 6:37).

Easter? Bring it on!

Whenever.

10 a.k.a. **Entitlement**

Christian unity?

There was once a large group of joyful people who understood that they were strongly connected to one another. It was like a family, except there were a great number of individuals involved and the relationships were formed by choice, not just by the happy accident of birth (or otherwise).

They were taught to care for each other and to look out for those in need, helping to feed those who were hungry and to support those who had no money. They knew about gifts of time and attention and financial ones too and they expressed their affection for one another in embraces and in words and acts of kindness. They enjoyed each other's company and spent lots of time together, eating and laughing. They also shared a set of values and beliefs, having exercised faith in God and his gift of love.

The people who opposed their beliefs referred to them with what they considered to be a derogatory, mocking name 'Christians'. Meanwhile, the faithful called themselves *followers of the way, disciples, saints, brothers* and *believers.*

But one sad day, a small group of them decided that they might honour and give more credit to one of their heroes of the faith, reflecting the name of his hometown. They created a small sub-set called *Tarsism.*

And thus began Entitlement (others use the term Denomination – but they both mean the same thing about gathering under a descriptive term). Even though they held everything in common, they were now divided. This seemed to be a backward step from the dynamic, friendly state they had been enjoying.

After a time, some became known by the name *Apollosians* (Apollos is our leader), others by the term *Rockers* (we follow Peter, whom Jesus called *the rock*).

What were the differences between them? Nothing much; just their preferences for the person who first introduced them to the faith... Then there were the ones who thought they were 'purer' than the others, who preferred the name '*WefollowChrist*', which was an unusual decision, but reflected their confidence that they alone had 'got it right'.

Divisions grew; sometimes groups separated themselves from others, when disputes and fine-tuning emphasized their differences, rather than their unity. This was mostly on account of language or translation difficulties in attempting to define how Jesus can simultaneously be both God and man which is clearly impossible and requires a miracle…

Some groups were born out of political expediency; others from a lust-filled desire to annul one marriage and justify another; some from disagreements on what might be termed secondary matters of how to conduct a meeting or to welcome a new member or to establish leadership, rather than philosophy or truth.

There were often groups who separated themselves from others who developed a new interpretation of the Bible or a divergent practice of worship or teaching. The new groups were sure they'd made a genuine discovery of truth, although the ones they left behind were equally confident in their orthodoxy.

So, by the time the faith had been around for two thousand years, the entire belief system was entirely fragmented: *Entitlement rules.*

Unity had been undermined by geography or arguments about practice (some of which were genuine pleas to return to spiritual truth).

One rare occasion when two groups decided to lay aside their differences and embrace one another's diversity gave rise to the *Collected Reconstituted Fellowship*, but not before many slipped away when the amalgamation was suggested.

And I haven't mentioned those that *Luth*, those that claim to exhibit *Greco-Veritas* or are *Soviet Standard*, or the group are very nearly *Am* (actually, the *Am* seem to have faded out now and just the *Almost-Am* are left behind.)

Key to Entitlements

Tarsism	we follow Paul of Tarsus
Apollosians	we follow Apollos
Rockers	we follow Cephas (Peter, *rock*)
Wefollowchrist	we follow Christ
Immersionists	Baptist
Wesleyites	Methodists (Wesley)
Protesters	Protestants (Anglicans)
Romish	Roman Catholics
Brothers (Stern, Ho!)	Brethren (Strict, Plymouth)
Wobblers	Shakers
Five-Expenses	Pentecostals
Gracious Groups	Charismatics (*Happy Clappy*)

Tremblers (Chums Club, or ChocFlapjack eaters)	Quakers or Society of Friends*
Luth	Lutherans
Greco-Veritas	Greek Orthodox
Soviet Standard	Russian Orthodox
Almost-Am	Amish
Tied Upgraded Family	United Reformed Church**
Entitlements	Denominations

Do you suppose this is really what God intended when he sent Paul and the other apostles out into the world to spread the good news of the Gospel to make disciples and plant churches wherever they went? I don't think so! I feel his first choice was for all the Christians to be united and not to form lots of separate groups – some following Paul, some Apollos, some Cephas, etc. Those who said 'We follow Christ' (see 1 Corinthians 1:12) were closest to a name God loves; but their attitude was not the best...

Entitlements have a favourite doctrine or distinctive approaches to worship or becoming a member or the way the churches are formed or connected to one another. Some of the so-called 'Christian' Entitlements have departed from mainstream theological statements to such a degree that they may be not 'Christian' anymore.

You see, many would claim that the groups called Christian Scientists, Christadelphians, Unitarians, Jehovah's Witnesses, Mormons (to name just the really big ones), started out reasonably orthodox and have since developed different beliefs or emphases that set them apart from most Christian churches.

My experience with folk from such groups has demonstrated idiosyncrasies which deny or underplay important Bible truths or emphasise practices to the exclusion of others and we need to show the wisdom of serpents while we are dove-like in harmlessness (Matthew 10:16). I'm deliberately being vague because this is not the proper place for detailed analysis.

---

* Quaker family businesses like *Cadbury's, Fry, Rowntree's* and *Terry's of York* imported cocoa to manufacture and market drinking chocolate to be a healthy alternative to alcohol; *Quaker Oats* is a brand name, chosen mainly because the believers known by the name *Quakers* were famed for integrity

** formed from the *Priesters & Pew-Fodderites* (Presbyterian Church & the Congregationalists)

But if a church group believes that Jesus Christ is the Son of God, who died for our sins and was raised to life again, that we should repent of our sins and put faith in him, our Saviour and Lord, then other issues (important, but secondary) fade a little.

In other words, if we can genuinely have meaningful fellowship despite our distinctives, then let's do our best to be eager to do so. Surely the important part is faith within, not any mere outward sign. Dancing, raising of the hands, kneeling, genuflexion – all can be empty form or of deep significance.

Perhaps you call the leading minister *Father* or *Vicar* or *Pastor* or *Jack* (if his name is Jack – oh, you know what I mean). You might even call your leader *Mildred*, if her name is Mildred. Consider that!

Or you may sing your songs of worship accompanied by an informal-sounding pop group, or an ancient wheezing Harmonium, or by a massive Wurlitzer, or some dreadful Coldplay tribute band, or a brass ensemble or by a swaying robed choir with Hammond organ or a not-very-skilled pianist who plays everything in Eb or just a fluffy-bearded bloke in sandals strumming three-chord tunes on a small acoustic guitar.

It's usually a matter of taste and preference, not a matter of important theology. After all, worship is directed towards God and comes from the heart, doesn't it? The content of the song matters more than the musical taste or lack of it, right? (See more from p140.)

My personal relationship with God is what really matters. And I think the apostle Paul would agree with me. That makes me a *Tarsusian*, does it? No.

And I'm certainly opposed to being called *Pauline*!

11 Escort to Wales

Jonah

The other day, (actually, it was quite a few years ago, which explains our lack of sat nav), I was trying to visit Lambrayne and Nancy, some dear friends I have mentioned already – the characters famous for the irritating incident featuring *Radio Llllllll* and Jesus the sightless cat. They happen to live on the Welsh border, for whatever reason.

I had arranged to travel with HD, another friend I've already mentioned (he has a beach hut and got caught up in the Fatboy Slim nonsense). We were going in his recently-acquired Ford Escort XR2, but after a fabulous breakfast in our favourite greasy spoon café (three bacon, two sausages, two eggs, fried slice, tinned toms, black pudding, beans, mushrooms, chips, two toasts and tea) we each had a couple of errands to run. HD needed to return three library books and I went to a trendy shop to upgrade my mobile phone (which shows, superbly, the difference in cool between us).

Anyway, we were soon ready to leave Brighton, so we filled HD's Escort with unleaded (not literally, just the fuel tank) and set off west. Based on previous experience, prevailing wind direction, shipping forecasts, economic strategy and ergonomic logistics, we reckoned it might take four hours to get to Abergavenny, plus a little more to allow for toilet breaks and the like, not forgetting a well-earned lunch.

So, we left plenty of time. Oh, plenty. We both preferred to travel in daylight, so we'd allocated the day to the journey and finally got on the road at 10.15am. Arrival time was estimated to be at about 3.30pm, after which we could relax and play cards; later, we'd perhaps have a beer and a game of snooker and then return to Jeff's house at the end of the evening for take-away curry and football on the telly. Top lads!

When we got to the first of the main roads on our route, we discovered that it was closed, due to an accident. This meant we had to take a dinky little detour, re-joining the A24 a couple of miles and three-quarters of an hour later. Once we'd got up to speed, we started to make a bit of mileage, which was nice.

But only too soon did we find that we were at the wrong end of a traffic jam, which held us up for a long time. HD was getting a bit stressed, but we carried on for an hour, sometimes crawling along at 3mph and sometimes completely stationary. Ho hum.

'Never mind,' I said cheerily. 'We've got all day to get there, so it really doesn't matter...'

How could I have known the irony of what I was saying or how those words would come back to bite us on the neck?

A few slow miles later, we were not quite in Guildford. HD's escort was getting a little overheated and HD himself was close to boiling. There was some danger of an eruption of liquid, but when it happened, it came not from within, but from above.

Suddenly an amount of water exactly equal to the contents of the Mediterranean Sea fell directly on us in a few horrible minutes (yes, I had it measured scientifically by boffins and the numbers add up). The resultant flooding led to several accidents that day, every one of which was in front of us and held us up for a considerable period.

Just after 2pm, after we'd been travelling for four hours, we nearly saw a sign for the M25 (usually about half an hour north of our starting place) but this was, of course, merely positive thinking.

There's a lot more tedium and dull episodes to this tale, but to cut a long one short, we reached Heathrow by 5.30pm. I'd normally expect to get that far well within two hours (and that's without really trying), so to have taken seven hours was hugely more than mildly frustrating. Reaching there at that sort of time meant we had become part of the busiest daily spell those roads encounter, so now we not only had the weather and accident delays with which to contend, but also the vast quantities of traffic that normally congregates on this stretch of road anyway.

I rang Lambrayne (using my shiny new mobile phone) to let him know that we might be late. There was no reason for him to be cross with us; characteristically, he wasn't. He shared our frustration but was cool about it.

'No rush,' he said. Oh, how right he was!

The M25 was completely rammed, so we turned off onto the A4 and tried to make some headway. But then rain fell again (most of the Atlantic this time) and everything slowed down, apart from the people having accidents, who went very fast, lost control and then slowed down suddenly, catastrophically and rather permanently.

It was 8.45pm when we spotted the sign for Southampton.

This depressed us completely, since we had been on the road for more than ten hours and Southampton is only just over one hour's drive from Brighton, if you take a direct route.

We felt like we had made no progress at all. That, of course, was mainly because we had indeed made no progress at all.

We talked it over and decided to try to calm ourselves and get out of the traffic, so we reckoned it would be best to abandon all hope of getting to Abergavenny for dinner, but that we should stop to eat now and join the traffic later, hoping the roads would be less busy later in the evening. So, we searched for a cheap restaurant for some time and then realized we should stop and eat in an expensive place since that sort was all we would ever find around here. There's great pleasure in eating together, usually, but on this particular day we were both tired, irritated at having to kill time like this, frustrated with the journey, resentful of the vast cost and disproportionately low quality of each mouthful, still unclear about how or when (or even if) we'd ever get to Wales. We were disappointed that our jolly jaunt away from home was starting so very badly; to say nothing of having become what some might call a little weary of one another.

Just about the only upside was that we now had an excuse to avoid the casserole Nancy had promised to prepare for us for the evening we arrived. She had been thinking 'it's easy to keep it warm if they're a bit later than expected', although us blokes were thinking 'curry is much nicer'. Ungrateful chauvinists, yes. With distinct preferences, too.

Anyway, we got going again by 10pm and found that the roads were starting to clear a bit. We drove steadily, concentrating and making sure we were navigating accurately – neither of us would have seen the funny side of making an unforced error now. But we didn't get Chez Lambrayne until past midnight, since his house is several miles beyond where we thought he lived. There was a brief but meaningful welcome, tea and toast, banter, recorded football highlights and that pleasant feeling that comes from being with special friends.

It had taken almost forever, been costly in terms of fuel, effort, stress, wear and tear on windscreen wipers and trusting one another's navigation skills, but at last we were there.

~

Jonah had a similar experience. Okay, so our journey was better than his and less eventful, too (nearly the same quantity of water, though). Admittedly, we weren't on the run from God, denying his call on our lives, or heading for a symbolically far-away place in Spain; and we didn't get ourselves thrown overboard by angry pagan sailors.

Neither were we swallowed by a great fish (that would have been exceptionally unlucky), nor spent three days being actively digested (which can only be described as severely inauspicious). To tell the truth, it was HD & I who were doing the majority of the digesting.

And the mild drama of our eventual arrival – turning off the main road into the quiet estate where Lambrayne lives, drawing the Escort alongside the kerb, engaging the handbrake and alighting, stiff of limb and weary of effort – could not by any stretch of the imagination really be described using the term *vomited*, either.

So perhaps it wasn't like his experience at all.

Except in this important way: we could have turned around and given up on our goal; we could have denied the purpose to which we had set our course. Jonah decided to travel in the opposite direction from the place God had called him.

We had to face distractions, minimise the detours, press through unavoidable numerous delays and exercise patience and wisdom when facing difficult decisions. Turn back or press on? Stay on the motorway or try to find minor roads? Become enraged with HD (because it was his fault) or think calm thoughts? Eat now or use self-control and then have to be polite about casserole? Finish the course or cut our losses?

There are a few spiritual lessons that can be learned, methinks. In life I am choosing to ignore the distractions and keep my eyes fixed on Jesus (Hebrews 12:2).

12 Wot, no wwwebsite?

identity and ministry of Christ

Who's your hero?

Perhaps you give attention to particular statesmen or political leaders like Churchill, Mandela, Gandhi or Washington. Or to significant scientists like Faraday, Curie or Newton. Or explorers and pioneers like Stanley, Polo, Columbus, Scott or Cook. Or religious figures like Mother Theresa, Mohammed, Guru Nanek or Buddha. Perhaps you're into inventors and engineers such as Edison, Brunel, Stephenson, Telford or Oppenheimer.

Maybe you respect sports stars like Rooney, Cracknell, Spitz, Rand or Owens; or musical performers like Clapton, Menuhin, Fitzgerald, Handel, Sinatra or Vivaldi.

Possibly it's military leaders for you, like Hannibal, Saladin, Charlemagne, Nelson, Caesar; or perhaps political high-fliers: Kennedy, Cleopatra, Benn, Walçesa or Perón. Or perchance you're a fan of super-heroes, for example Superman, Wonder Woman, Wolverine, Hulk or Black Panther; or other fictional characters, like Sherlock, Mary Poppins, Hamlet, Yossarian, Molly Bloom or Gandalf.

I ask out of politeness, not really because I want to listen to your answer, although that might in many cases be an interesting conversation, but because I want to tell you about my number one hero.

Can you guess? Of course, you're right!

I've freely adapted a well-known mini-biography of Jesus, entitled *One Solitary Life*, written by Dr James A Francis, a Canadian preacher. Originally published in 1546, it needs a bit of dusting off!

This is my version:

He was born in an obscure hamlet, among rumours of illegitimacy, to a peasant woman and her fiancé. Very early in life he had encounters with eastern mystics, religious figures and royalty, many of whom did not recognize him. He was a refugee in a foreign land in his early childhood, until his family could return to their home.

He grew up breathing sawdust, an apprentice carpenter, working in his fathers' business until he was thirty years old. He was never appointed to the board or given shares in the firm. He never married, nor had children of his own, despite his evident skill in winning their trust and befriending them.

Then he stepped onto the world stage as a traveling preacher. He never owned a home, a car, a smartphone, an iPad, a laptop or a personal jet, an office block, a fleet of lorries, a chain of shops, a distribution network, a denominational HQ or an international bank.

He never wrote a book or did a tv interview or released an album or won an award or starred in a blockbuster or had his picture in the papers or his own website dripping with Flash, soundbites and mp4 movies. He never went on a training course or to college or even to a big city. He never travelled more than two hundred miles from his birthplace. He never posted a selfie. He never did any of the things that usually accompany greatness or even mild celebrity. He had no credentials except himself.

He was still a young man when the tide of public opinion turned against him. His friends and followers deserted him and one of them betrayed him to those who were trying to silence him. A close friend publicly denied knowing him. He was arrested, falsely accused, illegally tried on trumped-up charges and sentenced to a savage, cruel, shameful death.

He was held up for public ridicule, subjected to a humiliating scourging and then nailed to a cross between two thieves. His executioners gambled for the only piece of property he owned, his loincloth. He was utterly misunderstood, undervalued, rejected and hated. The passers-by, the conspirators against him and even one of the criminals executed alongside him shouted abuse at him while he died. His broken body was hurriedly laid in the borrowed tomb of a follower.

Stories of his resurrection circulated briefly; they were never disproved. His followers regrouped and were at the heart of a few wild stories about fish and fire.

Two thousand long years passed and yet today he stands at the centre of human history. Today's date reflects his intervention and contribution to civilization and progress.

It's not too much to say that all of the paperbacks that were ever published, all the celebrities that ever aired their opinions, all the commentators that ever summarized, all the blogs and tweets that

> were ever posted, all the armies that ever went to war, all the navies that ever set sail, all the air forces that ever scrambled, all the parliaments that ever passed laws and all the monarchs that ever reigned, put together, have not affected the life of mankind on this planet with the impact of that One Solitary Life.

There is, of course, a serious weakness in my essay, like there was in the original. It omits any consideration of reasons *why* the life of Jesus has had such a significant impact over two millennia. I think there are at least three reasons.

1) Jesus was sent on a **divine mission** by Almighty God and exercised divine wisdom and compassionate miraculous power many times during his life.

2) Jesus was **far from an ordinary man**. Even the briefest examination of his life, activities, teaching and character shows that he was certainly the most together, focused, sane, determined, organised, relaxed, compassionate, purposeful, direct, loving, joyful, peaceful, patient, kind, good, faithful, gentle and self-controlled person that ever lived. He was empowered by the Holy Spirit of God and was a member of the trinity, pointing out on a number of occasions that he was God's Son, the promised Saviour, the Christ. He humbly laid down his glory but remained part of the Godhead. He sacrificed himself to win the lost. And his resurrection pointed towards his divine nature, too.

3) And Jesus **left more than just a set of memories** or philosophies: he established The Church. He appointed the apostles to be the founders of lots of local fellowships, all belonging to the one world-wide family of believers. He gives the people of God purpose, direction, help, a focus for their worship, a goal for their aspirations, a world to win and life to lead and a hope (that's the spiritual, certain kind of hope) of heaven. Jesus promised that although there would be serious opposition, even the gates of Hell itself shall not prevail against (defeat) the Church!

Keep this in mind. Examine the activity and teaching of Jesus in the light of his significance. Become an active part of the Church, where Jesus continues to influence, change, improve and empower!

13 Words of power

from the cross

Death by crucifixion is dreadfully slow and extremely painful. Breath is driven from the lungs by the agonizing weight of the body suspended by the nails through the hands and feet; repeat until exhausted and asphyxiated.

However, Jesus said seven things when he was being crucified. Making these statements cost considerable physical effort, at least. So, it is surely worth our effort to examine what he said.

None of the Gospel writers includes all these statements, which makes it hard to be sure of the order in which they were said.

Matthew backs up John and Luke in different places, but rather vaguely; it is clear each writer has focused on specific aspects of what Jesus said and woven a tapestry-like picture for us to consider.

We have a totally dove-tailed set of parallel passages in the Gospels only twenty times. Of course, they all, for example, mention Christ's birth, feeding the 5000, the last supper, his trial (amazingly, they all mention Barabbas by name), Jesus' crucifixion and his resurrection, but on other aspects Luke might take the lead, or let Matthew narrate. Mark provides three incidents that are unique to his testimony, yet more often choosing to create what we might call *edited highlights.*

Meanwhile John seems to have a very different agenda. Did you realise, for example, there are six miracles unique to John's gospel and yet absolutely no parables at all? John doesn't even mention Christmas!

So, I have taken the liberty of arranging the comments, prayers and declarations of Jesus on the cross in what I hope you will find to be a helpful order.

Firstly, there are three statements about others; the theologically-foundational and deeply shocking revelation that Jesus was forsaken; and finally three comments about himself.

Father forgive them,
for they do not know what they are doing Luke 23:34

Jesus pleads for the soldiers who hammered the nails into his flesh, crying out not in anger, but for their forgiveness. Despite the shameful and cruel treatment he was receiving, Jesus expressed his desire that God would forgive those who were taunting, abusing and executing him. If they didn't know what they were doing, what did they think they were doing? They thought they were executing a trouble-making Jewish rebel.

What were they really doing? Putting to death the author of life. They were hanging up for public shame the gentle, caring, wise and worthy Son of God. They were participating in the wonderful, glorious plan of God the Father to provide salvation for the lost, hope for the despairing, sight to the blind, life to the dead.

Jesus called out for their forgiveness and God smiled on this, because grace won a famous victory.

It is worth noting that Jesus was not responding to any cries of repentance or pleas for absolution. They didn't even acknowledge that they were doing anything wrong. The soldiers would probably have replied 'We were only following orders,' but the high priests and teachers of the Law would have claimed to have been motivated by their beliefs.

And yet Jesus called upon his Father in Heaven to forgive them anyway, despite their ignorance.

Today you will be with me in paradise Luke 23:43

Speaking to the thief who showed faith, Jesus reassured him that there is more to life than just the time between birth and death. Their short conversation included confirmation of an afterlife, of forgiveness and of Jesus's authority to make promises about such things.

Securing a place in heaven has nothing to do with 'hoping your good deeds outweigh your bad deeds'; Jesus never once mentioned balance scales. It's not about keeping a score of good works at all. Good works performed out of an attitude of pride or from trying to win God's favour are treated like 'filthy rags', says Isaiah 64:6.

Of course, God welcomes our worship and commends our acts of faith (Hebrews 11:1-2), but our behaviour doesn't win or earn our salvation. Eternal life is a gift (Romans 6:23), not a reward. If we received what we deserved, then we'd be in serious trouble! Just like the repentant thief, we receive the free gift of God – yes, a free gift. Anyone who tries to pay for a gift hasn't understood what a gift is.

Enough on what this is not: let's focus on the amazing statement Jesus makes. He responded to an expression of faith. The thief asked 'Jesus, remember me when you come into your kingdom,' recognising who Jesus was and showing faith in the powerful, forgiving Saviour who died to bring us to God. Jesus promised him a place in paradise, implied immediacy and required no religious acts of penitence, burnt offerings or pilgrimages. His raw faith was sufficient.

Being in paradise, a name meaning 'restored to Eden', is to be where Jesus is. The central theme of this wonderful promise is that we can be present with Christ both now and for all eternity. What a Saviour!

Dear woman, here is your son...
here is your mother John 19:26-27 *Matthew 27:55-56 refers*

Even in these circumstances, Jesus' focus was still on other people. He had nothing to leave to his mother, so he provided for her in the one way that he could. He knew his disciple John was willing to serve him and he knew she would welcome John's help.

Even during his crucifixion, Jesus showed love for his relatives and friends.

The writers of the New Testament speak about the church using picture-language: we are an army, a building, a body; and also a family. We are invited to become part of the household of God, to count ourselves brothers and sisters, respecting parents. The image of the extended family includes mercy shown to widows and orphans, special tenderness for those who are barren and a massive welcome for children.

Jesus' loving instruction to his friend and gift to his mother forms a family where there was none.

My God, my God,
why have you forsaken me? Matthew 27:46

Here's the important question: how can God the Father forsake God the Son? They are eternally united, surely?

God the Father, the holy God, cannot allow sin in his presence. Thus, when Jesus, for our sake, our substitute, was made sin so that we can go free (2 Corinthians 5:21), God reluctantly turned his face away from his son. Jesus took our place, settled our debt; became an offering; paid a ransom.

For the first and only time in eternity, the Godhead was not three in one. Truly a mystery, motivated by love deeper than the ocean.

God takes sin very seriously. For evidence, look at the many times when God judged sinners: the flood; the plagues, the Passover and the punishment of the army of Egypt; the destruction of Israel and exile of

Judah; the sudden deaths of Ananias, Sapphira and blaspheming King Herod; the ultimate destruction of Satan.

Jesus had to face the spiritual agony of separation from his Father. Suddenly, everything is different. The depth of aloneness must have been appalling. Notice that in this prayer, he does not use the intimacy of the name 'Father', but 'my God'. We will never understand it; but we should be greatly astonished by it and we can abundantly rejoice in it.

NB these words are a direct quotation from Psalm 22, a seriously detailed prophesy about the agonies of dying on a cross, written about a thousand years before Christ's death and hundreds of years before crucifixion, perhaps the most cruel form of execution, was devised.

I am thirsty John 19:28

This is not merely a simple comment about his physical needs. Surely anyone out in the Palestinian sunshine for several hours, with no shade and subject to extreme anguish and torture would welcome some cool refreshment? Of course, but this is also a fulfilment of prophecy.

Jesus was given wine vinegar, which is an ineffective thirst-quencher. It was traditional to give dying men drugged wine, which might provide a little pain relief, but he was denied even this courtesy. Check out Psalm 69:21 and of course, Psalm 22.

According to Jesus' parable in Luke 16, Hell is a place of thirst. Gloriously, Jesus promises the woman at the well that if she drinks the water of life, she will never thirst again (John 4:13-14). Revelation 7:16 reminds us that in heaven 'they shall no longer thirst'. There's also a promise that Jesus will drink 'of the fruit of the vine' in heaven (Matthew 26:29) So, when Jesus declares 'I thirst', perhaps he's showing us that he lacks the power of the presence of the Holy Spirit to quench his spiritual thirst.

When Christ was made sin for us, the Holy Spirit had departed. This must relate to forsakenness, too. Physical death, although awful enough, was only really the start of the agonies Jesus was suffering.

It is finished! John 19:30

This is absolutely not a whimper of defeat. On the contrary, it is a loud cry of triumph and accomplishment. What has been finished? The substitutionary work done by Christ. He was made sin for us and took the punishment we deserve, so that we can be declared forgiven and set free, that's what! In addition, the powers of darkness are defeated, the

Old Testament prophesies are fulfilled, his obedience was complete, his sufferings are ended, and the reign of sin is over. Death is defeated, the victory over the enemy is complete, the will of God is done. After all, Jesus prayed in Gethsemane 'not my will, but your will be done' (Luke 22:42) and now it is indeed done.

Three words, but oh, so theologically rich. Is this statement of victory about Jesus himself? Perhaps not at first glance; but when you consider who else might have said such a thing with any degree of truth, you'll be at a complete loss to name any names.

Christ has won the victory over Satan. Over the tempter, the father of lies, the evil one. Over the spiritual powers of darkness and deceitfulness; over jealousy, rage, bitterness, boasting, selfish ambition.

Satan has been disarmed (had his weapons of sin and death taken away) and shamed. His schemes are exposed and we live in the victory. Indeed, we are now, through Christ's death and by the power of the Holy Spirit, able to resist the devil (James 4:7), able to stand firm against him (1 Peter 5:9) and to defend ourselves against his schemes with the full armour of God (Ephesians 6:11).

Christ alone can stand in our place. Christ is victorious! Christ alone is the pure, perfect, spotless, unblemished lamb of God who has no need to take punishment for his own sin. He may well have cried 'I have done it!', which is exactly how other translations express this phrase.

Our salvation was won, our hope of heaven was secured. Jesus declares that nothing else at all is required. It is complete, it is accomplished. It is all done at the cross. The only way to the Father is though the Son (John 14:6), who won the way for us on the cross by his sacrificial, substitutionary, gracious death.

Can you tell I'm excited by this glorious news?

Father, into your hands I commit my Spirit

Luke 23:46 *Matthew 27:50 refers*

No-one took Jesus' life from him; he gave it for us.

God the Father had forsaken him and turned his back on him, but now the agony of body was drawing to a close and the greater agony of spiritual separation from God had begun. How dreadful an agony for the Father to be separated from his son, too… Christ's life was over and his only hope was that God would quickly pour out resurrection power and restore their union. Oh, that this dark day would pass and that the glorious light of new life would dawn!

As he died, he relied on the gentle, comforting hands of his Father (notice, not 'my God' this time) to protect his spirit.

~

The words Jesus spoke from the cross help to explain why he was willing to suffer and die in this barbaric, dishonourable way: it was for us and for our salvation. Obedience to his Father was key; completing the work for which he was sent was vital; becoming sin for us satisfied heavenly justice; perfect love motivated him; he won the victory; he was sacrificed in our place; he paid the ransom.

And now, when we confess our sins, God is faithful (he does what he says he will do) and just (the law is satisfied and the price has been paid) so he forgives us our sin (1 John 1:9)

In the famous words of the popular hymn:

And can it be that I should gain
An interest in the Saviour's blood?
Died he for me, who caused this pain?
For me, who him to death pursued?
Amazing love! How can it be,
That thou, my God, should die for me?

Charles Wesley (1707-1788)

14 Sunny climbs

God who preserves

Many of you may remember that I have a friend with the nickname HD. He's the one with the fully-inflated dingy and with whom I took all day to get to Wales.

Not long ago (2003, actually), we went to Portugal for a well-earned holiday for a week. Yes, I realise it seems all we ever do is take a break. It's not true, I tell you.

He had just changed jobs and had found the transition stressful. Additionally, I had not had a proper rest or time off work for a year or more, so we both thoroughly deserved to reward ourselves with a spot of sunshine, a little extra sleep, some lazy days and mild entertainment.

In addition to this, we also planned to hire a car and do some driving on the wrong side of the road – well, the correct side and the right side, but the different side from the side on which we usually drove, if you follow my meaning.

When got off the plane at Faro airport, our first task after baggage claim and customs was to find the coach that was going to transfer us from there to the apartments we had selected. Our instructions indicated that we needed to get onto Coach C and that this would be in the extensive Coach Area outside the airport.

Logical, so far. However, I thought this looked like a long walk in the heat and didn't really fancy it, so HD very kindly agreed to go and investigate, provided I stayed with the bags. This was a distribution of labour that suited me but one which I later realised was fraught with complication. I shall do my best to explain.

HD wandered off, making sure he had the booking confirmation print-out with him. His knowledge of the local language is, well, aggressively non-existent – in other words, he's proud and defensive about his ignorance. Actually, his grasp even of English leaves a little to be desired, but that's another story.

Anyway, he wandered about in the coach area (which was, like the instructions promised, extensive) for a quarter of an hour, minutely examining each vehicle for some indication of intended destination.

He made an important discovery; he didn't have a clue about the name of the town to which we were headed. Our details unhelpfully only mentioned the name of the apartment block and that Coach C was scheduled to drop us there. He was pretty confident he'd cracked it, however, when he found four coaches side by side, three of which had what looked like letterheaded paper displayed in their front windows, each bearing an identical logo to the one of the holiday company we had used. His stroll was self-assured now.

There was Coach A, here was Coach B, then an unmarked one, and at the end of the row, Coach D. Could it be? It was enough to confuse a simple person, but HD was a bit more self-sufficient. He wasn't going to make any assumptions, (as he explained, to assume makes an *ass* of *u* and *me*) but then he wasn't able to check any information very easily.

Fortunately, some drivers were standing around, having a smoke, like many Portuguese coach drivers do.

So, HD sauntered up with vast British colonial confidence and authority. He pointed at the unmarked vehicle between Coach B and Coach D and asked the drivers 'Is this Coach C?'

No 'excuse me,' no 'good afternoon, fine fellows, well met!' and certainly not even the slightest chance of '*Favor confirmar que estou correto em concluir que este autocarro me levará em poucos minutos ao destino detalhado aqui na carta em papel timbrado correspondente.*' TRANSLATION: Greetings! Please confirm, if you'd be so very kind, that I have correctly concluded that this coach is the one which will, in a few minutes' time, take me to the destination noted here on this matching letter-headed paper.' The drivers were perhaps not ready for HD's abrupt and English-tourist interruption. One murmured 'H'mm?'

NB please remember that I was not present to add words of advice, so the only version of this incident I ever heard was HD's. You can see I have had to piece together what must have happened from his explanation.

HD repeated his question, this time a little louder, with a slightly more Oxfordian style and with a grand theatrical gesture towards the unmarked vehicle. 'Is this Coach C?' It was almost a criticism, like he was chastising them, saying 'You chaps should have put the correct notice in the windscreen, for the information and assurance of paying customers. I'm right, am I not?'

Anyway, the most helpful driver said one word. The most confusing word he might have said. 'Si.'

HD's untrained ear, of course, heard 'C'.

Now, I do not know why HD thought for one moment that these stout-hearted working-class residents of the Algarve would even begin to understand his question. Neither do I suppose that it ever occurred to HD that their reply could possibly be the Portuguese for *yes*. The entire issue of how foreign nationals pronounce the names of letters of the alphabet had never before nor since occurred to him. Of course, Portuguese-speakers pronounce the third letter *seh*. But HD didn't know this. Admittedly, I wasn't sure, but I knew *si* was *yes*.

I agree, it had indeed been dangerous to let him wander out of his comfort zone, roaming freely among the natives.

He was blissfully unaware, of course, that this was not necessarily a reliable confirmation, but may simply be a reply in the positive or even an invitation to repeat the question in Portuguese.

Initially, I was impressed when he returned, since he was certain he'd identified the right vehicle and we set off with all the bags on the trolley. There they were: Coach A. Coach B. Blank. Coach D.

'This must be it,' he said. No uncertainty in the expression, nor any lack of confidence in body language.

I wasn't entirely convinced. 'It doesn't say C, you know.'

'I asked and they said it was.'

'You asked?' I was starting to be less than assured. 'How did you ask? Did you ask the Portuguese people in Portuguese?' I knew he hadn't, but I didn't like to challenge his legendary ignorance too aggressively – after all, this was still the very start of our holiday and there was going to be plenty of time over the next few days for arguments, mockery and recriminations.

'I asked *Is this Coach C* and they said it was.' He was slightly cross, I think, that I should have taken this line of questioning.

'Those Portuguese people answered your English question in English, using the word *Yes*, did they? Or did they say *indeed I do most wholeheartedly concur, English gentleman?* Or what?' It is possible that a hint of sarcasm was creeping into my tone. It does from time to time.

'Pretty much…' he defended. I suspected some of his certainty was starting to drain away now. Wisely, he reverted to the unvarnished truth. 'I asked *Is this Coach C?* and the bloke said C.'

It might have been one of those lucky coincidences, but I was still not entirely sure. 'Could he have said the Portuguese for *yes*, perhaps?'

'What?'

'Their way of saying *yes* is *si*. Your question may have seemed to him to be very much like *This is a Coach, yes?* so he just said *yes*.'

HD was cross now. 'I think you're being a bit technical.'

Born-and-bred indigenous Portuguese coach drivers deep in the heart of Portugal, speaking monosyllabic native Portuguese is HD's idea of technical. 'Well, if you think you can do better…'

I stopped for a moment and tried to frame a question for the drivers to which the only possible answer was the confirmation we sought. I needed to eliminate the doubt and to say the letters of the alphabet in the local lingo. Education in my day being what it was, I could confidently list the days of the week in French or numbers from one to one hundred in French, but all I could muster was a tentative grasp of how to pronounce the names of the letters in French. It was worth a try. I approached the drivers.

'Hi!' I pointed at Coach A, clearly marked A. 'Coach *Ah,* si?'

They nodded and said 'Si!'

I pointed at the Coach unambiguously marked B.

'Is Coach *Beh,* si?'

They nodded and said 'Si!' although I would have forgiven them for saying 'We've got a right one here.'

Undeterred, I worked the magic. I pointed next at Coach D, unmistakably marked D.

'Is Coach *Deh,* si?'

One of them said 'Si!' The others exchanged glances which were the Portuguese for 'Foreign looney.'

This now, here, was the moment of truth; my master card; if this didn't work, I was out of options. I pointed to the unmarked coach. I shrugged. 'Is Coach *Seh,* si?'

'Si!'

Bingo! I punched the sky and said to HD, 'Let's get these bags loaded.'

HD was unrepentant, irritated at this timewasting and annoyed at my lack of trust. 'Told you.'

'You're very welcome, old friend. Get on the bus and let's hope someone knows where we're going.'

Happily, it was Coach C and these blokes knew exactly where they were going. HD crowed about it for the rest of the day and has done so more or less ever since, but at the time I let it go, since we were on holiday to have a good rest, rather than falling out over this sort of minor hitch. Little did we know, things would get much worse.

My storytelling technique may lack subtlety, but HD's approach to every language except English was going to get us into a great deal of bother.

Meanwhile, we were dropped off at the most splendid private apartments. It was a single-storey two-bedroom villa with an open-plan kitchen/living room and a modern bathroom, set inside a walled garden, with just four other villas inside the courtyard, surrounding, on three sides, a lovely private swimming pool. There were shaded areas, suntraps, excellent facilities and the promise of a week of extremely pleasant relaxation.

Within a few minutes of our arrival, the car hire bloke turned up with our vehicle and we had wheels! I confess I was tempted to fashion a big sign to put in the windscreen, saying *Car C*, but I thought better of it, since HD might not have found this amusing.

So, during that week we sat in the sun, played cards, swam morning and afternoon, drove on the right side of the road (in both senses of the expression) and ate out at every opportunity. We tried the local cuisine and some English-themed pubs and cafés. At one Bavarian-style restaurant, we sent our steaks back, saying they were insufficiently well done, which was somewhat arrogant and ill-informed of us, but no-one seemed surprised that these English were throwing their weight about.

We even found a couple of places that were offering a two-course meal (starter & steak or steak & afters) for £2.50. We piled in to one of them and had prawns followed by steak. Having paid up, we went next door and had another steak and some profiteroles. That was a good evening, eating fabulously for just a fiver!

We decided to upgrade our hire car for the next model in the range, to get one with a cassette player in (it was long ago, before we owned any of those new-fangled CDs), since local radio was taking a severe toll on our joie de vivre. The car hire place turned out to be a launderette, too, which seemed an odd mixture and it set us trying to imagine other unusual twinned businesses, like a ship's chandlery & dog kennels, a Christian bookshop & off licence or *Pedro's Hand-Made Caramel Bonbons & Urine Analysis While-U-Wait One Stop Combo Mart.*

As you may have been anticipating, HD's attitude toward European vocabulary got us into serious trouble one day. We had decided to travel on the motorway system, the quicker to arrive at a major city we wanted to visit. We planned to take photographs there and then look for a curry restaurant. Such establishments are not easily located in rural Portugal, we had found, but we were in the mood for a plateful of spicy lamb or chicken with a tangy sauce, plus rice, poppadums and/or naan bread and that delicious mango chutney.

So, we set off. HD was driving and I checked the route from time to time until we reached the motorway. 'Can't go wrong,' I said, folding the map, my duty done. I still hadn't worked out what was signified by all the little numbers printed next to the roads; some were clearly identification numbers, including for example A2 or A17 (A must represent what they call *Autoestrada*, I guessed) and then there were what seemed to be mileage counters between waypoints. But the other tiny figures didn't mean anything, I concluded. At least, probably nothing important. It was pure guesswork.

Mile after weary mile (sorry, kilometer after weary kilometer) flew by and the combination of heat, rest, HD's fave pop tape (more than a little samey) and holiday relaxedness had the usual soporific effect. I must have dropped off for a few minutes, because when I awoke, we were much closer to the destination than before.

Less pleasingly, we had slowed to join a small queue of vehicles passing through what looked like a toll booth area.

'What's this?' I asked.

'Toll, I think,' HD said.

'How much is it?' I asked, fiddling in my pocket for coins.

'Don't know yet. The signs are all in foreign.'

'Well, they would be, I suppose.'

'Because they never have any tourists in Portugal, do they?' HD's sarcastic tone can be a little acid.

When we reached the booth, HD wound down his window and smiled at the bloke. 'How much is it?' he asked.

'Que?'

I tried to help. 'Combien?' Not a lot of help, I agree.

'Eenglish?' It was a sign of pain from the man in the booth, not an exclamation of understanding. But, entirely professional, he soldiered on. 'Ticket?'

I grasped the situation immediately. 'Yes, we want a ticket, please.'

Apparently, I had comprehensively failed to grasp the situation. 'No, you have ticket?'

Fortunately, there were no vehicles behind us, waiting to get through the tollgate. So, we were able to try to get to the bottom of the problem.

'H'mm?'

The tollbooth man sighed. He was used to tourists, I expect, but we were being especially complicated. 'Ticket. You took ticket when you drove onto autoestrada, yes?'

'I don't understand, sorry.' This made no sense to me at all.

'Okay. When you drive onto autoestrada, you take ticket, yes?' Being able even slightly to rephrase his question was an impressive language skill but moved us no closer to an answer.

HD, of course, hadn't followed the conversation. 'What's his beef?'

I attempted to explain. 'He says when we joined the autoestrada, we got a ticket.'

'Joined the what?'

'The motorway. When we joined the motorway, we should have got a ticket.'

'Oh, a ticket. Yes, I wondered about that.'

'What?'

'Well, you were asleep, so that was no help. I was busy driving.'

Somehow, whatever the problem turned out to be, it was starting to sound like HD considered that it was my fault. I sought further clarity. 'Yes, well, it might not have been the best time to doze off; although you could have given me a nudge. Anyway, tell me more about this.'

'About what?'

'When I was asleep, you were driving and you first got onto the auto… motorway,' I said, with deliberate care. I was working hard to keep any tone of accusation out of my voice and any defensiveness out of my choice of words.

'There was a ticket machine and lots of signs, all in foreign,' HD explained, with mild xenophobia. 'The car in front just drove on, so I reckoned those signs didn't apply to me, either. I ignored them and drove through.'

The bloke in the tollbooth chipped in. 'Many local drivers have a pass. They pay in advance.' His English was far better than we had any right to expect. He was actually providing a degree of clarity now, not just making demands and repeating himself. I had a suspicion that he was enjoying the encounter.

I smiled at HD. 'That might be what you saw, then.' He shrugged.

I spoke to the tollbooth chap again. 'We do not have a ticket. How much do we have to pay?'

'No ticket?'

'Didn't know we had to have one,' said HD, slightly aggressively.

'Let's not wind the bloke up, eh?' I suggested, calmingly.

'No ticket, you pay full price,' the boothgent said.

'Okay,' I said, with a shrug.

What else could I do? We couldn't exactly offer to turn around and go back, since presumably there was someone at the other end who would also want money. We could, I suppose, stay on this stretch of motorway for the rest of our lives, never passing through a tollbooth and thus never having to pay. The only alternative was to choke up the spondulicks.

Knowing the sort of toll we would have to pay for places like the Severn Bridge or Dartford Tunnel, I was imagining a fee of perhaps a fiver or just a little more. It was just a road, after all. No structural engineering or waterproofed bits, after all.

The ticket man rattled off some hugely complicated Portuguese expression, which left me unimpressed and thoroughly uninformed. 'Huh?'

He wrote it down. €53.75.

I looked at the number and waited for the decimal point to move somewhere sensible.

'Nice,' I said to HD.

'What?' he said, aggressively.

'This trip has cost us a small fortune.'

'How much?'

'Fifty-three €uros 75pee.'

'Oh.'

I asked the ticketchap to explain why it was so much. 'You have no ticket, so I charge you for whole network of road. You have ticket to show where you enter and leave road, you pay for that road. No ticket? You pay for all autoestrada in Portugal.'

I sighed and reluctantly passed him my Visa card. He did the business. He gave me a tiny scrap of paper that entitled us to drive all day on roads throughout the country, including several which were 550 miles away, we later realized. It would take a concerted, well-planned effort to use each of the roads in the whole Portuguese motorway network in a single day. It's the sort of challenge HD & I would have relished. But we only wanted to use the little stretch between where we were staying and the big city. Oh well.

'How much was it then?' HD asked when we drove on.

'Fifty-three €uros and odd.'

'How much is that in real money?'

At the time, the exchange rate gave us 1.45 €uros to the pound. 'Thirty-seven quid.'

'Oh. And how much would...'

'...how much would it have been if we'd slowed down at the first tollbooth, looked at the sign, checked with the bloke in the booth and paid for the little bit we wanted to use? Is that what you're asking now? That's what you want to know? Now, when it's ridiculously too late, I say, now, you have a thirst for knowledge?'

I have to confess that I was starting to become slightly cross and may have allowed my irritation to show. I checked on the map. Suddenly I understood what the meaningless little numbers next to the motorway routes meant; the ones that weren't road numbers or mileages.

'€4. £2.75.'

HD remained silent. Hopefully he was feeling guilty.

I couldn't help myself. 'Did you really say *The signs were in foreign, so I assumed they didn't apply to me?* That's very colonial...' I shook my head in disbelief at the severity of the financial punishment I was suffering for having fallen asleep.

The atmosphere in the vehicle was a little uncomfortable, but HD changed all that. 'So, do you own that bit of road now?'

Fortunately, I could see the funny side of it.

Anyway (and this gets us slightly closer to the point of this tale) on the last day, we had some time to spare before the flight home, so we wandered around in the town.

We noticed a scaffolding tower that was rigged up with harnesses and ropes. One face of the tower was boarded up, with handholds and footholds and at the summit was a bell for successful climbers to ring.

HD liked the look of it and I knew he fancied his chances, but we observed that it was being used by children. So, I used my smattering of Portuguese (mostly gestures, shrugs and lip-gymnastics) to ask the people in charge if HD was able to have a turn. 'My friend – *cavaleiras* – would like to try,' I said. 'Is okay?' (No, this isn't a translation to make it easier for you. This is my smattering of Portuguese. And I know now that *cavaleiras* isn't *gentleman*, like I'd hoped; it's the term for a ladies' toilet. But somehow these people saw through my blunder. 'Inglês, obrigado,' they said.)

They looked him up and down and agreed it would be nice. 'You're next,' I told him.

He put on the harness and got ready for his ascent and I sat down on a nearby bench. I encouraged him with well-chosen words. 'Go HD! Like a rat up a drainpipe!'

He did very well for a man with neither experience nor technique and within less than a minute he'd hauled himself to the top. He rang the bell and then abseiled down to the ground. His fingers were sore, but he was really pleased with his triumph. He did it twice more, but each ascent took longer, because he had used most of his energy the first time. I congratulated him on this achievement.

Later, we talked about the physics. HD is a lot heavier than the little fellow who was holding the other end of the rope, so I wondered, why wasn't the lightweight pulled into the air on the occasions when HD slipped and lost his grip? Oh yes, there were several of those moments. I wasn't going to say, but then your pesky science questions dragged it out of me. What I had not realized from my distant position on the bench was that the safety rope was slightly elastic (they call it bungee), so the rope itself was taking some of the strain of his weight, which allowed the boy on the pavement to remain on the ground.

~

We all need friends who have their feet on the ground to provide security and balance to our adventures. HD needed the Portuguese climbing expert to hold the rope and he needed me to buy him a glass of refreshing Vimto afterwards, to steady his nerves. If memory serves, it was almost certainly Vimto. Or Fanta.

Similarly, there are many times, I am certain, when we are being supported by God in ways we do not realize. Check out these verses:

If you make the Most High your dwelling – even the LORD,
who is my refuge – then no harm will befall you,
no disaster will come near your tent. For he will command
his angels concerning you to guard you in all your ways;
they will lift you up in their hands,
so that you will not strike your foot against a stone.
You will tread upon the lion and the cobra; you will trample
the great lion and the serpent. Psalm 91: 9-13

Yes, this is one of the ways the Devil tempted Jesus in the wilderness; but our Lord recognised the sneaky test in the enemy's intent (Luke 4:9-12). Instead, the Psalmist is celebrating God's protection.

God routinely keeps us from nasty surprises, from harm; he faithfully protects us, calms our fears, shields us from attack, saves us from more diseases than we realise, shelters us from harm… His loving kindness even extends to granting us courage and confidence and also a powerful sense of belonging. How marvellous!

He silently keeps us safe, despite our vast ignorance, groundless assumptions, crazy schemes and risky behaviour. Throughout, God is providing friends, help and loyalty (and, sometimes, miraculous healing).

Now, there are occasions, of course, when we fall ill or are harmed in some way – often through our risk-taking or deliberate disobedience, or because of the hurly-burly of life – but this does not undermine the truth that God has been (in the background, usually unseen and unacknowledged) sparing us from far more frequent disasters and hideousness.

For example, if HD and I had made a poorer choice of holiday destination, then his 'the signs were all in foreign' attitude may have lead us into a somewhat more dangerous 'I didn't know what signs said, so I assumed the armed guards weren't shooting at us until the windscreen shattered and you died on the spot' or even 'all the signs seemed to me to be so much Arabic scribble, so I thought it would be fine to wear these lycra shorts and have a can of lager with my bacon sandwich, simultaneously photographing this public building' scenario.

Yes, really, you read all that rigmarole just so I could make that important point about God's unseen (and often unrecognized) presence and faithfulness.

15 Privet lives

with acknowledgements to Jerome K Jerome

Have you ever been in one of those real-life mazes, with tall hedges? No, many people haven't. Let me try to persuade you never to experiment should the opportunity arise; it's not worth it. You only have one life and it is more valuable.

A privet maze (like the one at Hampton Court Palace) is almost entirely unlike any maze you've ever followed on paper, because with those you get to see from above and only need to use a pencil to trace your path – or a pen, if you're feeling confident or don't mind scribbling out.

Similarly, you can give up without suffering any great loss, except perhaps pride. Or simply turn to the answers page to find the solution.

But with a real maze, you don't see the plan from above and giving up isn't an option, once you have started. Either you find the middle (or, more helpfully, the exit) or you must carry on being in the maze. Unless you happen to know the phone number of someone with a helicopter who can stage a rescue, lowering a bloke on a winch to fetch you out. But I bet you don't, so that's you stuck, matey.

Doubtless you're already reading between the lines, so I'm going to short-circuit that by telling you what happened to me at Hampton Court upon my first encounter with a privet maze.

In my naïveté (which was and still is, in many ways, almost comprehensive) I rushed into the maze with enthusiasm and began to seek the middle. The hedges towered over me in a way I hadn't expected, even though I realised before I began that I was considerably shorter than these famous hedges, planted originally in 1690.

It's an experience like few others and I wandered around for a while, chuckling at my errors and hoping that I would not encounter yet another wall of privet but a fresh route to explore. I tried to convince myself that the maze had a middle, since the designer had deliberately made it a bit tricky to find.

No matter which way I turned, I kept on discovering a dead end (which, I suspected, may have been the same dead end several times over, since they were identical).

All the other people in the maze seemed to be going the other way, so I assumed they were looking for the exit.

'Perhaps in a minute or so, I too shall seek the exit. But let's find the middle first, eh?' I said to myself, in jocular tone, failing admirably to convince myself I know what I'm doing.

After about half an hour or so, I tried leaving a crisp packet on the ground at a particular dead-end, so that I would know I'd been that way before if (when) I found the same dead-end again. And that, of course, is the last time I ever saw the crisp packet, despite constantly finding dead ends. This meant either I'd found a different dead-end or I'd found several dead-ends that all look the same; they were all intimidating privet-hedge dead ends, so they were hard to distinguish from each other. Or perhaps someone had tidied up.

Then it occurred to me that I could navigate by the sun. No-one can clear that away. Brilliant! At last, there was hope. Well, at least until dusk.

So, I tried to head north, keeping the sun behind me. This was superbly effective, except that I spent ages gazing into the sky, trying to remember how many times I had turned around.

Minutes later, however, it struck me that the trouble with astral triangulation (cosmological navigation?) is that I needed to know where I was, in order to get to where I wanted to be and I had no longer any way of telling in which direction the middle lies. I might have been one turn from success, or hundreds of yards away from it; I had no idea at all.

The middle might be to the north. I used to know where the entrance was, but I'd wandered around for so long that this memory was now lost in the mists of ancient history.

So, to summarise, I didn't know where I was and I had no clue about the location of either of the places I was keen to find. Yes, you're right, dismay would be a good descriptive word to choose to express my emotional state.

Who can tell? 'Only someone with a map,' I muttered, abandoning this idea.

Thus far, I'd been diligently ignoring the great unwashed masses rampaging blunderingly through the narrow alleyways, but it seemed the right moment to wonder if they might have possibly known something I didn't.

'Even if their ignorance matches mine,' I reckoned 'it's preferable to perish in company, probably, than to die alone.' This seemed exceptionally morbid for someone who, less than an hour before, was blithely chattering about 'nipping around this simple maze and then checking out Ye Olde Gift Shoppe for a souvenir for Auntie Beryl'.

Well, I people-watched for a few minutes and selected a group who looked like they had a plan. 'Three turns to the left and then one to the right. Follow that pattern and this maze is easy!' they said to each other in a self-congratulatory, Jerome K Jerome-esque manner.

'Hah!' I snorted to myself, 'arrogant fools!' But I followed them anyway, just in case. Their strategy didn't work, of course, mostly because after the third left turn they were facing a dead end, with no right turn or left turn. When they realised their idea was a dud, they improvised randomly, ineffectually, frustratingly and hopelessly.

All seemed lost. Me, included.

Soon afterwards, I noticed that some of these formerly confident people had latched onto me. Although I thought I was following them at a few discreet paces, the truth is that they were watching my moves and doing their best to follow me. On the balance of probabilities this was unlikely to be successful, since neither party knew where the middle was, or how to get there. No-one was taking responsibility for leading anyone else. This is only marginally worse than someone who doesn't know what they are doing striking out with bravado and taking full responsibility for achieving nothing at all.

'Ah, even a stopped clock is right twice a day!' I said to myself. (I seemed to be doing an alarming amount of under-the-breath muttering on this journey, which cannot be a good sign.) It took me what I can only call an embarrassingly long while to realize that this proverb bore no relation to the conundrum with which I was currently faced.

I sat down to rest, to weep and to compose a short farewell note to my silver-haired mother, expressing my love and regret at not ever seeing her again.

What a fool I have been, Mama, a fool, I tell you! I was idiotically credulous; I believed the people who claimed it was an easy maze. I am defeated, I wrote, in my head, finding a measure of solace in the quality of composition. *I shall never be able to make up for all the broken windows and promises, or for the regrettable incident with the sponge pudding. I have always thought of you with warm affection and hope, somehow, you will not be too sad at the news of my complete disappearance.*

I was becoming somewhat morose and perhaps slightly hysterical.

Now, I should make it clear at this point, for the sake of readers of a nervous disposition and those of an empathetic gift, that there is ultimately no need for alarm. My peril was short-lived and even before we reach the foot of the page, the unfolding begins showing how I eventually emerged from this ordeal reasonably unscathed, armed with the wisdom of experience. I trust this reassurance enables you to read on without panic or undue concern.

Beware, however, the tale takes a number of twists yet before a happy ending; these are for dramatic effect and should not be interpreted in sinister ways. To continue.

In the midst of my despair, a child of no more than perhaps four approached me and offered to take me to the middle for 20p. I paid up gladly, but the boy trousered my coin and immediately disappeared, with a scornful laugh, through a tiny hole in the hedge behind me. The hole was too small for me (or any adult) to follow and suddenly I was both lost and diddled.

I rushed about, fired with a new motive. I was keen to find the little child and rapidly extend the five-knuckled cudgel of justice, or at least demand my money back – and then, by accident, around a corner, stumbled, with considerable surprise, upon the middle of the maze.

Oh, what glorious, bountiful waves of relief washed over me!

I quickly recovered my composure, allowing a smile to play over my lips, trying to make it appear that I had planned all this. 'Ah, yes, the centre,' I said half-aloud and continued to mutter about 'this ridiculously easy maze I thought I'd stroll around to fill in a few minutes before lunch.'

Having reached the middle, I sat down for a more relaxing, less gloomy rest than the one I had a few moments before. Trouble is, I didn't have the first clue how I got there and I was rapidly reaching the conclusion that there was very little chance of ever finding the way out. I was resigning myself to spending the rest of my life in this maze, or at least having to wait until the entrance kiosk was closed for the night, when I'd be chucked out.

I wistfully pictured a friendly park keeper escorting me (and many other fellow travellers) to the exit as I wept tears of grateful relief. And I consider an alternative scene, in which the park-keeper climbs up on a step ladder to get that bird's-eye view needed to guide us, shouting clear instructions. These imagined rescues have equal appeal, despite featuring a closing time which was yet some six or seven hours away.

It was around then that I started to feel the need to find the public conveniences. Ah. Right.

Then four of my friends arrived, with ice creams, having 'done' the maze seven times already, grown tired of waiting for me to join them and gone to watch a movie, to play five sets of tennis and then come back to see where I could have possibly got to.

Oh, I was so pleased to see them! I stuck close, watching them slurp their way through overpriced 99s, sorbets and cornettos, and when they decided to leave, I followed them blindly. They confidently lead me out and left, left, left, right and… into the middle again.

'Funny that,' said one of my friends. Not all that funny. 'I was sure I knew how…'

After another three equally futile attempts to find the exit, yet always returning to the middle, I reached the sad realisation that my friends were using the three left, one right method. I suggested that on the way out, shouldn't that be three right, one left?

'Of course!' they said. We all set off with renewed hope and returned, relentlessly, unsurprisingly, wearily, on nine occasions, to the middle.

Feeling hopeless and foolish, I had another sit down. At least the benches here in the middle were more comfortable than sitting on the path at some long-forgotten but oft-visited, crisp-packet-free dead end.

Suddenly I spotted that small child again. All feelings of violence towards him have evaporated in my desperation; I dared hope he knew the way out and was prepared to sell his knowledge. After some questioning, he claimed to have the answer I required. His price for finding the exit was £1 per person per trip, because he's a smart kid and can recognize desperation when he saw it. I paid up but kept hold of his sleeve to prevent him getting away again. I emerged from the maze, slightly delirious, forty-five seconds later.

I had almost given up on ever experiencing such feelings of liberation. Was this how Prisoners of War felt when they were finally released by friendly troops? Or Nelson Mandela on his Long Walk to Freedom? Or the Children of Israel stepping away from Egypt on dry land across the Red Sea after 400 years of slavery… Perhaps I was making a little more of this than was appropriate.

I noticed the small child had pocketsful of coins. He had showed me through the exit, although I had briefly considered either mugging him or following him, learning the route and setting up in competition.

But I was foot weary, feeling slightly claustrophobic from high hedges and overabundantly endorphinated with the joy of being free; free at last!

I have provided a bird-eye view of the maze to demonstrate that it is indeed extremely complicated; that 'three left turns and one to the right' is worthless twaddle; and that 'nipping round before going to the gift shop' was destined to have involved Auntie Beryl in an exceptionally long wait.

Anyway, I enjoyed the simple pleasure of allowing my eyes to focus on the middle and far distance much too much ever to return to the daunting narrow corridors of the privet trap from which escape had seemed impossible.

Standing in that very convenience, I took that day a solemn vow never again to enter another maze – reckoning this would demonstrate my grateful attitude towards the merciful heavens for sending that rather

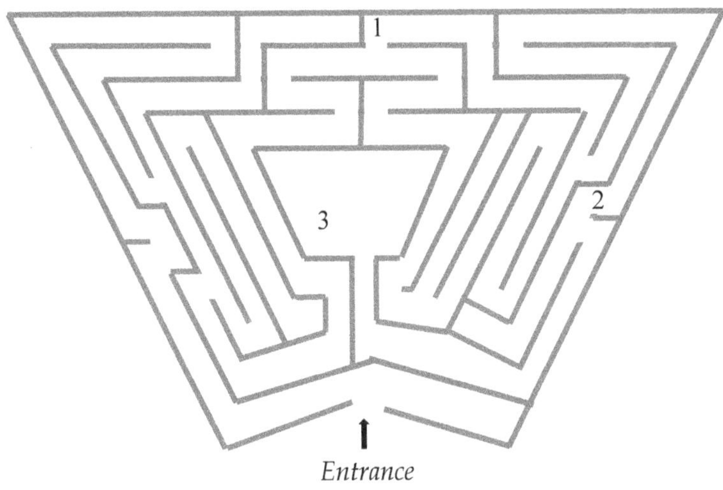

The layout of the famous Hampton Court Maze, showing the multiple dead ends, designed to confuse, since they look identical from between the hedges. It was in the upper central portion of the maze (indicated 1, approx) that I began to give up hope; on the long straight down the right-hand side (probably, indicated 2) where I first encountered the wealthy kid; and deep in the middle of the maze (shown 3, certainly) where I started to feel the need for a visit to the gents (not shown)

well-disguised guardian angel (in the form of a small, financially encumbered yet surprisingly uninjured boy) to rescue me.

I also felt inclined to keep away from privet hedges of any kind for several years, too.

~

In the parables Jesus told in Luke 15, the sheep that went missing was lost by its very nature; lost like me in that maze, hopelessly unable to find the way to the fold until the shepherd rescued him and carried him home rejoicing. (See also chapter 19)

The coin was lost by circumstances, hidden away somewhere in the room – like me in the maze and coins that had once been mine, now secreted in that boy's pocket – until the woman of the story set to with diligence, systematic thoroughness, a lamp and a broom, to find it.

And the self-centred, walkaway, wild-spending son was lost like me in the maze, too. He found himself in a desperate state, despairing of ever returning to his home, on account of bad decisions, foolish choices and overconfident self-assurance until glorious revelation brought him to his senses, he laid down his pride and went home humbly.

Jesus' parables encourage us that even when we are lost, despairing, feeling cheated and yet completely responsible for the state in which we find ourselves, he came to this world to rescue us by his a-**maze**-ing mercy.

Here is a trustworthy saying that deserves full acceptance:
Christ Jesus came into the world to save sinners
– of whom I am the worst. 1 Timothy 1:15

16 Oh yeah?

miracles

It's very easy to allow ourselves to fall into cynical unbelief.

Take bits of the Old Testament, for example. What about when the spies who went into the Promised Land came back with far-fetched stories about vast bunches of grapes so big that they needed two men to carry them (Numbers 13:23)? And that the inhabitants were giants (Numbers 13:32-33)? Or take the story about the mighty walled city of Jericho, besieged by worshippers and brought crashing to the ground by a loud shout accompanied by a brass section (Joshua 6:20). None of those stories can be true, surely?

And then there's the hard-to-believe tale of the day the sun stood still when Joshua prayed (Joshua 10:12-14). After all, modern science tells that the sun doesn't move at all anyway, so it must have been the earth that stopped moving. However, we have sufficient grasp of rudimentary rotational physics to draw an alarming conclusion. If the world stopped revolving, momentum would cause all the people and animals (and anything else that wasn't firmly secured, like cars, trees, buildings and bridges etc) to fly about uncontrollably at about 1000mph (1600kph) for a time, until friction slowed everything down.

And don't forget that the atmosphere would suddenly be rushing about too, like the worst-ever hurricane. The oceans would also slosh at high speed, like a mega-tsunami.

Well, either that, or the earth's rotation's centrifugal force, which constantly flings us away would be suddenly reduced, so we'd be crushed, squashed flat against the ground by gravity, which would be revealed to be far more powerful that we ever considered.

It's evident it didn't happen, so surely it can't be true.

I'm not even going to mention the Old Testament story when the sun actually reversed (well, the shadow which climbed the ten steps on the stairway of Ahaz moved back down again) simply to be a sign that God was going to heal the King's boil (2 Kings 20:1-11). The global implications of the sun going into full reverse makes the Joshua story pale into... well, that's why I've decided it's best not to mention it.

Moving on, there's the hopelessly implausible yarn of Gideon's three hundred soldiers who scared off three massive armies with a minor surprise involving broken pots and a few firebrands (Judges 7:8,22).

No, surely, no-one could possibly imagine that these are literal stories based on fact? Of course, they may have important spiritual significance like fables or parables, but they didn't really happen, did they? We should reckon that these are teaching tools, not historical documents, right?

Well, consider this for a moment.

Way back in Genesis 12:1, God hinted at a land that he had set aside for his people. Then, at regular intervals, he continued to remind folk that he had set aside a promised land for them. Just think about that expression: promised land. Sounds like a land that had been promised, doesn't it? And God's promises are sure and certain and are always kept, because his character is totally good and he'd neither break a promise, nor make a promise he couldn't keep.

So, we can be confident that he intends to give them a land for themselves.

But look again. The land that God promised to his people had been invaded by a crowd (several large nations, actually) of interlopers – other ethnic groups who were not God's people; they had stolen the land for themselves. They had no right to stay there.

It seems to me quite likely that God would help the Children of Israel throw out these thieves. And knowing what God's like, it's not surprising that he uses his supernatural power to assist them.

Since God is God, he could manage to make big grapes, couldn't he? Or to knock down a wall in whatever way he chooses? Or to arrange for a slight change in the earth's revolution around the sun, or place fear into the hearts of enemy soldiers, so that they ran away at the sight of Gideon's tiny battalion?

When you put it like that, these amazing miracles don't seem quite so far-fetched. Amazing, yes, of course, but not impossible.

Frankly, if your faith in God's power is so small that you think he can't make big grapes, then you're missing the point and your fruit is way too puny, friend. Doing the impossible is what God achieves before breakfast (and he tucks into Alpen with extra-vast raisins). It's our lack of faith that makes us think things are impossible and our lack of imagination that means we have a fry-up or porridge or Shreddies or marmalade on granary toast or whatever each morning.

Where were you when I laid the earth's foundation?
Tell me if you understand. Who marked off its dimensions?

Oh yeah?

Surely you know!... Can you raise your voice to the clouds and cover yourself with a flood of water? Do you send the lightning bolts on their way? Do they report to you, saying 'Here we are'? Who endowed the heart with wisdom or gave understanding to the mind? Who has the wisdom to count the clouds?... Will the one who contends with the Almighty correct him? Let him who accuses God answer him! Job 38:4-5, 34-37; 40:1

Can you sense the rich, warm, smiling but sarcastic tone in God's voice?

You're right, these are God's accusing but gentle words, correcting the cynicism and disbelief of Job and his friends. They made the mistake of thinking they could put God in a box or set limits on his ability. Oh, please make sure you don't have a small vision of God's greatness; he is mighty and able to do far more than we ask or imagine.

Collapse the walls of Jericho? Doddle! Frighten an army with a few torches? Piece of cake! Raise Jesus from the dead? Mighty, mighty potency, but certainly within the range of such a powerful God!

Change the heart of a school bully or a mean boss? Fast-track a house sale or provide finance from unexpected sources? Heal cancer or offer the gift of salvation to wicked sinners? Yes, and much more!

Never fall into the trap of looking at the problem so much that you take your eyes off the one who provides the solution. God is abundant in power and love and ability and willingness to bless his people.

True, you will not always get what you think you want precisely when you think you want it, but you can trust God that you'll always (yes, always) get what he knows is best for you, and for his glory, in his perfect timing (check 1 John 5:14-15)

So, let your cynicism go, dear friend, and walk by faith.

17 Losing the syrup

ten commandments Exodus 20

Sad but true: when I was a boy, the Christian Life seemed to be filled with the phrase *Thou Shalt Not*. That's because when I was young, the main translation of the Bible that was used was the Authorised Version and not because I am so ancient that people actually spoke like that!

The phrase comes, of course, from Exodus 20 where the Ten Commandments are listed. But some of the commandments I had to follow went way beyond the ones God spake unto Moses.

Mostly they related to Sundays, the so-called *day of rest*.

When I was a lad (let's say about ten years old), Sundays were frantic with activity; not restful by any description; although I now realise that's not what 'day of rest' should be taken to imply.

Anyway, these were the extra-Biblical rules during my childhood:

1 Thou shalt not speak to others in church; but signalling with thine eyebrows is okay.

2 Thou shalt not ride thy bike on a Sunday, for that would be A Poor Witness.

3 Thou shalt not disobey the FHB rule during Sunday teatime (Family Hold Back and let the guest gannets swoop first).

4 Thou shalt not even consider, let alone request of thine mother, wearing any other raiment on the Lord's Day except thine Sunday Best clothes, even though they itch and squeeze and rub, yea, even unto much chafing, despite manifold applications of the finest of talcum powders.

5 Thou shalt not have any time to thyself, since the Lord's Day hath an strict schedule thus:

8.30am	(latest) get up, wash, dress; downstairs and ready by
9.15am	leave the house and travel to church meeting, for both thy parents doth love with vast vigour arriving at such events most grievously enthusiastical and abundantly early, since it seemeth to them meet and right so to do
10.15am	Church with Sunday School
12.50pm	lunch
2.45pm	Crusaders Bible Class *(see introduction)*
4.30pm	thine house brim-filleth; yea, copiously with most exceedingly random visitors for Student Tea Ceremony

6.10pm	Dad & students depart for church Evening Service
7pm	bathtime (once a week, whether I needed it or nay)
7.20pm	bed; read a book
8pm	sleep, for tomorrow is An School Day; and no radio under the covers, or there'll be trouble.

Some of the rules that my parents applied to us seemed difficult to comprehend. Admittedly, they subjected themselves to the eyebrow-waggling rule, so I can't really moan about that.

There was one old lady in our church who had her forehead technique down to a fine art. With her it was practically semaphore (the signalling code which uses flags), but unfortunately, she had a very cheap wig. When she said 'hallo' (both eyebrows up together, twice) her wig was flung back and forward with alarming force. 'How are you?' (left up, with a blink and a frown) had little effect, to be honest, but she nearly lost the entire syrup when she attempted 'What are you having for lunch? We've got roast pork with carrots followed by rhubarb crumble.' It would have been far easier to stand up, remove the wig and reveal the question and full menu tattooed on her skull.

Of course, I exaggerate, but the 'no talking in the house of God' rule meant that fellowship was reduced to practically nothing. Yes, there is perhaps some wisdom in establishing an opportunity for people to prepare themselves for entering the presence of God in worship, but it is only natural that when God's family meets together, the people have a desire for joyful greeting, fellowship, news, conversation, even praying for one another and so on. Okay, lots of loud chatting and laughter might lack reverence, but is certainly more friendly.

In recent years, many church meetings begin or end with fellowship over warm dishwater and a ginger nut or stale custard cream, but this is hardly a motivation to hang around. Our church has recently experimented with providing Brunch after the meeting. It became a good reason to attend the early meeting, which finished at around 11am. Bacon or sausage sandwiches using fresh, crusty granary loaf, plus quality filter coffee; this seemed a top-drawer idea to me.

Sadly, this experiment was discontinued, not because it failed to provide friendship and fellowship opportunities, or an excellent place to invite guests, or even following a complaint from the vegetarian mafia (becoming ever more vocal in these parts), but on account of an alteration in the timetable. The positive effects of this adjustment are that those of us previously attending the early meeting now enjoy a more civilised start time and we now can share fellowship with those who had been attending the later gathering.

On the downside, the end of the meeting and traditional Sunday lunchtime are now much closer together, rendering the bacon sarnie option surplus to requirements. Shame. But it does mean my occasional suggestion of slipping away for a Carvery Roast with Yorkshires, stuffing balls and a good number of precariously-balanced spuds has once again become an option.

Anyway, to get back to my original theme of parentally-enforced additional Sabbath-observance rules: I wondered how riding a bike could possibly damage the eternal truth of the gospel. I reached the conclusion that either the gospel truth is exceptionally flimsy, which it isn't, or the bike ban was hopelessly ill-considered, which it was. Even though I was still young and not experienced in theological debate, I challenged my mum on the topic (I challenged Mum because she always seemed far less dictatorial in matters of church practice than Dad – she even allowed us to slum it in t-shirts and jeans one Christmas morning, for heaven's sake; I suppose it wasn't a Sunday, so the usual rules didn't apply. See what I mean? Fast and loose with traditional interpretation. Some might call it woolly-headed liberalism).

Anyway, the bike thing and the challenge. She reckoned it this way: just suppose, she said, one Sunday afternoon, the man next door was staring out of his kitchen window, thinking about his sin and the state of his eternal soul, when I rode past on my bike and distracted him. He might accidentally forget about God. So, she concluded, bike-riding was 'A Poor Witness'.

I didn't get it then and I still don't follow the logic.

But when I get to the afterlife, I really hope the bloke who lived next door is there, staring out of the heavenly portal, because that would make all those reduced-fun Sundays worthwhile.

I have recently spoken again to my dear silver-haired liberalotrix about this odd ruling.

Unsurprisingly, the lame rationale concerning the neighbour had been forgotten; now she claims that banning the bike was her way of helping me keep Sunday special. After all, she says, I could ride the thing any other day of the week, so to abstain on Sunday is part of honouring the Lord's Day.

There is a rather significant difference between these explanations. One is focused on a neighbour's journey towards salvation; the other is rooted in obedience to a commandment. I suggest mother's memory is at fault (not unusual these days) and her reasoning in both explanations flawed (never been all that rare) and rammed with weaknesses aplenty.

To start, it denies the possibility that the easily-distracted neighbour may consider eternal truths on any other day, which is plain silly.

Busy weekday traffic creates additional danger on the roads, so I was already pretty much reduced to weekend travel on my bike anyway. With just Saturday and Sunday available, another fifty per cent of my bike-riding options were now removed at a stroke. My experience and confidence in busy traffic was minimal, since we lived on a quiet cul-de-sac, where rush hour amounted to two cars and a mobility scooter. Indeed, my brother and I regularly played football in the road for hours without interruption from a vehicle. So, given that bike-riding, for me, was not so much a form of transport, but a healthy hobby, this ruling which limited my opportunities to gain balance, grace, wind-in-my-hair etc and indeed much-needed confidence, was nothing short of harsh.

Can it really be what God intended when he commanded us to set aside the Lord's day – to inflict an unreasonable restriction on a charming, handsome child? I wasn't honouring anyone; I was simply having a law imposed upon me. Okay, maybe I was honouring my parents, but it's a stretch. Almost certainly the counter-balancing sin of resenting enforced Puritanical strictness (oh, let's not deny it) was nullifying any treasure in heaven I may have been accruing.

Riding my bike past the bloke next door could only possibly qualify for the criticism of A Poor Witness if he was made aware that this unfeasibly stringent rule was being flouted, because I would then be seen to be in breach of Parental Obedience and this might reflect poorly on the way they were bringing me up and suggest that having a Christian faith wasn't making much of a difference to them or their skill in raising submissive progeny. So, I'll only buy that one if they were prepared to let him know that the rule had been laid down in the first place. Otherwise, the entire premise was built on the ridiculous assumption that his thought-processes were hopelessly flimsy. Grand questions of eternity and beyond were apparently able to be dissipated by the gentle tinkling of a bell or the sight of a young lad enjoying healthy exercise in a safe environment.

But the truth is that he couldn't have guessed, he hardly ever looked out of his window and probably never thought philosophical thoughts during Sunday afternoons, when he was, if he had any sense, asleep or taking a leisurely bath or watching a film on BBC2, or mowing his lawn, or being a Sunday driver or visiting his relatives or buying stuff at Homebase, nowhere near his front window. Or out for a bike ride!

Meanwhile, I could have been safely and gleefully riding my bike between lunch and Bible Class and maybe again between Bible Class and teatime.

My mother apologised to me decades later for giving me what she mockingly termed 'such a deprived childhood'. Of course, I smiled in the way a grown-up son does, not particularly wanting to have a fight about it.

Other rules: the 'day of rest' myth (some say *misunderstanding*) never stood a chance when Sundays were crammed with action and activity.

Our house was manic on the Lord's Day, especially when a crowd of University students, many of them Christians, arrived for my mum's legendary home-made Sunday tea, which always featured sausage rolls, sandwiches (perm two from tinned salmon & cucumber; ham; ham & tomato; corned beef; corned beef and cucumber; egg and cress mushed up in salad cream). Then came home-made Victoria sponge, fruit cake, Dundee cake or 'butterfly' cakes; Battenberg; millionaire's shortbread; madeleines; or, a special treat, McVitie's Ginger cake), fresh baked scones with cream and home-made jam, flapjack, chocolate teacakes, orange Club biscuits and gallons of PG tips. Standard rules apply: FHB, except on the boring sandwiches.

Bertie's enigmatic shoes contrasted with the dark suit preferred by Charles, who was, frankly, nondescript and went on to become an accountant. Enough said.

Other students were Bible scholars, evangelistically enthusiastic or otherwise Christ-like. I remember very few wise, spiritual or scholarly conversations, but then I was only a nipper.

My younger sister wasn't old enough to know any better, but always tormented the guests after tea by insisting on playing a dreadful board game called *Cat & Mouse*. In this, you threw a dice to see if your little marble (mouse) escaped down a mousehole before the big marble (yes, of course, the cat) could catch up with you. The game usually ended in tears, either because my sister (who liked to be the cat) didn't win and she wasn't emotionally stable enough in those early years to cope with games of chance, or because it was such a shockingly tedious game that everyone else lost interest. The game was biased towards the mice escaping, since the small marbles could fit through the big holes in the board, while the cat – well, you get the idea – but my sister never twigged. I say never, but I expect she gets it now. She retired last year.

It was usually a relief when time came for the students (why didn't we ever have female students? Perhaps there were fewer in those days or these particular male students were so busy being enigmatic, nondescript or spiritual that they didn't attract girls at all) to pile into Dad's car and be wheeled off to the evening church service. When they noisily stumbled out of our front door, I would prayerfully hope the bloke next door wasn't doing his deep and meaningful stare from his kitchen...

Sundays were not even slightly like a rest. No-one explained that 'rest' didn't mean 'lazing about' but 'being refreshed by focusing on God.'

Clothes, as already mentioned, have to be different on a Sunday. They are supposed to be uncomfortable, or you won't feel adequately righteous. They have to itch and pinch so that you will be constantly aware of the sacrifice you're going through for the Lord's sake. But the clothes I was required to wear made me so bad-tempered that any miniscule amount of sacredness gained was more than countered by my under-the-breath annoyance. The Christmas Day previously referred to was such a departure from the norm that the memory of the guilt I felt about being so casual has remained.

Please note that we're talking here about traditional old-fashioned Sunday Best, not the holy underwear so beloved of American cult cyclists; purity pants, virtue vests or legalistic long-johns.

So, what am I concluding? Commandments are bad?

No, of course not. It's just that the additional commandments my parents bolted on to God's were an attempt to provide some boundaries for my behaviour or limits to how I should act. I suppose they were right to do that, but there was more than a slight danger of them adding to my burden. Jesus criticised the Pharisees for a similar miscalculation (Matthew 23:2-3).

These days, it has to be said, Sundays in my house have a rather different look about them.

I do my best to be on time for church, to make sure I get to speak to friends before the meeting starts; I often chat to someone sitting near me when the collection is taken; and I usually hang about at the end to see other friends, catch up and put myself about, hoping for a lunch invitation. There is almost no eyebrow semaphore; so far I've not spotted any obvious wigs.

Riding a bike to church is an ecologically sound decision. I don't think it's a Bad Witness, but then neither is it officially witnessing, unless the cyclist tows a large neon sign with Bible verses on. Sometimes I catch a bus or get a ride. I have even been known to walk to the church meeting.

Many of these options represent for me a new-found freedom and a fresh understanding of the reason God want us to Keep Sundays Special, not just Especially Unpleasant.

I'm afraid the days of chocolate-coated flapjack or of home-made scones with cream and jam are long gone. These days, it's going to be a healthy apple or perhaps a small glass of mineral water, or maybe some fresh air and a cloud.

I wear regular clothes on a Sunday. Who puts on a suit to catch a bus?

I have understood a little more about the purpose of setting aside a day for worship, reflection, fellowship and honouring God.

Obeying the Ten Commandments is only possible with God's help; they enhance our understanding of what God is like and the best way for us to live.

But surely, ten's enough, eh?

18 These three remain

lesson learned in lockdown 1 Corinthians 13:13

Doubtless all of us have anecdotal evidence of how we survived the 2020 Covid-19 enforced lockdown.

Perhaps you feel it went on too long, or started too late, or was insufficiently fierce, or lacking in compassion or cost too much or was some sort of divine reckoning – whatever your opinion, I'm sure none of us imagined, as the virus began to flourish, that its effect would have such long-lasting and wide-ranging impact.

But I am keen to testify to the God who preserves and comforts. My experience during 2020 was deeply spiritual as well as almost entirely lived in physical isolation.

One of the politicians tried to convince us that the guidelines applied equally to everyone by suggesting 'we're all in the same boat' but this wasn't even slightly true in my opinion. We were all in the same storm, but some were in much larger boats, ships, clippers, galleys, windjammers, steamers, sloops, galleons, corvettes, frigates, cutters, minesweepers, battlecruisers, dreadnaughts, aircraft carriers or ocean-liners.

Passengers on board large sailing vessels live very differently to those of us in a small rowing boat, a dhow, a canoe, a coracle, a surfboard, on a punt or in a makeshift paddling pool that leaks. Unless the storm is severe, large ships can make way without the five-star restaurant below decks being affected; while even the slightest touch of inclemency utterly changes the experience of a boat that is at the mercy of the wind and waves.

~

It was several years ago that I began to live on my own.

I moved out of home at the age of twenty, leaving my parents and sister (my older brother had already finished University and had remained away from the family home). I was off to London, to live in shared accommodation with three other single blokes, all of whom were unknown to me.

The training centre for *Campus Crusade for Christ* (now *Agapé*) required the ups and downs of flat-sharing. This was partly for financial reasons and partly for fellowship. I suspect it was also partly to test us and prepare us for similar living conditions, as the lifestyle we were choosing wasn't likely to lead to great riches.

What I hadn't expected, however, was that the flat we were sharing had just two bedrooms, so I didn't even get a room to call my own. The experience was mostly positive, but I certainly learned to treasure 'alone time', as there was precious little of it.

The first-floor flat in built-up north London (situated between Regent's Park and Hampstead Heath) was high on a hill, across the road from a fire station and had high ceilings. It was very blandly decorated, so we decided that we'd add a splash of colour by dyeing the lounge carpet. This was 1978, so naturally, we chose orange.

We emptied the room of furniture, threw several cakes of dye into a bathful of water (approximate proportions) and set to with scrubbing brushes and brooms. We must have added more than 30 gallons of liquid to the carpet, which was made from acrylic tufts embedded in a spongy plastic backing. Then we thought we should add more, as our poor technique had left the colour a bit patchy. This may not have been our first mistake, but it was certainly one of them. Using dyes of a darker hue for the 'second coat' was another.

How to dry the carpet? We raised it up off the floor by positioning furniture underneath, letting it drip into washing-up bowls, buckets and similar receptacles. Once this slowed, we added all our electric fires, convector heaters, fans and hairdryers; we turned them all on and closed the door.

It took three weeks to evaporate the moisture in the carpet. We could tell the work was complete when the rainbow faded away. Of course during this time the murky orange, light-red, pale orange and light brown carpet had dried into the contours provided by the warm air and the furniture over which it had been draped. It was very far from satisfactory, but we were utterly fed up with living without a lounge (and without any of the kitchen chairs we'd used in the lounge. We were also concerned with the way the little disc in the electric meter was rotating at high speed, fatiguing its bearings.

We surveyed our attempt to beautify our living conditions.

What we had achieved was a nasty, stained, multi-coloured blotchy floorcovering with strange hills and valleys all over (I was going to write *lumps and bumps* but it was much worse than that). We tried to stamp them down, but to no avail, so we returned the furniture and tried to live with it.

For the rest of the year, the lounge featured several significant tripping hazards and a permanent assault on the eyes. When our tenancy ended, the landlord was displeased that the carpet in the lounge no longer fitted the 'off-white' description written on the inventory.

He agreed it had displayed one or two minor stains when we moved in and was probably prepared to accept a little 'wear and tear', but this was taking the mickey, so our deposit was not returned. I think we got away lightly, as the flat downstairs didn't make any fuss about having a soaked and/or collapsed ceiling, which may or may not have happened, but we hadn't even considered the risk.

Next, I lived in a house of multiple occupancy in Cardiff, and when I returned to Brighton, found lodgings with an elderly missionary couple. I was not made very welcome, which wasn't my fault, so I left them and rented a room in a house with several students. This was better, except the configuration of the house meant we lacked a living room, so I was the accidental host most evenings, when the guys crowded into my room to watch my telly. After a couple of years, I decided I should share with a professional, rather than my recent experience of being with students.

Despite Simeon being a Leeds United fan and having several boisterous friends who came to stay, I liked the flat in Brighton near the sea front. Following a season as lodger, I became co-owner and eventually owner, when Simeon moved on to get married.

I enjoyed having lodgers myself, as this made financial sense, but the flat was very small. HD stayed for a short while until he bought a bedsit flat which he had refurbished.

Once I'd relocated to Birmingham, I continued to live alone for a while. But the need for financial stability induced me into finding several lodgers over the years. Some kept themselves to themselves, which was fine, while others maximised the opportunity to cook dinner for themselves every evening and then watch commercial channels on my telly, in my lounge. The last of these left early in 2018 and since then I've lived alone.

So, when the announcement was made in March 2020 about staying indoors, working from home and the closure of cinemas, pubs and restaurants, I was isolated. My church cancelled in-person meetings and began to upload worship, notices and sermon videos, which were pretty helpful, although the part I liked best was the section on Zoom where we could send messages to one another and see faces. The Community Group to which I belonged also met on-line and maintained good fellowship.

What no-one realised, of course, was that the initial four weeks were just the beginning of a long, long lockdown. The Community Group began a series of meetings based around wellness – exploring physical, mental, relational and spiritual health. These sessions were advertised on the church website and several people who were not members of the church or of any church joined in, which was hugely encouraging and a joy to get to know them.

But the key to my survival in the midst of all the aloneness was my Bubble. One of the church elders and his wife invited me to be in what was termed a 'social bubble' with them. This meant Adam, Danielle and I were able to meet up indoors and to consider ourselves one household, even though they lived several streets away.

I jumped at the opportunity and felt immediately included. Their daughters (aged 4 and 1) were delightfully welcoming and I almost immediately learned about the depth of parental training in *how to lose a game graciously* that had been provided to the older girl, Marlene, which was almost none.

Invited to play draughts with her, I asked myself 'Is it better for her to win every game or should I show her what real life is like?' Arguably, this should not have been my decision. In the end I went with the easier approach and chose to let her win. Following my plan, I made several deliberately poor moves and she took my pieces with glee. Eventually, I put myself into a losing position, but she didn't spot a chance to take one of my kings. However, the resulting *huff* move I made (because, surely, standard draughts rules apply?) would create sufficient space for her to clean up.

Sadly —and her parents are entirely to blame for this – no-one had told little Marlene about huffing, so there were tears and vitriol, all aimed at me, some of which came from Adam, who assumed I had chosen the 'real life' approach to games. I tried to explain that if her piece was removed from the board, I could only make one move; this would jeopardise all my pieces; thus Marlene would be able to chalk up a glorious victory. But no-one was listening, which was disappointing and possibly the closest we came to bursting the bubble.

Happily, we were able to move on, although I don't play draughts there anymore.

Instead, I've been subsequently forgiven (why? - I did nothing wrong!) and invited by Marlene to listen to her reading her oracy homework and sign off on the sheet and to several games of *Guess Who?* This turned out to be an execrable *Disney Characters Created Long After Disney Stopped Being Any Good Guess Who*? so I was confronted with princesses, undefined beasts and strange fish. I didn't recognise any of them and most were nondescript in terms of the regular *Guess Who*? distinctives – big lips, white hair, eyebrows of note, cleft chin etc – which in the past have given me an edge. It seems my questions, such as 'hat?' and 'showing their teeth?', were insufficiently standard.

We've also played several games which come with a full set of rules (most of which Marlene dispenses with) and additional bonus decrees, such as 'Marlene is the winner'. I may start sounding a bit grumpy unless I curtail this theme, but I suppose the point of the exercise is to spend time together attempting to wring whatever educational value these games provide. I don't mind losing every time, but it's tough to remain cheerful when 'Marlene beats all-comers' is not only the objective of the game, it's also the immutable over-riding imperative.

Her younger sister Marie, on the other hand, is far more easy-going. We celebrated our birthdays together (born on the same date, 61 years apart) which was great fun, as wrapping paper abounded and she took great pleasure in unwrapping all the presents. Danielle learned quickly to explain to the child 'this one is for Andy, but you can unwrap it. Not your present, but you can take the paper off…' Otherwise, the misunderstandings could have become a lot more awkward.

My visits to their home sometimes coincide with times when Danielle is either working (she's a medical specialist) or preparing for a night shift (or recovering from one). This means I can closely observe of how Adam interacts with Marie.

It's been an eye-opener for me to observe Marie's development over an extended time - from week to week her vocabulary grows and her ability to express herself, in phrases at first and now in complete sentences, is quite remarkable.

She seemed to gain ability from one week to the next. I think this was to her own advantage, since when she was presented with a plate of freshly-prepared lunch, rather than saying 'thank you' or 'ooh, this looks lovely!' or even 'Daddy, how remiss of you to have neglected once again to enrobe my torso with an apron, all the better to keep my clothes from food spillages', she was focused primarily on the anticipation. The ham wrap/cucumber/carrot stick/houmus platter was a merely prelude to what she knew was coming as a follow-up (and what she really wanted) – 'blueberries!'

It's been testing to walk through a difficult season during which Marie used her developing language skills loudly to express disapproval of activity suggestions made by her father such as tv viewing, painting, lunch, going to the park, taking a nap, using the potty, clearing up some playthings before emptying the third toybox onto the carpet, talking not shouting, etc. Seeing her being unable to tell us what was wrong and watching Adam try to get to the bottom of each storm was sad and noisy. The 'terrible twos' hit the household with fury, but the worst is over and it's now not so fearsome.

I could say 'I knew it would come to an end', but I am not a parent, so I keep my cakehole firmly closed. I only witnessed a few hours at a time, while her parents had to cope round the clock. Of course, Adam also knew it wouldn't last forever, but his was the greater pain as he watched his frustrated daughter raging. Particularly when she stopped crying and wailing long enough to explain her preferences, because to give her what she wanted at that point felt like giving in and allowing the tantrum to be an effective manipulation tool - a lesson he was understandably eager not to teach.

It's been such a privilege to be treated as part of the family. No, I don't live there, but the time I spend in their house is relaxed and inclusive.

I no longer feel like a guest, but like someone who belongs there, has a place, mucking in like everyone else. Now, don't be silly - I'm always going to remain seated when the dishwasher's being loaded, since it looks laborious, I've not been trained and I don't want to be responsible for incorrectly positioning a bowl, thus incurring the wrath.

Similarly, when I'm offered coffee (sometimes within an hour of arrival!) there's either the warning 'it's only instant' or it's coffee which has been sitting in the cafetière for several hours and needs microwaving so that it scalds my lips and the roof of my mouth, so I have learned to plump for the instant. I treat their home with respect but have been known to fetch my preferred plaything from the toybox and hope one or both of the girls join me. I know I should always clear up after me, too.

I am certain I belong, because when Adam and Danielle have an argument in front of me, they don't take a breath to put on a united front for their guest. Indeed, they each attempt to enlist my help to help them win their side of the disagreement. This I handle with characteristic charm and diplomacy, naturally.

I've also witnessed occasions when there has been giggling and cuddling as they express their love for one another with appropriate freedom in their own home, with family present.

The favourite part of my visits to their home is the moment or two when I'm left to myself - Marlene is at school, Danielle's at work or sleeping it off, Marie needs her nappy changing and thankfully, this takes place in private. So, I have a few minutes which I make the most of by hiding chocolate around the house.

Adam let slip in a sermon that he has a weakness for Yorkie bars, so I add three of them to my Tesco order each week (discounted), wrap them up and put them in various places: behind the toy box; in the spice rack; down a wellington boot; balanced on top of a picture frame; secreted within a lever arch file… My best ideas include recycling a used frozen peas bag, popping a Yorkie inside and adding it to the collection of similar-looking partly-used vegetable bags in the freezer; putting a bar inside a flat box, adding it to the books on the bookshelf such that the side of the box appears to be another spine; and my pièce de résistance, using double-sided sellotape to position one under the dining table. Recently, it has become necessary for me to put name labels on them (I use the *Open Air Campaigners* typographic style), because it came to my attention that whenever Adam finds one, he accidentally forgets to share. The addition of name labels (chocolate clearly marked with names not his own but of his loved ones) does not, I hear, affect his behaviour in the slightest, but adds a soupçon of guilt, because his conscience is not entirely lifeless.

Recently, he spoke about Narnia in his sermon, mentioning that he knows I have some hesitations in treating Lewis' fantasy as allegory (see Chapter 30). Anyway, that week, one bar remained undiscovered until I gave a massive clue; I practically told him where to look and that it was a Lion bar – his excitement wavered slightly until he discovered it – a Yorkie but named for Aslan.

I surprised myself one day when sitting on my sofa, alone in my house. I was thinking about solitude, trying not to concentrate on the negative aspects, using words like *loneliness,* or *boredom,* or to allow myself to linger upon the darker sadness of not having anyone alongside me. I chose instead to count my blessings and list some of the many benefits.

For example, things are where I left them, not 'tidied' or thrown out; whatever provisions come into the house remain available until they are consumed (or disposed of, if I don't get round to them in time); I don't need to ask anyone's approval or opinion if I want to open a window or increase the heating; the place is quiet, unless I turn on the tv or activate my playlist. They say an Englishman's home is his castle – I can pull up the metaphorical drawbridge, let down the figurative portcullis and keep myself to myself behind a rhetorical moat. I take pleasure in this sort of control and have the option of making appointments for socialising.

As I mused, I discovered that the contentment and sense of companionship that my bubble supplied was continuing to satisfy me, lessening the downside of solitude. In other words, the topping-up of my love tank which takes place on a Monday was continuing to keep me refuelled for the rest of the week!

I admit I was relying very heavily on those precious hours in Adam's home. Sometimes, it was simply having different walls at which to stare that refreshed my soul; other times, it was the delight of meaningful conversation. We'd discuss the vacillations in the fortunes of his beloved Wolverhampton Wanderers, the complications of locked-down church life, the latest announcements from the Chief Medical Officer, or insights either of us had discovered from our reading of the Word. We'd pray together sometimes. I cannot express enough the enthusiasm I had for those oases of fellowship punctuating my isolation.

Despite all this gratitude for my bubble, the long weeks and months of the lockdown eventually took something of a toll on my wellbeing. I was tuned in to yet another on-line sermon, trying to concentrate. One of the verses drawn upon on that occasion was

And now, these three remain: faith, hope and love.
But the greatest of these is love. 1 Corinthians 13:13

Of course, the preacher went on to make what I can only assume were insightful comments about love. I assume that, since it's the primary focus of the passage. I like to listen to preachers who recognise the importance of preaching what the word says, not just what they wish it says or some other variation. However, this time, I had to make that assumption, because I'd stopped listening, I'm afraid. I do that, sometimes, during sermons, especially when the person at the lectern passes over something which seems to me to be far more interesting than the main theme of the talk. Is that wrong? I know the preacher feels they have 'a word from the Lord' for the congregation and they may be right, but they may not realise that some of us are being spiritually arrested by something they say or refer to in passing. They keep going, of course, because others in the crowd are receiving the blessing originally intended. This is one reason why preachers should quote or refer to more than one verse when they make their points.

My attention had been distracted, as I say, by a different part of the verse about faith, hope and love. How was I doing, I wondered, on these three essential elements of spiritual life?

Starting, then, with the one the scripture declares to be the 'greatest of these' – love. I received so many messages and gifts from a wide range of people that I never lost my confidence in their affection for me. Indeed, this encouraged me to cling firmly to the love of God; this hardly wavered throughout the period. He kept on reminding me about his tender mercy; spoke to me from the scripture; embraced me, metaphorically speaking, with his kindness; and gave me every assurance of my place in his family. Love wasn't an issue.

Neither was faith. My certainty in divine purpose remained strong and I felt drawn close to God in worship, in prayer, or through various passages of scripture. Dear friends reminded me of wonderful ways God has protected me, blessed me and ministered to me over the years.

Then I stopped to think about hope.

My church used to meet in the school hall which was the location for the final scenes in the 1986 film *Clockwise*, where John Cleese plays Brian Stimpson, a headteacher who has to meet a deadline; this evades him throughout, of course. At one stage he gives up and makes the remark 'It's not the despair, Laura. I can stand the despair. It's the hope!' Constantly having his hope dashed has resulted in his conclusion: he'd rather accept failure than keep on thinking there's some tiny possibility that he might succeed somehow and then finding that likelihood taken away, once again. This is primarily because he is using the term 'hope' to refer to a vague optimism, an aspiration, wish or chance. In the Bible, that's not how the word is used, particularly when referring to our expectation of glory.

Biblical hope is not the same as our vague wish for good weather tomorrow, nor a cheerful but insubstantial wondering how nice it would be if circumstances turn out for the best. It's certainly not some ill-considered warm cheerfulness that whatever route we take, we'll end up where we want to be – that's called disorienteering (made-up word, but it strikes the right tone) or failure to trust in the sat nav.

In scripture, hope is far more substantial. It's not built upon a desired outcome or wishful thinking. Biblical hope comes with God's promise.

Now it is God who makes both us and you stand firm in Christ.
He anointed us, set his seal of ownership on us,
and put his Spirit in our hearts as a deposit,
guaranteeing what is to come. 2 Corinthians 1:21,22

It's firm and certain, like all God's promises, because he never lies, never fail, never forgets. Try this for size:

Therefore, since we have been justified through faith,
we have peace with God through our Lord Jesus Christ,
through whom we have gained access by faith into this grace
in which we now stand. And we boast in the ***hope***
of the glory of God. Not only so, but we also glory in our sufferings,
because we know that suffering produces perseverance;
perseverance, character; and character, ***hope****. And* ***hope*** *does not put us*
to shame, because God's love has been poured out into our hearts
through the Holy Spirit, who has been given to us
Romans 5:1-5 [my emphasis]

Nothing woolly or wishy-washy there; it's concrete, flint, mahogany, marble. So, no problem, you might guess. The book of Psalms contains thirty-four references to hope, most of which are packed with confidence, assurance, certainty. The New Testament contains more than sixty references to hope in the sense of a reliable certainty of a future blessing. When God repeats himself, we should take notice!

My trouble was, I guess I must have taken my eye off the prize and allowed the isolation of lockdown to undermine my positive view of the future. It was a time when there was no point in making plans, as no-one knew when restrictions might be lifted; indeed, some people had lost confidence in the government's announcements, thinking that there was such an eagerness to reopen shops and offices (as well as pubs and restaurants) that this would be (for once) too much, too soon.

When there is little to anticipate with any degree of certainty, hope takes a beating and begins to shrivel. Unlike the Cleese headmaster Mr Stimpson, I wasn't hoping fervently against the evidence. I was in an even more desperate state: I'd begun to think hope was gone. I acknowledge I should have been more confident, more reliant upon God, more determined to see it through. But I wasn't.

Putting my faith in God was not called into question and I was even more sure of his love than ever. But hope was being eclipsed.

I had allowed doubts and fears to cloud my thinking and obscure my vision, bringing harm to my emotional wellbeing. Focusing on the world had taken my attention from eternal benefits that were still available to me, if only I'd taken hold of them! I was suffering, yes, but God says this can (if only I'd co-operate with him) produce perseverance. And the determination to see it through can result in a more noble character. And then, we're into hope; hope does not disappoint us or put us to shame, because it's firm and certain. Which is where we came in and where I could have been, if only I'd remained steadfast in the first place.

I'd allowed myself to plummet the depths – not a good place. 'What about all those decades of walking with the Lord?', I hear you ask, with an appropriate tone of rebuke in your voice. 'Have you learned nothing?' Now you're getting a bit too fierce, but I needed something to shake me out of self-pity and distraction.

And, of course, God came to my rescue the moment I turned my attention away from how sad I was and turned instead towards his faithfulness. He was so much more gracious than certain harsh critics I have just quoted. His questions came with Holy Spirit conviction, which always leads to life, repentance, fellowship, restoration.

What particularly struck me from the 1 Corinthians 13 verse was that 'these three remain'. Here's another of God's firm, unbreakable promises. Love, for me was strong. Faith, for me, was about right. But hope was reduced to a teeny tiny level. But God says it remains. And it wasn't gone.

The words that flooded into my consciousness were the negative, disastrous ones, like lost, departed, eviscerated, vanished, expired. None of them applied; yes, hope was beaten down, diminished, fading, lessened… but not completely gone. God had not allowed it to be eliminated.

But we have this treasure in jars of clay to show that
this all-surpassing power is from God and not from us.
We are hard pressed on every side, but not crushed;

perplexed, but not in despair; persecuted, but not abandoned; struck down, but not destroyed. 2 Corinthians 4:7-9

Observe the words *hard-pressed, perplexed, persecuted, struck down* – Paul was truly going through a difficult time. But he was not crushed, not in despair, not abandoned and not destroyed. He denies these words which signify defeat or an inability to rise up and try again. He leans hard on all-surpassing power of God and embraces the victory. This jar of clay was bashed, bruised, chipped, cracked, leaking even; but still just about intact. Still a jar, not just a handful of broken pieces of stoneware.

Faith, hope and love, then. They interact – hope gives you faith and love gives you hope. Faith enhances love. Can we distinguish between them? This may not be easy or necessary, but I was trying to get by on two out of three. God says 'these three remain' so I took him at his word and fanned into flame the hope within me. The embers were cool, but by his Spirit, I sensed a renewal of confidence. Forward-looking, I was viewing temporal things as less important.

19 Lost Again

woolly walkabout

Luke 15:3-7

Quite some time ago, inspiration fell upon me as I watched someone give a talk using chocolate bars as illustrations. 'What was the talk about?' I hear you ask. It was the Parable of the Prodigal Son. The inspiration was to see if there were other ways I could tell that story, using a range of constrictions. You'll be aware of how successful I was if you've come across my book *The Lost Son*.

After more than three hundred retellings of the prodigal's story, I now turn my attention (much less comprehensively), to the Lost Sheep; an animal lost by nature and rescued by love. With a final revelation.

Then Jesus told them this parable 'Suppose one of you has a hundred sheep and loses one of them. Doesn't he leave the ninety-nine in the open country and go after the lost sheep until he finds it? And when he finds it, he joyfully puts it on his shoulders and goes home. Then he calls his friends and neighbours together and says, "Rejoice with me; I have found my lost sheep." I tell you that in the same way there will be more rejoicing in heaven over one sinner who repents than over ninety-nine righteous people who do not need to repent.' Luke 15:3-7

Let's examine this tale of instinctive astrayment, compassion, rejoicing and community, featuring a marginalised, poor, possibly non-Jew.

Alliteration

Lenny looks longingly; lacking! Locates little Lambikins lies, languishing. Lovingly lays lamb-like lengthwise lapel – legs lodgingwards. 'Look, locals. Lost Lincoln Longwool liberated!

Old Oscar obfuscated; one of ours out o'order! Off on outing, observing… outcome! Organises overjoyed Oktoberfest.

Summation shortages shock shepherd Simon; sets south seeking single sheep. Searches… success! So, shoulders Swaledale. Says 'Shout 'static, satisfaction!' Spirits sing, specific soul saved.

Tom tallies, tells tale that total's trimmed. Tours through territory, tracks, trots though tolerating Teeswater transport. Tells tenants

'Thanks! Thumping tremendous testimony/theology!'

And I couldn't resist

Careful custodian counts: curse! Calculates complement close. Crosses countryside, conquering. Cruises cottage-wards; celebrates: combining cousins, citizens.

Considerable commemoration (celestial city), concerning conversion, comparing continuation.

Alphabet Games

Lipogram (*avoiding the letter e*)
Say a man adds up, but finds his woolly flock's count is down by a singular animal. Actions: judging ton minus Larry shall stay okay on a plain, looks vigorously for lost individual. Found, man puts it on his back, walks into his town and throws a slap-up lunch for family and all who know him. Christ says spiritual city has party on noticing total turn-around by a bad man, but not so much on account of abundant saint.

Acrosstic

A man, who had a hundred in his flock
L ooked and noticed with considerable shock
O ne was gone, vanished. So, he left the rest
S afely and searched for the stray, distressed.
T ook him a while, but he found his sheep
S houldered the beast and with heart a-leap,
H eaded home for a party with his friends and
E veryone who knew him. It was grand!
E ven in heaven, repentance brings celebration,
P erhaps more than when there's already salvation.

Key words

Post-Victorian UK Prime Ministers
An elderly farmer known as Old **MacDonald**[1] (husband of Jo) noticed the wind blowing o'er the **heath**[2], past his four mills (labelled A to D) and saw this as a thre**at. Lee**[3]ward hillsides sometimes created absent sheep hideouts or lost lam**b lair**[4]s.

There was indeed a sheep missing, so he went to find it, recognising his bi**as: quit h**[5]is responsibility? No chance.

The sheep was one of an African breed, with a distinctive bleat.

Soon he heard the **call. A Ghan**[6]aian was caught in a bush in the valley of Arla, near the **church. Ill**[7]? No, but very tired. His heart sang at the sight of **that cher**[8]**ub on Arla**, **w**[9]hen he placed her on his shoulders.

His return journey was wind-assisted; this was good kar**Ma.**

C Mill, an[10] old building, appearing over the hill's **brow, n**[11]ear the tree, was the first structure he spotted on his return. He sought permission from the Lord **Chamberlain**[12], clashed his cym**bal four**[13] times and at the sound of this enig**ma. Jo r**[14]an to greet him and cried 'Celebrate with me!'

Many villagers visited his home but several played away: **Lloyd; George**[15]; **bald Win**[16]; **Douglas (home)**[17]; **Cameron**[18]; **May**[19]; **John's on**[20]ly daughter Arla; and the famous **Wil, son**[21] of his father **Campbell-Bannerman**[22].

Restoring the sheep made this a new **eden**[23].

		Prime Minister	*term(s)*	*party*
1	Ramsay	**MacDonald**	1924	*Labour*
		second term	1929-1935	*Labour/National Labour*
2	Edward	**Heath**	1970-1974	*Conservative*
3	Clement	**Atlee**	1945-1951	*Labour*
4	Tony	**Blair**	1997-2007	*Labour*
5	HH	**Asquith**	1908-1916	*Liberal*
6	James	**Callaghan**	1976-1979	*Labour*
7	Winston	**Churchill**	1940-1945	*Conservative*
		second term	1951-1955	*Conservative*
8	Margaret	**Thatcher**	1979-1990	*Conservative*
9	Bonar	**Law**	1922-1923	*Conservative*
10	Harold	**Macmillan**	1957-1963	*Conservative*
11	Gordon	**Brown**	2007-2010	*Labour*
12	Neville	**Chamberlain**	1937-1940	*Conservative*
13	Arthur	**Balfour**	1902-1905	*Conservative*
14	John	**Major**	1990-1997	*Conservative*
15	David	**Lloyd George**	1916-1922	*Liberal*
16	Stanley	**Baldwin**	1923-1924	*Conservative*
		second term	1924-1929	*Conservative*
		third term	1935-1937	*Conservative*
17	Alec	**Douglas-Home**	1963-1964	*Conservative*
18	David	**Cameron**	2010-2016	*Conservative*
19	Theresa	**May**	2016-2019	*Conservative*
20	Boris	**Johnson**	2019-present	*Conservative*
21	Harold	**Wilson**	1964-1970	*Labour*
		second term	1974-1976	*Labour*
22	Henry	**Campbell-Bannerman**	1905-1908	*Liberal*
23	Anthony	**Eden**	1955-1957	*Conservative*

Languages

Franglais

Un homme qui regardez les sheep numero cent mains un. Ils abandonné les autres dans pays non-ferme, et allez dans search d'une qui est disparu. Discoveré, ils back-pack le sheep et entre le maison. Il invite tout le monde pour mange et boire dans les hours minute-wee.

Jésus dit 'Ils sont plus celebré sous un homme mal qui repenté than pour quatre-vingt-dix-neuf personné salvationné.

Aussie

Lookin' arfta floxiz almost seconatcha to us. But this Bruce loses wunch eepsoweep anicsand goes off afterit. Bonzer! Findsa, putsa ova-is-sh older and goes ometuis Sheila. Throws another coupla prawns on the barbie, invie tsallis mates for a few tubesa Fosters and ane'sup. Ripper!

There's more celebratin' upstair sover one sinna who repents than over ninety-nine what don't needta.

Pastiche

Pseudo-Shakespeare

SCENE ONE *right near an brook*

SHEP'D [*counts*]

BOY [*watches*] Master, pray tell, what numbrest thou?

SHEP'D Oh, forsooth, I've lost count! If can'st not see furrow-brow mindfulness, then thou art grossly thicker e'en than a Tewkesbury mustard. Drawing all my enscratched marks from end to beginning, mine fruitfulness hangs low upon the bow'rs o'rithm'tic. And so, from one, again I shift my eyes.

BOY My lord, my lord, my much-addled head do I hang in deep shame – than it ne'r wast in mind betimes to cause distraction upon thine. So humbly hath I hereby taken this request within my yearning breast…

SHEP'D Angels and ministers of grace defend us! Hold thy whisht from all thy rambling!

BOY Yea, my lord.

SHEP'D [*counts*]

BOY [*watches*]

SHEP'D [*concludes*] Alarum and haroo. Tis pity, tis, tis true. Regret doth truly fill my chest; I have no more but ninety and nine, mine counting-rod declareth.

BOY Tis but an small loss, my lord. What carest thou?

SHEP'D Thy words hang leaden upon pustulant pock-faced lips, thou pribbling folly-fallen boil-sore on a carbunkle!

BOY Hath thou not a care what pain and hurt such poison words scour across mine visage?

SHEP'D But ninety and nine is too great a loss. I'll make quickly fourscore miles (or more as doth mine foot entread) to seek this singular woollen bleater. Vouchsafe he'll be hid 'neath an thornbush, yea, I'll warrant, lest he drowneth in an brook or lies of wounds in yon meadow, waiting in vain for his fleece-white flockish companions to show wither he might follow, right quickly. An brief diversion can make much gap, or stumbling caper, or tarry to o'er concern w' verdancy… I'll sojourn not here, not loiter; I shall make haste; I'll seek, hunt, indeed!

BOY Will yet I remain? Corporate I'll lay on guard.

SHEP'D Aye, wi' all this flock G'ist me mine staff. [*exits*]

SCENE TWO *upon the heath*

SHEP'D [*enters, searches*] All I hath found thus is what appearest to mine wits to be where a fire burned right recent. Mayhap weird sisters hath found my lost one and made broth-potions… but bone I find not, mere ash and clinker, marry, with discard eye of newt and toe of frog. Confound the whining hedge-pig withal and scorched earth where hath that cauldron bubbled [*exits*]

SCENE THREE *same*

SHEP'D [*enters, searches*] And many hours do I wander, may yet… but wait! What ist I spy? Sheep? Yet best doth murder sheep? Fie on't. A bramble hath not legs, a bush doth not wear a beard, thickets hath not a mouth to bleat – marry, gambol and jiggish dance! Lo, 'tis mine lost sheep, sought out with sweet care, discovered here before mine eyes. [*places sheep on shoulders*] Mine woolish-rounded quarry, thy breath and spirit hath returned, so much better than reportingly! [*exits*]

SCENE FOUR *village*

SHEP'D [*enters, carrying sheep*] Full haste and come all ye! Gather hither! Merry make and celebrate! My sheep that was lost is found!

BOY What meat providest thou upon yon griddle? Hath we an fatted calf to kill, or red salmon that springeth o'er waterfalls far and yon, or clucking feathers to pluck? Or even yet –

SHEP'D Yea, call hurrah, yet make not thy voice to any vile dark-cornered thoughts of mutton on a spit, for that fools surely makest of us all.

JESUS [*for it is he*] Heav'n sings great joy o'er one sinner. Ninety and nine are pastoral vouchsafe, but glory fresh upon return'd ones. [*they prance and frolic*]

Plot

What if?

• **Suppose a hundred of you have one sheep and it gets lost?** Perhaps you were distracted, or left the responsibility to someone else, who was leaving it to you.

• **Suppose you have a hundred thousand sheep.** You'll never know that one got lost. Your hired men may not care sufficiently; may not count very often; may fear telling you bad news.

• **Suppose you have a hundred thousand sheep**. You never know that one hundred got lost. Your hired men may never realise, either.

• **Suppose you have a hundred sheep; none are lost.** You'd learn no lesson and set no example.

• **Suppose you have a hundred sheep and one got lost**. You've read the appropriate management manuals and happily say to yourself *my initial and ultimate responsibility is to the majority; in my heart, I'm grateful to the Lord for the ninety-nine.*

• **Suppose you have a hundred sheep and one got lost**. You leave the ninety-nine and go after the one that is lost. You never find it and you perish in the wilderness.

• **Suppose you have a hundred sheep and one got lost**. You leave the ninety-nine and go after the one that is lost.

You find it and return with it; however, meanwhile wolves have attacked your flock, which is now scattered over the open county. Fifty-seven are slaughtered. Now you have forty-three sheep, but it takes you more than a fortnight to gather them together. Some would call this a net deficit.

• **Suppose you have a hundred sheep and one got lost**. You leave the ninety-nine and go after the one that is lost. You find it and you return with it; you invite the villagers to rejoice with you, but they have read the appropriate management manual and disapprove of your desertion.

• **Suppose you have a hundred sheep and one got lost.** You go and find it. In the same way, there is more seeking in heaven than pastoral care.

The Quest

The trebled-checked count was disappointing; indeed, one sheep was missing. A tiny percentage, some might say, but only if not employed as a Shepherd in New Testament Palestine.

No, this was Lano-Lynne Bigfleece III, a much loved Charoliais – missing, sadly fate unknown. Ensuring the rest of the flock were secure, with safety in numbers and fine pasture, this crook-bearing fellow retraces his steps in seeking L^2B^3. He crossed miles of meadow and many streams, checking between bushes and in thickets; he searches hedgerows and remote barns. Tiredness is set aside, such is his compassion for the lost one.

Eventually, he spots L^2B^3, caught in brambles, distressed, fearful, harming herself on thorns. The shepherd tenderly sings to his loved one to calm her (his sheep know his voice) and gently retrieves her from the grip of the blackberry bush. He hoists L^2B^3 onto his shoulders and joyfully shrugs off weariness, striding purposefully back to his flock; the ninety-nine are restored to one hundred!

He calls on lots of village folk inviting them all to celebrate with great festivities. Some didn't understand what all the fuss was about, but once they'd realised there was free drink flowing, they turned up just the same.

Jesus explained that each one is precious and heaven rejoices over repentant sinners.

Poetry

Haiku

Sheep lost by nature
Sought and found; taken homeward
Rejoice; heaven too!

Iambic Pentameter

Where are you now then, my favourite lamb?
I counted thrice, almost ad nauseam;
How many sheep of all those that are mine?
The answer was short, just ninety and nine.
Can't be right; oh but yes, my blood ran cold,
Too few here to call it a complete fold.
I considered you, bright as a button –
I want you to grow up to be mutton!
I quicken my steps; I leave all the rest,
My heart's fit to burst right out of my chest.
I wandered to find the one that was lost;
I travelled afar; you're so worth the cost.
I called out your name, knowing you know my voice

Then saw you – oh, glory, did my soul rejoice!
A worthwhile journey, favourable trek,
I gathered you up, placed you over my neck,
And rushed back to town in old Palestine
To party with mates and drink lots of wine.
Heaven is glad at these predicaments
Angels all sing when one sinner repents!

Senses

Even before he started counting, the shepherd could **smell** a rat; he could **see** there was one sheep missing and **felt** sorry for it, so he went to search for it. He **heard** the sorrowful bleating and the sheep **heard** his voice. He carried the sheep home. 'Rejoice with me, villagers; I've **tasted** success and found my lost sheep!'

Style

Operatic Libretto

(Overture)

CHORUS Bleat, we bleat, yea we bleat and baa/yes, baa and baa/and bleat and baa!/It's an onomatopoeia!

(Recitative)

SHEP'D We wander the hills both day and night/to find blades of grass we rejoice at the sight. We flock together and act with one will/as we wander down dale and over the hill. Centurian we, with fine wool on our back/we're counted each day to ensure we don't lack. One, two, three, four, five, six, seven/and then comes eight, nine, ten and eleven; And every day we reach ninety nine and one more/to make up the full and appropriate score.

Count, count, count, count; upon this green mount/count, count, count, count; the correct amount/Count, count, count, count, accuracy paramount!

(Aria)

SHEP'D It's always a joy to be sure that the flock/is full and entire and not missing in stock/not missing, not missing, not missing in stock/our full and complete and entire woolly flock! It's always a joy to the sure that the…shock! Ninety-nine is no fun/We are down by one/My care this is dissing/one sheep now is missing. Oh, oh woe is me/now there's no guarantee/ That this flock is complete/this is so bittersweet/I shall wander afar from this threshold/My mission to return the lost one/yea this lost one/unto the fold/yea, unto this my fold.

(Intermezzo)

SHEP'D Where are you, dear one? Where? I seek thee with all of my might. I have satisfied myself that the rest were secure from attack and foul weather and safe in a fold, to come thus a-hunting to find you.

Yes, ninety and nine are all settled down, but my soul has a hollow void where you belong – oh where will I find thee? Many miles and many more will I ramble in hope of hearing, seeing you again, my dear loved, dear loved, dear loved one. [*spies sheep*] My soul thrills fit to burst with serious compassion; I'll carry you home, even though you are not injured or tired! I'll put myself to yet more trouble – I'll support you on my shoulders.

(duet with chorus)

SHEP'D Hurrah and hooray/ This glorious day/ My search hath born fruit/ Proving joy absolute!/ My actions have been astute/ Love that will not dilute/ No lamb can substitute!

CHORUS Found! Found! Found!/ Far from home ground/What a great turnaround!/ Found!

SHEP'D [*calls on villagers*] Feast with me, let ale be downed/ Celebrate, this lost sheep is found!/Drink, dance and make merry/(I'm no mercenary)/For one who went missing/there's no reminiscing/returned to be with us/we're ninety-nine plus/(not superfluous)/no, we're family complete/eternally upbeat/story so bittersweet/to hear your bleat!

(reprise)

SHEP'D Centurian again, fine wool on our back/I'll count you each day t'ensure no lack!

(finis)

Gourmet

A **shepherd**, sporting **mutton chops**, discovered he'd been a **chump**, **overdone** the wandering and lost one of his **sheep**.

So, he decided to **leg** it and seek the stray; 'let's be clear**cut**; **let's** be thorough', he said.. He might as well be hung for a sheep as a **lamb**, he thought, **rack**ed with guilt.

When he found the lost animal, put it on his **shoulder** and went home to his house, which was called **Knuckle End**. The party he threw featured **kleftiko, shank, doner kebab** and **mint sauce**, along with **shepherd's pie**.

There's more joy in heaven over one sinner who repents than over **ninety-nine** saints.

Viewpoint

Sheep

With a start I noticed that I had somehow become separated from the crowd. Usually, this would just mean looking about and finding them all again, or, in a worst-case scenario, bleating until rescued.

But for some reason, it didn't work this time.

I cried out until I was nearly hoarse yet still no ram or ewe came to find me. I had just about given up when – yes, such joy and full-on rapture – the shepherd came into view! He gathered me up in his strong arms and rested me on his shoulders. With a song and a purposeful stride, he carried me back to the fold. He gently put me on the ground and I quickly found my mother.

The shepherd celebrated with his pals, which was nice.

Neighbour

Parsley Pete we used to call him. Daft old chap, earning his living looking after a bunch (okay, okay, flock) of dozy sheep. *What's so difficult about that?* we thought.

Until one day, PP comes rushing into the village and throws this enormous party. Balloons, streamers, music, wine, beer, Pepsi Max, chicken wings, scotch eggs, sausage rolls – the whole lot. Apparently, he'd lost a lamb from his flock and gone off to look for it; now he's found it and was really pleased with himself.

That showed real determination and pastoral care if you ask me. So, he wanted to rejoice. It was very kind of him to include us, when we'd perhaps been a bit mean in the past.

Party Pete we call him now.

Wordplay

Monosyllable

A man who tends sheep counts, yet finds eight times ten, ten more and nine – one less than the full count. He leaves the rest where they are safe on the hill and goes in search of the one which is lost. When he finds it, oh, he sings with glee, puts it on his back (up near his neck) and walks back home. He calls on those who live near him and on those who have blood ties and asks them to eat, drink and be glad that he has found the stray. Christ made the point that there is great cheer where God dwells on high in the midst of those who serve him (with wings and harps), when a man owns up to his sin, turns from it, seeks and puts his faith in the Lord; more so than a large crowd of saints with no need of such change.

Polysyllable

Shepherd observes missing animal. Any number below double-fifty strongly suggests deficit. Leaving others safely, searches enthusiastically everywhere until discovery complete. Returns, carrying, rejoicing, inviting family, acquaintances.

Party! Jesus remarks: Greater rejoicing over sinners repenting, compares favourably against already righteous people.

Wordsearch

The usual rules apply. However, rather than merely providing a list of words, they've been incorporated into a narrative. In the grid, find the words within the narrative below which have been highlighted in **bold type**. These may read forwards or backwards, up, down or diagonally. The letters left over (reading from the bottom right) will express the angels' attitude when someone who was lost is found. Salvation-tastic. (Solution p265)

S	H	E	P	H	E	R	D	T
R	A	G	R	S	N	E	I	S
E	C	F	I	O	H	P	Y	E
D	S	O	E	J	M	E	T	R
L	J	U	S	I	N	N	E	R
U	O	E	S	K	R	T	N	P
O	Y	S	E	E	U	S	I	T
H	A	E	T	R	J	E	N	R
S	S	G	N	E	V	A	E	H

A **shepherd** discovers one **sheep** is **lost**; making sure the **rest** are **safe**, he will **seek** the stray. Finding it, he will **return** with the sheep on his **shoulders**. **Jesus** declares: There is **more joy** in **heaven** over one **sinner** who **repents** than there will be over **ninety-nine** righteous people.

20 Two ways to make custard

25th December

Radical, possibly unpopular statement: the main trouble with Christmas is that it comes around every year.

This has the downside that we can so easily fall into the trap of tradition and repetition, rather than making sure that we celebrate the birth of Christ every time and not something less.

Take my family, for example. When I was young, my Dad woke us up every Christmas morning, without fail, by playing his *Massed Bands of the Royal Marines* record at top volume, marching up and down the corridor outside our bedrooms, pretending to be the Drum-Major, twirling his imaginary mace and conducting the military bandsmen. It was all there: *A Life on the Ocean Wave; Anchors Aweigh!; Radetsky March; Land of Hope and Glory*. Dad alone enjoyed this. My mum tolerated his indulgence. My brother pretended to sleep; my little sister (at the time not old enough to know any better) played right into Dad's hands by moaning loudly. I was zen-like: I appeared calm but inside I was raging.

My parents always took us (sometimes dressed sloppily) to church on Christmas morning, for several carols and a mercifully short sermon and then it was back home at top speed in readiness for the distribution of armfuls of presents from under the tree.

An orgy of gift-unwrapping followed. My brother and sister and I always enjoyed that bit! Our protocol was to take turns, so we could see what others were receiving and also so we could watch when the gifts we had given were being under-appreciated, welcomed or something in between. The reality of unexplained popularity meant that my little sister either had twenty-five turns to herself at the end, or even alternated with everyone else, effectively taking four times more turns that the rest of us, just to get though the vast heap of brightly coloured presents in her pile.

Then Mum would call us in for lunch. Somehow, she always made this happen seamlessly, with very little waiting time. Perhaps she'd got up early or something and had it all sizzling, steaming, roasting, baking, bubbling, browning and thickening away merrily during our time in church. I still don't know.

Anyway, there was always a magnificent spread, complete with crackers (the ones with bad jokes and silly hats), a light starter of perhaps melon or paté and then a roasted bird of some sort with sage and onion stuffing, pigs-in-blankets, loads of sprouts, roast potatoes and mash, thick gravy (just the way we liked it), bread sauce, several forgettable vegetables and all the trimmings. My sister was always disproportionately happy if there were some smashed-up plain crisps sprinkled over the whole plate, but I think that's just one of her many endearing peculiarities.

When we asked (we always did) what bird had been roasted, Mum would tell us it was a capon. She explained that Dad wanted something more special than just chicken and she was reluctant to cook turkey because she believed it to be 'too dry'.

My guess is that it's primarily errors in cooking style that renders a bird's meat too dry, but in those days of only Craddock and Floyd I wasn't aware of anything called 'cooking errors'. My mother's expertise was unquestioned, with good reason. But I have (only very recently) discovered that my mother was economical with the truth each year when asked to explain what a capon was, since she told us (in her *and let there be no more discussion about it* voice) that it was a cross between a chicken and a turkey. In the absence of Google (this being in the 60s & 70s), we didn't know any better. Perhaps she'd believed this bowdlerised twaddle. Crossbreeding was hardly a suitable topic for the dinner table. I later discovered most attempts at doing what doesn't come naturally between chickens and turkeys, were unsuccessful, as were unions of turkeys and chickens. I'll withhold unnecessary detail.

The truth, of course, is even less suitable for children, wether (see what I did there?) at the dinner table or not.

But the lunch always tasted fantastic, which was the whole point and Dad said, every year 'the meat was beautifully moist'; we were all happy. The spuds were always excellent and so were the pigs-in-blankets, although I have since discovered infinitely superior ways to make stuffing. I fear my mum may have misread the packet the first time and forever afterwards continued to use far too much water, producing a sloppy offering. It was a very forgivable, extremely minor chink in her culinary armour and since in those days stuffing only made an appearance at Christmastime, she didn't have enough opportunities to hone her skills.

Truth be told, none of us was foolish enough to criticise her food, because we all realised that encouragement and positive endorsement would result in continued hard work; indeed, I believe she expressed her love for us very tangibly in the effort she poured into providing food for us. Speaking of which, let us now turn to the highlight of the Christmas lunch: Christmas pudding and custard! Not for us any nonsense about alcohol-infused butter or white sauce. And flambé wasn't an option.

No, this was a special day and so Mum's custard was what was required. After all, you don't mark special celebrations by 'indulging' in sub-standard rations. No, you ensure everything's maxed out on quality; especially the sweet course.

There are two ways to make custard: my mum's way and the wrong way. Yes, other people may be content to settle for thin, runny, insipid yellow dampness. But in our house, we always had a delightfully thick, viscous, velvety, vanilla, warm, sweet (but not too sweet), slippery coating on our puddings. Oh, it was perfect! It didn't really matter much to me about the darkness, fruitiness, spiciness or stick-to-your-ribs solidity of the actual pudding, or even any financial surprises; provided the *crème anglais* was top-notch. And with my mum, there was culinary dependability; all was well.

Then came cheese – one yellow (firm, waxy, mature), one white (creamy, soft, foreign), one blue (speckled with tasty mould) and lots of crackers (the other sort) – and superb fresh brewed coffee.

Now, Dad was entirely responsible for the percolation of this production number and he would prepare the carefully selected brand of beans, grind them, decant them into the machine, then set it into burbling, warming, steaming, brewing action during the break between main and afters, so the piping hot beverage was ready in good time. The resultant dark, fragrant, glorious liquid was poured carefully into tiny cups with or without hot or cold milk or cream. Even the sugar was special: either demerara or an odd-looking large crystal formation. It almost spoiled Dad's day when I made it evident that I preferred my coffee black, without sugar or alternative sugar and without cream, or milk of either temperature. Luckily, Mum always wanted hot milk, my brother liked to play with the floating cream and my sister was willing to experiment with the sugar. With coffee came After Eights, even though it was not yet two o'clock (my Dad's middle name was Pedantry, but on this one day of the year certain rules could be relaxed).

Then we would all help with the washing-up. My brother always preferred to watch the James Bond movie on telly, but the rest of us went off to the local cancer hospice to dish out tea and cake to the residents, their visitors and the nursing staff. Mum and my sister helped take the trays around to each bedroom and the lounge; Dad and I stayed in the kitchens and did the tea-pot cleansing ceremony with scalding water and much laughter, washing and sterilising all the china and stainless steel. We had to stop to watch the Queen's Speech (yawn) in the staff room and then we carried on with the work.

Returning home to the end of the Bond film and a roaring log fire, we'd settle down in front of the telly with teatime treats of cold meats (capon and ham, as a rule), piccalilli, home-made sausage rolls, crusty bread and more crisps. This would be followed by a long evening of properly decent telly, regular dips into the big tin of chocolates, at least one round of nut-cracking and either a generous helping of yule log or a hefty slice of Christmas cake (perhaps with a piece of Lancashire cheese to accompany it).

Stuffed witless and exhausted with laughing at the *Morecambe and Wise Christmas Show*, the joyous season had been celebrated.

How can I remember this so vividly? Simply because (as I'm sure you have realised) it was the same, every year, for decades.

It's a good tradition, I suppose and although it's far from healthy, it's relatively harmless. We never felt more like a family than when we were completely comfortable with the routine, doing things we all enjoyed (or considered valuable and charitable).

But one year, when I was bit older, the pattern was changed. I still celebrated Christmas at my parents' home, but the leaders of my church invited me to run the Christmas morning service. What, me? I was stunned! Instead of just letting the festive season happen, I could actually have an influence over what happened during my Yuletide!

Not many people came to that meeting, compared with the crowds that normally packed into our church gatherings, but those who were there seemed to enjoy themselves. We sang a few carols (it's always a good idea to sing *O Come All ye Faithful*, because it's got that verse with the line *Yea, Lord, we greet thee, born this happy morning* and there's only one window of opportunity each year to sing it). I was tempted, briefly, to include a few slightly left-field Christmas songs, since I was in charge.

I considered *Rudolph the Red-Nosed Reindeer, Fairytale of New York* and *I saw Mummy Kissing Santa Claus,* but wisdom prevailed.

I invited the children to show everyone the presents they had received. There were probably a few notices. And the sermon I preached was the shortest ever heard in our church, by a considerable margin. My sermonina (tinier even than a sermonette) was based on just two words: *but now.*

Therefore, no one will be declared righteous in God's sight by observing the law; rather, through the law we become conscious of sin. But now, a righteousness from God, apart from law, has been made known, to which the Law and the Prophets testify. This righteousness from God comes through faith in Jesus Christ to all who believe. Romans 3:20-22

Therefore is a word that brings the conclusion of an argument or thread of reasoning, so it's only sensible to look at what the writer has been saying up to this point (see also chapter 31). Paul has been quoting from the Psalms and other Old Testament verses emphasizing humanity's inability to live Godly lives; thus, none of us will be declared righteous. The law only makes us more aware of our sinfulness. Bad news. Indeed.

But now... the word *but* indicates a change or new direction. Before Christ came, our state was dreadful. God's people were powerless to live righteously.

On the other hand, *now* carries a strong sense of immediacy; it's current; previously, things were like this... *but now* the old reality has gone, the new has come, all has changed. Our current circumstances are different to what they were; they were changed in the twinkling of an eye and they are not only different, but a lot better! *But now,* God has sent his Son to a lost world to shed light, hope, purpose, salvation, forgiveness and righteousness. God has solved our problem.

Yes, you're right; it was indeed a magnificent sermon and it only took five minutes! This means I occupied about ten per cent of the time usually allocated to this part of the meeting.

And yet, it packed one hundred per cent of the punch.

The lead elder of the church (quite a famous preacher, actually; I expect you'll have heard of him) sat in the front row and smiled encouragement at me throughout, which was really very kind of him, because he must have known that his presence could otherwise have been rather intimidating. I worked out later that his heart for the meeting was not to catch me out or to make a fool of me – I was perfectly capable of making a fool of myself without his help – but to celebrate Christmas, encourage and envision the people and properly to exercise his fatherly leadership role. He looked rather taken aback (pleasantly surprised) when he grasped that suddenly it was all over bar the final carol *Hark the Herald Angels Sing* and that he was free to go home and share the day with his family. If it had been one of his sermons, by this time we'd have only just got out our notebooks and made ourselves comfy (well, the cheap plastic chairs helped to keep us all wide awake) for the duration. I even dared hope he might follow my example. But the truth is, some thirty years later, there's no sign of him trimming even a few minutes off his average sermon length.

That year (1991), I honoured God properly at Christmas. In following years, however, I'm afraid that I often fell back into easy routine, avoiding awkwardness for the family's sake. But this glimpse of how things could be different inspired me to plan more thoroughly and make alternative arrangements, so I could choose sometimes to celebrate the day in my own setting, with a lot less indulgence. I have even been invited to spend the day with other families, with their own traditions and weirdness, which were wonderful, even if bewildering.

And on a few occasions recently, I've chosen to remain by myself (on purpose), with cold beer and medium-rare steak and peace and quietness. I'm undecided just yet which is my favourite form of celebration. I haven't been invited to preach at the church again. Perhaps it wasn't such a good sermon, after all…

The chances are that you'll not be asked to preach a sermon or direct the meeting on December 25th. But you definitely can learn the lesson I learned; Christmas is not only about giving and receiving presents, consuming industrial quantities of wonderful food and drink, following dubious and/or positive traditions or overspending.

Christmas is a time to thank God for his wonderful gift, Jesus Christ, Saviour, King, Redeemer.

And to reflect, gratefully, on custard made The Right Way.

21 Embrace the love

responding to God's affection

Some recent developments in the way we express our worship and practice our outreach have impacted my relationship with God enormously.

Yes, of course I still sing content-rich hymns; current favourites include *Up from the Grave He Arose, And Can it Be?, On Christ the Solid Rock I Stand,* and *When I Survey the Wondrous Cross* in addition to more-recently-written belters like Stuart Townend's *In Christ Alone,* Israel Houghton's *I am a Friend of God,* or Matt Redman's *Blessed be Your Name,* which are similarly packed with scripture and celebration.

And of course, I choose to talk to God with reverence when I spend time on my own in worship. I also love to read scriptures that encourage me, build up my faith and strengthen my belief in a mighty God who has been unfolding his plan all through history, saved my soul and has even graciously permitted me to play my part, too.

But I have discovered the Christian life is so much more than just getting the theology right and ensuring your lifestyle matches. Those things are hugely important, of course, but there's more.

What could this possibly mean? Watering down eternal truth? May it never be! Defying God in order to live in a more chillaxed manner? Forbid it, Lord! Maximising theatrics and loud music, overlooking flaws like showmanship or inaccuracies? A thousand times, *no*! Rather, what I mean is the recent introduction of a range of worship songs that don't particularly focus on restating Bible truths in poetic form.

Now, please don't get me wrong. I'm always going to be a firm advocate of block-busting classic nose-bleed-inducing rip-snorters when it comes to a worship session. See the list above, for example, plus *Blessed Redeemer, Great is thy Faithfulness, How Deep the Father's Love for Us, Before the Throne of God Above, O Jesus I have Promised, Ten Thousand Reasons, What a Beautiful Name It Is,* etc, etc. Bring them on and often, or at least be assured that they will feature in my own personal times of devotion.

However, some songwriters have recently developed a style of lyric content for their worship songs that expresses their devotion to the Lord in a way I can only describe with the word *romantic*. Now, I don't mean soft or fluffy or ephemeral or temporary, like a romantic relationship, which might start with warm fuzzy feelings, whispered 'sweet nothings', an exchange of meaningless gifts and the joy of the innovative which could develop in different directions. Perhaps such feelings will lead, sadly, to rejection, either to be replaced with the next novelty or with hollow emptiness. Alternatively, of course, the fuzziness could deepen into something more solid, long-lasting, real and tough enough to withstand the hard knocks of wedding preparation classes, marriage itself and commitment.

I have little time for the *Jesus is my boyfriend*-style of song, since he isn't and I desire a deeper relationship than that. And if I get married, it will be to a female, whoever the lucky woman turns out to be.

No, no (clears throat, composes himself, gets hurriedly back to the point) what I'm highlighting here is that with some sorts of worship song there is an opportunity to spend time enjoying the affection of Father God, revelling in the warmth of being with Jesus, the lover of my soul and welcoming the sweet presence of the Holy Spirit.

My failure to understand the intention of many songs initially caused me to be unfairly dismissive of them; now I have learned to meet with God through their gentle tunes and rhythms. They provide a setting for congregations to experience the radical love of God.

I have firm opinions on the subject of how a worship time should be constructed. There is a biblical precedent for us to declare eternal truth about God (objective praise), then to rejoice in our personal engagement with that truth (subjective praise), then to revel in it with love songs (adoration and worship) and to end (sometimes) with declarations of God's sovereignty and victory (prophetic songs).

What do I mean? I suppose I'm trying to steer our singing towards being definitively truthful, warmly responsive and affectionately reflective, rather than soppy or all about me or overly repetitive. Yes, I confess, I'm a wrinkly and I like rhymes that rhyme, but that's mostly because that's what makes the poetry more memorable.

Consider these lyrics from the National Anthem:

Send her victorious, happy and glorious,
Long to reign over us God Save the Queen; anon ©1745.

Strange grammar, very odd requests and deep subservience, I agree, but poetic, visual, purposeful and unforgettable. Later verses of this song drift alarmingly towards themes of war-like disdain or worse for our neighbours over the Scottish border.

Never gonna give you up, never gonna let you down,
*Never gonna run around and desert you;**
Never gonna make you cry, never gonna say goodbye,
Never gonna tell a lie and hurt you
Never Gonna Give You Up *performed by* Rick Astley;
Stock Aitken Waterman ©1987 RCA

This is the kind of soppy tosh no woman is ever going to swallow, agreed, but it's memorable due to the rhymes. The tune rattles along, but you keep up since the lyrics scan and rhyme, thanks to the polish that the songwriter bothered to apply.

Compare and contrast these with the intense but apparently unrefined lyrics deployed in a lot of Christian songs produced recently. I have seen or read a number of interviews with writers of worship music who genuinely believe that the Lord inspired them with their repetitive, unrhymed, theologically flawed or weak songs. I am sure they really do think God delivered a finished song to them; I'm not convinced He's so slapdash. I suspect the truth is that God provoked them with an idea which, crafted with skill and creativity, might have become a song.

Consider these contrasting words from a worship songwriter. 'My new song has taken two years and required a lot of perseverance. I love the process: the chewing, the meditating, the journey I've been on. It's a challenge to study huge themes, trying to distil theology into language that fits melody, but also provokes a response at a heart level. But I love crafting and digging for gold. Eventually, after several versions, I've realised that this song is a simple heart cry in response to truth.'

Doesn't that sound more valuable than a freestyler's spontaneous but somewhat dodgy rapping declaration that 'God the Father died on the cross/ to help you behave better 'cause you're men of the cloth'? One 'composer' uses the deny-it-if-you-dare phrase 'God gave this to me'; the other uses (less spectacular, more Biblical) words like craft, persevere, meditating, study, digging, persevering labour, theology…

Perhaps I'm complaining about songs written specifically for the younger generation and I'm really not supposed to understand or appreciate it.

---

* See Psalm 147:3, John 6:37, Hebrews 13:5. God is similarly faithful

But can someone tell the worship musicians in my church, please, that we're not all of the same demograph? My passion is to see the younger generation grow up with a depth of understanding and appreciation for Bible truth and I am saddened that some of the young men in my discipleship group lack the confidence and bedrock provided by hymnody, having only songs of recent years from which to draw.

So, where is my focus in worship? Declaring truth, reminding myself about the cross and its significance, using songs with depth and worth, expressing a strongly thankful attitude?

Or is it upon my feelings, my warmth towards God, working towards a warm and fuzzy sensation, 'having a great worship time' and coveting a spiritual experience?

Please do not misunderstand me; I know God does graciously meet with us in the holy place and it's never wrong to seek to have an encounter with God, obviously. But worship must be primarily about God, not centred on how I'm feeling and certainly not about what I can get out of it. We seek God, surely, in order to find him, not so we can feel great or get goose bumps or decide that the morning wasn't wasted. If my primary goal is to feel good, then my attitude betrays me. Honouring God must come first.

And when I meet with God, it may very well result in conviction of sin or challenge about my attitude or behaviour. It's likely in such a case that I come away from the meeting feeling worse (or at least, meaningfully confronted), rather than better. Meeting with God is almost always a serious business and very rarely a vague fuzzy feeling.

Just a thought.

Worship should be about declaring truth – Bible truth – in addition to praise, prayer, exercise of spiritual gifts, readings from scripture, testimony, etc. Within this, there is a place for expression of love and devotion, of course. And only some of this needs to be accompanied by music, so let's not get side-tracked by the size, volume or attractiveness of the band or the light show or the flag-wavers or the dancers or those who repeatedly shout 'Hallelujah!' or those who sink to the floor or kneel in the aisle (which surely must flaunt health and safety rules about tripping hazards and clear gangways).

I suppose I am droning on, pleading the case for a redressing of the balance here. Please be patient; God's not finished with me yet.

Like the journey into the temple in Jerusalem, in our times of devotion we pass from outer courts to inner courts and then approach the Holy of Holies – you know, the place with the curtain that was torn from top to bottom when Jesus died (Mark 15:38). In a similar way, these are the various stages of entering the presence of God. Our song choices can reflect them and even help direct us from one dimension of worship to the next.

A session can progress through elements of

• Celebration and **praise** (objective): *enter into his courts with praise* Psalm 100:4. Examples: Majesty, Worship His Majesty; All Heaven Declares; Come, Let us Sing for Joy to the Lord; Praise to the Lord the Almighty, the King of Creation.

• Heartfelt **response** (subjective): *I worship you with all my heart* Psalm 119:10. Consider: In Christ Alone; My Hope is Built on Nothing Less; Father God I Wonder; Just As I Am; Love Divine, All Loves Excelling.

• Songs of devoted **adoration**, plus receiving from God: *let us draw near to God with a sincere heart in full assurance of faith* (Hebrews 10:22). Try: Here I Am to Worship; Be Still, For the Presence of the Lord; Jesus, Jesus, Holy & Anointed One; Amazing God; There is a Redeemer.

• Prophetic or missional **declarations** via songs such as: You're the God of this City; Great is the Darkness (Come Lord Jesus); Let Your Glory Fall in this Room; The Church's One Foundation.

So, we need to have the right attitude to praise and worship sessions and to be focused on God. Similarly, let's ensure we are exalting the name of God the Father, loving his Son the Lord Jesus Christ and have an openness to the activity of the Holy Spirit. Since it is part of the Holy Spirit's role to give honour Jesus and assist us in worship, we need to be aware of his presence, making space for his direction and gifts.

This could mean the use of gifts of tongues and interpretation, some prophecy, words of wisdom or of knowledge and so forth. I think the activity of the Holy Spirit includes inspiring folk with Bible verses, songs, or prayers (including that awkward feeling that you should leave your seat to go and pray for someone privately. Why are they always on the other side of the room?) It is marvellous to be in such a meeting, knowing that God himself is loving it, that Jesus is being honoured and the Holy Spirit is directing the traffic.

Talking of which, I heard recently of some Christian youth workers who were eager to help some of the young people in their group wrestle with the question of the existence of God. They engaged the young people in an activity called *treasure hunting*. This involved asking the Holy Spirit to reveal names, places, special circumstances, clothes and other clues. Once the list was compiled, the group set out to find people who match the clues. Risky, eh? Forgive me if I've misremembered some of the finer details but consider the main point.

So, on this occasion, after a few minutes' quiet, everyone was invited to mention impressions or pictures or whatever they felt God was putting into their mind. Someone mentioned *the 99p shop*. Someone else added *red stars*. Also on the list were *flowers* and *a flower display* and the name *Julia*, along with some personal details that may or may not mean something to the right individual.

'Okay,' said the leader, 'I think we should head off towards the shops by the Square, where the 99p shop is. And we should keep a look out for red stars and flowers on our way…'

They set off to the 99p shop. When they got there, they noticed right next door was a supermarket with a display in the window, featuring red stars, suspended over a stand packed with bunches of flowers. Boxes were being ticked. What could this mean?

They went into the supermarket and saw a young woman with her partner and their baby, waiting under the red stars, by the flower stand. Amazed, but slightly uncertain how to approach her, the group wandered to the back of the shop and had a quick conference.

'We should ask her if her name is Julia.'

'But we've found the flower stand, though.'

'Yes, I know.'

One of the leaders wanted to add another item to the list. 'I feel God's told me we should check out Boots the Chemist too.'

'What for?'

'I can't be sure, but I think we should.'

'I suppose it won't do any harm…'

They returned to the front of the shop, but found that the family was gone, which was a bit of a blow. Perhaps the group had missed them by being too cautious?

Anyway, they decided that two of them should go to Boots the Chemist and the rest of them should stay in the shop, in case the family should return. No-one could quite explain why they thought this was likely, but they stayed nevertheless.

The pair selected to go to *Boots* did so and saw nothing there of any interest, so they came back. When they walked into the supermarket again, they saw the same woman standing under the same red star display next to the same flower stand. But where were the rest of their group? They quickly found them, still at the back of the store, still undecided about risking contact or conversation.

'It's definitely a woman.'

'And she's right under the red stars.'

Eventually, one of the females was selected to speak to her. She sucked up her courage and approached the woman. 'Er, hallo,' she said, nervously. 'Excuse me for interrupting, but is your name Julia?'

The woman nodded. 'Yes… how did you know?'

'Well,' (emboldened by this bullseye, the others took a step forward) 'we were praying and God said we would find these things on this list.'

She was impressed. 'Where did you get this list from?'

'We prayed and asked God to speak to us and that's how we got the list. And here you are and you're standing under the red stars, by the flower stand, right next door to the 99p shop, which is the only reason we came in this direction at all.'

'How did you know my name? That's so strange…'

'We think God was speaking to us when we prayed. We are confident he loves you, Julia and has some of these things on our list to say to you too…'

The young mum explained. 'We only came out to buy some flowers. When we got here, we did some shopping and ended up accidentally spending all our cash but hadn't got any flowers! So, we went to the cashpoint down the road – you know, the one next to Boots. My partner took the baby home and I came back to buy these flowers. Aren't they nice?' She was practically babbling by this point.

It was evident that God had led the group very specifically to Julia and that he knew, in incredible detail, all about apparently insignificant things and wanted Julia to know that he loved her.

And so, the young people withdrew to give space for the female leader to show some of the personal details on the list to Julia and share the good news of Jesus with her. Finally, she asked 'May I pray for you?'

'Okay, yeah, if you like,' Julia replied.

'I mean right here, pray for you, just now?'

'Oh! Well, alright then.'

And they prayed there and then to Almighty God for Julia, holding her flowers.

Afterwards, probably slightly bewildered, but definitely thinking about God more than she had been earlier in the day, Julia thanked them and left.

The young people in the group were amazed that their list had proved to be so accurate and detailed. Those who had previously been unsure about God and his care for each of us began to reconsider their doubts; some were clearly moved by the impact of what they had witnessed.

The group was still chatting animatedly a few minutes later when Julia came up to them again. 'I still can't get how you knew my name!' she said. 'Can you tell me those things again, because I was reeling a bit from you discovering me when you mentioned them the first time.' The leader was only too pleased to go over it again. In fact, she wrote them down so Julia could take them with her.

On the way home, the young people in the group were clearly astonished that a quick prayer, some inventive scribbling and half a spoonful of faith had generated such a ridiculously accurate list of precise details. Every item on the list was right there.

God was saying 'I know all about Julia and I love her,' and 'I know all about you and I love you, too,' to each member of the group.

You see, God is almighty, magnificent, eternal, powerful, wondrous and creative.

God is also friendly, kind, loving, devoted, gentle and a Father.

And he has a sense of humour, especially about Boots the Chemist.

So, in conclusion, let's be ready for personal encounters with the Holy Spirit, but let's make sure that we are engaging with God and worshipping Jesus, not ever merely chasing after experiences or signs and wonders. Agreed?

22 Fleece of cake

guidance

My experience of seeking God's will for my life is rich and varied, mostly because I have been alive for a fairly long time and had a number of important decisions to make: jobs, location, romantic relationships, big purchases, etc. To explain ways in which I 'felt led' would be lengthy and probably varied, but mostly fruitless.

One conclusion I arrived at quite early on, however, was that the 'laying out a fleece' model is largely flawed. In case you're not sure what I mean, check the story of Gideon (he of the winepress hiding place, a proto-barbecue and, eventually, the ever-reducing army). The Spirit of God came upon him and he summoned the armies of five districts to stand against the invading Midianites. So, it would seem that God was calling Gideon to fulfil the name given him 'mighty warrior'. But then we have this strange passage.

So Gideon said to God, 'If you will save Israel by my hand
as you have said – look, I shall put a fleece of wool
on the threshing floor; if there is dew on the fleece only,
and it is dry on all the ground, then I shall know
that you will save Israel by my hand, as you have said.' And it was so.
When he rose early the next morning and squeezed the fleece together,
he wrung the dew out of the fleece, a bowlful of water. Judges 6:36-38

'Mighty miracle!', we may say. 'There's powerful confirmation!' But is Gideon setting up a valid method of checking the will of God? Is he asking 'did I hear you correctly?' Or is he trying to find a test that even God can't pass, which would let him off the hook?

My feeling is that he's a bit behind schedule. The time to question the will of God (if there is a time for such a thing) is before you blow the trumpet and start gathering five armies to fight the battle.

Some see the fleece-laying in terms of Gideon giving God the opportunity to build faith and confidence in him.

Gideon's heart attitude is betrayed in part by the opening word 'if', implying doubt relating to God's intention to deliver his people. Has Gideon not been paying attention? This is the people of God he's talking about. And the One True God who has so far delivered them from the flood, the Egyptians, the waters of the red sea and several cycles of the judges. I know, it's easy for us to see the pattern, knowing the end from the beginning, but really, are these the words of a 'mighty warrior'? Or a feeble worrier? Gideon also shows a doubting attitude by what he does in response to the miracle of the wet wool – he effectively admits his lack of faith and makes the test even harder.

> *Then Gideon said to God, 'Do not be angry with me, but let me speak just once more: Let me test, I pray, just once more with the fleece; let it now be dry only on the fleece, but on all the ground let there be dew.' And God did so that night. It was dry on the fleece only, but there was dew on all the ground.* Judges 6:39-40

'Do not be angry with me' is a give-away request. Clearly Gideon realises that God's annoyance would be well justified. But such is God's grace that he does what Gideon asks, thus showing his gentle attitude towards his people. It is clear to me that an entirely faithless, unbelieving, time-wasting challenge of this sort is exactly the wrong approach to clarifying the will of God.

Armed with this interpretation of scripture, I wasn't about to 'lay a fleece' when the time came for life-changing decisions. I chose to interpret this story as a how-not-to and to exercise my (admittedly) meagre faith rather than expressing doubt and disbelief.

~

By 1984, I was twenty-six. I had made a pretty lame attempt for a year or so at being an office clerk and left in order to serve in schools' evangelism, working with *Agapé*, an evangelistic agency where the arrangement was for each worker to raise their own funds by developing a support team. 'Living by faith' was a bit hit-and-miss for me, but God preserved me through the experience.

After several years, I stood down from those duties and took a temporary job with a research company for a few months. I was conducting interviews, compiling data and proof-reading some of the resulting publications.

I reckon I was doing well enough at this job, because the boss offered me a permanent post, with a bit of a pay rise. It would also give me considerably increased job security. Easy decision? Yes, but office was more than an hour's commute from my home and the 'sensible' thing to do would be to move closer. I was unwilling, however, to walk away from my local church.

I sought the counsel of a church elder. He very patiently listened to me laying out the advantages of this attractive job and continued to give me attention while I listed a few of the reasons why I hadn't bitten off the hand of the boss when he made the offer.

The elder looked at me and asked 'What do you want to do?'

I must admit, this wasn't what I was expecting. I knew he wouldn't try to tell me the right answer, command me to spend three weeks in fasting and sackcloth until I saw a neon light in the sky, or even suggest a change of wallpaper for my hallway (there were rumours about church elders being a bit dictatorial in those days).

Taken aback, I said 'I want to be a part of this church and I don't think I can do that if I move away.' I was involved in a number of church activities and had many friends there.

He smiled, sat back and opened his hands in a gesture of 'well, there you are then'.

It really was that simple. He helped me see what was of greatest importance to me. Nicer job, more money, bit of security for my future… or recognising that my church membership meant more to me.

On reflection, it was, of course, a good decision. A more appealing job was soon on the table, less than fifteen minutes' drive away.

The 'right' decision? We may never know, but God certainly showed me a lot about what I thought of church life and I remained for twenty-five years; fulfilled, busy and surprisingly loved.

~

The new job I'd taken developed and morphed into working for the church, serving in the publishing department (actually, being the publishing department). We produced weekly notice-sheets to save the congregation from lengthy announcements each Sunday, a regular church digest with testimonies, articles, news etc, and a quarterly magazine for the family of churches with which we were associated. This gave me the splendid opportunity to learn about publishing and to work with several bosses within the staff, each of whom was responsible for the various items I was producing.

I loved the variety and particularly enjoyed having my skills appreciated.

After learning the ropes with traditional *typewriter/mark-up/take it to the typesetters and wait 24hrs to get it back and find you made a misjudgement and have send it back again and wait another 24 hours* method, I discovered it was possible to obtain a computer (loaded with the right software) which could take what I had typed and print it out in seconds. I could produce corrected pages for the magazine far more efficiently. Desktop publishing was in its infancy at the time. I was eager to learn.

So, I requested (and was delighted when I was granted) a Mac-II, which was, at the time, (1988) a top-of-the-range powerhouse with enough processing punch to achieve all the ambitions of my bosses. The £5K laser-printer was not forthcoming, so we settled for an ancient, slow, second-hand piece of kit which used a lot of toner cartridges. I made the most of finding out how to use the software and everything ran reasonably smoothly.

After three years, these bosses of mine revised their ambitions and it seemed skilled specialists were needed. The CEO suggested I could maintain my journalistic and proof-reading contributions to the projects, but from the comfort of my own home; this would amount to about two days per week, thus giving me ample time to pursue my own projects and find new clients. It all seemed like a good idea, but how could I afford to tool up with the tech I was going to need?

Along comes Macintosh again, having just launched the PowerBook 140, highly suitable for my needs (it was a laptop complete with a 20Mb hard drive, which was more storage space than anyone could ever imagine using). The CEO generously sweetened the redundancy package by supplying the computer and software for me to be able to sub-contract to him and to be able to do my own thing independently. Very nice.

Now, all this might sound like I was being shown the door, but it felt at the time like the chance to be become self-employed, independent and no longer subject to the silly rule about wearing a tie every day. But was it the will of God for me to make such a dramatic change in my working life, finances and self-determination? Did I have the discipline to work from home, when all that toast and telly beckoned?

I certainly felt excited about the prospect of striking out on my own (especially with the security of a decent-sized client already on the books). My sense of peace was considerable. I knew it would be an adventure, but then I knew a little bit of risk was required to help me develop beyond the role I'd carved out for myself.

Was I right to take the package, make a fresh start and celebrate with an extra round of toast on the first morning? Of course, I was! Was it the will of God?

Well, that's a much harder question, because it implies that there is just one way to go that meets with God's approval. But I had reviewed my plans to expose any weaknesses.

Was there anything sinful about what I was doing? No. Would doing this dishonour my parents or covet my neighbour's ox or mean working on Sundays? No. Had anyone wiser than me or in spiritual authority over me counselled caution or significant adjustments? No. Did I feel a check in my spirit, warning me that this was too great a risk or going to lead me into sin? No.

I asked myself all these questions (except the one about coveting, because my neighbour had recently sacrificed his last ox, so that wasn't likely to be an issue). Christian friends with whom I discussed the possibility were either non-committal or mildly positive about the idea, since no-one knew what the future might hold for me.

I have been self-employed (on and off) since that date and enjoyed a great deal of freedom and toast, along with some troubles caused by being my own boss, too.

~

I know things change and people move on, but it was so hard to say goodbye to Sean and Kate when, in 2004, they moved to Birmingham so he could work for a world-famous car manufacturer. The three of us had been close friends and served together with the youth of the church, sharing famous holidays in Wales and lots of wonderful times (with the exception of that dreadful evening featuring Slimboy Phat).

Anyway, on the day they were leaving we had a small gathering, with food and a short speech. We opened a bottle of cheap sparkling wine to celebrate the new start they were making, but unfortunately I'd forgotten that Kate wasn't drinking on account of being eight months' pregnant and Sean wasn't drinking on account of being the designated driver due to Kate's inability to reach the steering wheel. But the rest of us raised a glass and drank to their future, to adventures and to all kinds of fruitfulness.

Once they had left, I found myself uncharacteristically emotional, knowing I'd said goodbye to people close to my heart. The celebration had been about their adventure, their new opportunity, not about our sadness; but now they were on their way, the tears flowed.

After they went to Birmingham, I avoided making contact, on the false premise that it would be harder for them to leave the past behind if folk from the past kept on contacting them. Eventually I made a call and they invited me to make a visit to meet the baby, which of course I did. I made sure I had the opportunity to attend their church and I was delighted to find they met in the school hall featured in the film *Clockwise*, starring John Cleese.

Time passed and they became increasingly indispensable to the church they'd joined; so much so that Sean dropped the split-diff and suspension engineering job (the fruit of his efforts were featured on BBC's *Top Gear*, no less) and he started working for the church, running the busy office and setting up procedures to assist elders and interns.

I visited a few times over the next five years, each time greatly appreciating the warmth and vibrancy of the church meeting. Their congregational style was refreshingly different to the celebratory approach at home, with many contributions (prayers, songs, prophetic words, scriptures etc) and was far riskier, with greater possibilities for excitement. And the preaching was always accessible and relevant.

Anyway, the first big crunch came one day at a Christian conference I attended where the speaker invited us to pray aloud together for our city, asking God to make us an active part in evangelism and expanding the kingdom of God. I joined in but realised quickly that my previous passion for Brighton had, somehow, waned.

I wondered what was wrong, but over the next few days I found I was no longer enthusiastic about the south coast at all. It felt odd, after living, working and serving there for nearly fifty years – a strange indifference seemed to have overtaken me.

My insides were still echoing with this unaccountable emptiness when the time came for a scheduled working visit to Birmingham. I spent a very special Sunday morning with Sean and Kate in their church meeting, which concluded with me talking to the preacher, who was a senior leader in *Agapé*, the evangelistic organisation I'd worked for decades earlier.

He surprised me by revealing he recognised my name. I had been one of the visitors to his school who came in to speak his class about Jesus. Apparently, I'd asked the class to indicate if they were church-goers and this question provoked a response in him since he wasn't sure if he was willing to raise his hand and reveal this in front of his mates. He said it was a turning point for him!

I was still reeling from this extraordinary encounter when Kate (still very strong in hospitality gift and culinary expertise) plied me with

Yorkshire puddings and innocently asked how things were going in Brighton. I tried to explain about feeling neutral; she was smart enough not to suggest I should consider Birmingham.

But the next time I saw them, when they were on a visit to Brighton a few weeks later, they gave me the 'move to Birmingham' speech hot and strong, declaring how much they'd love it if I would check the place out and pray over the possibility.

I readily agreed because this dispassionate feeling was less than welcome. I planned a couple of what are called 'vision trips' and made appointments with estate agents to see what was on offer in the housing market. I had been told my Brighton seafront flat near the hospital was likely to be of considerable value, so I had an idea of how much I could spend.

But when I went to view the properties that had looked promising on the well-known website, I came away disappointed. The only one worth considering was on a quiet estate, but I was a bit put off by the sight and smell of a burned-out car at the end of the road.

I was driving home, thinking over the desire for Birmingham that seemed to be growing within me and considering the tiny, unsightly and disappointing houses for sale I'd seen (and one in particular, which was particularly small, ugly and dispiriting).

I felt overwhelmed by all the decisions that were waiting to be made, so I decided to stop at the service station, try to find something else to think about and to put Birmingham out of my mind for the rest of the day. I parked up and went to the loo before buying a newspaper and a strong coffee. I took a seat from where I could do some discreet people-watching. I read the newspaper headlines, looked at the chess and bridge columns and turned to the crossword on the back page.

One down: *Heartless man; I grab him wandering in city* (10). Now, believe me when I say that I'm not usually fast at these cryptic clues, but this one took only a couple of seconds for me to untangle. *Heartless man* suggests removing the *a* from the centre (heart) of *man;* and *wandering* hints at rearranging either *in city* or, more likely, *I grab him.* Looking at these letters (*mnigrabhim*) took mere moments to form them into the name of a *city*; of course, it was *Birmingham*!

I sat there in the motorway services laughing aloud at the wonderful sense of humour of my all-knowing, all powerful Father in heaven, who had organised the crossword puzzle in the Daily Telegraph for that day to be exactly on topic, out of a possible 25,652 crosswords published to date, each with at least forty clues; over a million in total. What are the chances?

Now, it would have been exceptionally foolish for me to take this on its own as a clear prophetic indication from heaven that I was to move.

But alongside other pointers, like my growing feeling of warmth towards the place, the church, the friends I was making, the presence of the preacher who had been a schoolboy and the encouragement of my Godly friends Sean and Kate, it was starting to build towards a picture. I added the significance of the incident to the much more important scriptures which were provoking me at the time.

> *This is what the* LORD *Almighty, the God of Israel, says to all those I carried into exile from Jerusalem to Babylon: 'Build houses and settle down; plant gardens and eat what they produce. Marry and have sons and daughters… Increase in number there; do not decrease. Also, seek the peace and prosperity of the city to which I have carried you into exile. Pray to the* LORD *for it, because if it prospers, you too will prosper.'* Jeremiah 29:4-7

Yes, I realise I wasn't being carried into exile and I know I have no sons or daughters, but the principle of becoming established, thinking long-term, belonging and making a contribution all struck me.

> *Trust in the* LORD *with all your heart and lean not on your own understanding; in all your ways acknowledge him and he will make your paths straight.* Proverbs 3:5-6

> *The* LORD *will guide you always; he will satisfy your needs in a sun-scorched land and will strengthen your frame. You will be like a well-watered garden, like a spring whose waters never fail.* Isaiah 58:11

Despite the consistent mention of gardening, which did not appeal to me at all (NB I had lived in a first-floor flat for twenty-five years) I could see the value of what these scriptures were saying about self-sustaining places of calm and about rest and growth and opportunity for barbecues and gathering a crowd. I also realise that the West Midlands is hardly a *sun-scorched land*, either.

Over the next few weeks, I found out that I had slightly more finances available than I'd originally calculated, so I spent a little more time looking at that website. I visited again and had a historic meeting with an elder from the church in Birmingham, letting him buy me a curry and tell me about the church and how well I'd fit in. I explained my desire to make a fresh start and my willingness to learn and grow.

Earlier in the day, I'd looked at some much nicer properties than the first selection and found one I really liked. I booked a second viewing for the next morning and this time Sean was available to come with me. We had another look and I liked it even more. We stepped outside to have a few moments away from the estate agent, to discuss the merits and drawbacks and to pray. Sean's patience with me, Dithering Champion of the Year, must have been wearing a bit thin, but he didn't let it show. We went back indoors where I put in an offer. During the few minutes in which we were waiting for the owner to call back with a decision, the agent selling my flat called me to say I'd received an offer – one I was happy to accept.

My confidence was greatly boosted and after a tiny bit of negotiating (for the first and last time ever in my entire life I used the phrase *would they accept another two grand?*), it was all settled.

Returning to Brighton to begin the tedious process of making financial arrangements and packing up, I realised I hadn't done everything in the right order. So, I set up a meeting with an elder of my church, explained how I felt God was leading me and submitted myself to his wise counsel. He immediately and wholeheartedly agreed it was clear God had brought about my change of heart and I'd found a church where I could grow spiritually and make my contribution.

This adventure in guidance relied on lots of hard work, many hours of travel, exciting conversations, several prophetic provocations and the courage to spend a lot of money.

Almost immediately after moving in, I felt certain I'd made the right decision. I was assured God was on my side, cheering me on, parting the water, making his entertaining contribution in the Games and Pastimes Department at the offices of the Daily Telegraph to make sure his little joke appeared on the right day, and giving 'oh this place has great potential' vision to the property developer who was keen to buy a flat between the English Channel and the Sussex County Hospital.

In summary, I'd strongly suggest that finding the will of God isn't a conundrum or a series of difficult tests and rarely includes dew-soaked wool. He's a God of revelation who loves it when we are willing to be obedient and walk in his way.

Make sure it's not sinful; see if there are direct instructions in the Bible; check you're not running away from or denying something; consider if your expectations are unrealistic; listen to your feelings; ask yourself questions about peacefulness; talk to quality, mature Christian friends; seek the wise counsel of church leaders with a pastoral gift; buy a newspaper; leave your phone on if you're doing a second viewing. Simples? No, but remember, God is eager to bless you.

Additional anecdote flowing out of the experience of moving: it was excellent fun, a few months after I settled in Birmingham, to visit Brighton on business. The streets were familiar (of course) but I didn't feel connected at all, which was odd but reassuring.

I noticed that the flat I'd lived in for twenty-five years had been completely refurbished and was on the market again, at a greatly enhanced price. I cheekily booked an appointment for a viewing. I was fascinated to see what they'd done with the place, to check out the way they'd rearranged the bathroom (a great improvement), installed shiny new cupboards in the kitchen (not sure) and built wardrobes into the bedroom (wasting a lot of space).

Amazingly, during the ten minutes I was in the building, the post arrived – and there was a letter for me. Remarkable.

23 The names of the meals

Last Supper

These days it seems that there are many moveable feasts, but there is still one vast gap. Follow me carefully now.

Breakfast is one of those anything-goes meals which (apart from the all-day breakfast, of which more later) can be served at any time from approx 4am to 10am or even a tiny bit later, especially if you own a smoking jacket, a sideboard and have dainty waiting staff to replenish the silver salvers, platters and dishes with or without cloches. Key features: croissants; cereal or muesli with ice cold milk; eggs (fried, soft-boiled, poached or scrambled); smoked salmon, kippers; at least six types of bacon, five or six types/sizes of sausage, black pudding, beans, tomatoes, fried mushrooms, hash browns, fried bread; a wide variety of fruit, yoghurts, Danish pastries and of course tea, coffee, a range of toasts and at least four kinds of marmalade.

Some prefer porridge or kedgeree, but I feel they are missing out on the main event.

One of my dear friends runs a Breakfast Café and specialises in what she calls the *Widowmaker* (a magnificent serving salver spread with six fried eggs, six rashers, six sausages, four portions of black pudding, four hash browns, double portions of beans, tomatoes and mushrooms, two slices of fried bread, six slices of toast and a mug of tea and if you finish it you can have another). I dare not visit very often.

10.30am to 12noon is **brunch** territory, which usually turns out to be a cut-down version of breakfast, or a similarly-reduced lunch menu. The main ingredients include door-step bacon sandwiches, sausages, hash browns and top-quality coffee, or even soup and crusty rolls. Often followed by pastries or muffins.

A genteel and spontaneous variation is termed **elevenses**. With Winnie-the-Pooh it was always *time for a little something*, but I think that was more to do with a horological problem. This excuse for an appointment with the kettle dovetails excellently with the famous 'a drink's too wet without one' advertising slogan recommending Rich Tea biscuits (other brands and varieties are available, including Digestives, Hobnobs, Bath Olivers or even Jaffa Cakes, Custard Creams, Bourbons, Nice, or Petticoat Tails). It would not, by the way, take a great deal of persuasion for me to allow the concept of half-past ten-ses.

After this comes **lunch**, which seems to slot neatly (generally speaking) into the noon-2pm zone. Lunch can mean a multitude of options, ranging from a miserable piece of fruit or granola bar eaten at one's desk to a full-on meal with appetiser, amuse bouche, hors d'oeuvres, starter, fish course, palate cleanser, main course, sorbet, pudding/afters/sweet course, coffee, chocolates, brandy. A great deal depends on budget, naturally, but it seems odd that a name like 'lunch' can mean anything from a lonely bag of crisps to a proper blow-out with several wines (although perhaps a true English gentleman would call such a substantial feast 'luncheon').

There is such a thing as a **late lunch**, which almost fills the next hour, featuring any amount of delights, but usually with a smaller number of the kinds of dishes found at luncheon. There has to be a watertight excuse for a late lunch, because it has strong connotations of being accidental.

Then we run into a dark empty, tummy-rumbling abyss between about 2.45 and 4.15pm. What can be done? There's almost no-one in polite company or even the furthest reaches of Christendom who feels comfortable cooking or serving any sort of a meal at this time, which perhaps explains why there are no names that can be properly applied to it, even if you overcome the sense of guilt.

However, in some parts of India, in a bygone age of British occupation, a 3pm snack known as **tiffin** was introduced, with a selection of sandwiches with the crusts cut orf, biscuits or cake and a cuppa (always served in the finest bone china or similar). A version of this snack features biscuits with or without chocolate coating, although this is the ideal opportunity for speciality biscuits like the hard, expensive ones from Germany or the buttery/crumbly swirls from Austria, or the chocolate-coated shortbread that comes wrapped in coloured foil. This is probably reflecting the fridge cake now called *tiffin*, made with crushed biscuits, held together with sugar, syrup, raisins, cherries and cocoa powder, covered with melted chocolate

By 4.15pm, **tea** can be taken, although test-match cricketers take a break they call *tea* from 3.40pm to 4pm, which perhaps give further credibility to the distinction often drawn between gentlemen and players. Anyway, for those of us with any class at all, tea features a selection of sandwiches. Usually there are enough for each diner to have two or three delicate triangles, with a range of fillings: cucumber, egg & cress, smoked salmon, ham & salad, cheese (but strictly not marmite or sandwich spread or jam & peanut butter, since such concoctions are usually reserved for low-quality snacks and/or picnic environments). Sandwiches are accompanied by various delights such as sausage rolls, scotch eggs, crisps and even salads, plus a variety of cakes, pastries and many kinds of biscuits, plus plenty of tea with which to wash it all down.

The high-class option is the **cream tea**, which features scones with cream (whipped or clotted) and jam on top or, if you're from even further west, jam with cream (clotted or whipped) on top.

Depending on content, the time for tea turns swiftly (at about 5pm) into **dinner**, unless you are one of those awkward customers who call lunch *'dinner'*, (which is fundamentally confusing) and can happen from then until a late hour: 9 or 9.30pm.

Dinner is essentially a delayed version of what has already been described above in terms of *lunch* or *luncheon*, except the wines are fruitier and traditionally, port and cigars are served to the gentlemen after the final course once the ladies have retired. It is impolite (unwise) to indulge in dinner if one has already had luncheon, although this may occasionally be permitted. Once it becomes a regular habit, trouble looms and the midnight feast will often be foregone in favour of a couple of Rennies.

In addition, I submit, m'lord, if I may be so bold, that the very name 'brunch', being a portmanteau word combining 'breakfast' and 'lunch' and occurring when it does, establishes the correct name for the mid-day meal as 'lunch', leaving the later slot to be filled with 'dinner'. No-one, I say, no-one ever speaks of 'brinner', do they? I rest my case.

The working-class option is the **high tea**, which is an early supper by another name, often featuring a main course and a pudding. In contrast with tea – which may occur in a drawing room or lounge, perhaps with individual side tables or trays on laps, but almost always with china cups and saucers – high tea is taken 'up at the table'; thus, it is 'high'.

When the start of dinner is delayed beyond 9pm, (shocking consideration), it becomes **supper.** The implications of this term include fireside or candlelit intimacy with sweethearts, rather than entertainments for relative strangers. Both dinner and supper are contexts for romantic assignations. The lateness of the hour sometimes hints at supper being a smaller meal, although a hearty stew with crusty bread, followed by a generous slice of sponge pudding with thick custard, is always welcome.

Even later than that (anything after 11pm) and you have to admit you're larging into a **midnight feast**. This can take the form of an all-day breakfast, even though it's not long until breakfast time for real. It's most definitely night-time, which seems an odd choice of occasion for something called 'all-day'.

And then it's just a mercifully short snooze until **breakfast** time again.

So, here I am at 3.45pm, having missed lunch and feeling most decidedly righteous but considerably more than a little peckish. It's much too late for elevenses and, since I am not a test match cricketer, far too early to have tea.

It would be decadent to start cooking up soup or a stew or anything substantial, or to call anyone using speed-dial, like Mario D'Angelo, Deelip Patel or Lim Sum Tak – and they're smart enough to be not firing up the wood-burning stove, the tandoor or the wok until about 5.30pm anyway. So, is decadent off-limits, then?

Must I wait until teatime to have dinner? What about a doner kebab and chips in the middle of the afternoon? What would you say to that? Or a bag of custard donuts with a mug of hot chocolate? What's your opinion? Should a meal's name be defined by the time at which it is served, or by the food choices it offers?

I feel honourable mention should be made of **feast** and of **banquet**.

Any oversize lunch or dinner may be called a feast, since this is descriptive of volume in addition to quality. However, when the term is applied in the specific context of the midnight feast (mentioned earlier), it seems to take on a different set of connotations. A midnight feast (with the exception of the all-day breakfast variation) is rarely particularly lavish and almost never a sit-down meal with plates and cutlery. Often, it's just a Mars Bar and a bottle of Coke. Or a plain chocolate Bounty with a can of Fresca. Perhaps a CurlyWurly with Sunny Delight. Packet of Wotsits, couple of Freddos and a Lilt. The 'feast' element is that it's illicit, rarely taken alone, often by torchlight or in darkness and a stark contrast to the traditional 'fast' of slumber.

Meanwhile, the term banquet is reserved for very special occasions: an extensive meal with lots of different courses, large joints of meat, many diners, much celebration and perhaps, in some circumstances, music, juggling, fire-eaters and dancing girls. Or even swordfights.

An exception to all of these rules I've listed above applies to the meals taken by those who work night shifts. They go to bed after the rest of us have breakfast, sleep through elevenses and lunch and wake up during the afternoon. They probably have the equivalent of lunch at teatime and a sandwich to keep them going when they clock on later in the evening, with a main meal halfway through their shift, at about 3.30am. The only times I've worked to a schedule like this, I quickly rewrote the rulebook and had breakfast when I woke, lunch after I'd been awake for six hours and dinner in the wee small hours. I may also have had a midnight snack at 7am, before falling into bed. It was radical, I know and didn't suit the folk around me (although it was in perfect tune with the half of the world on the other side of the globe…). The only difficult bits were the first and last nights of the week-long series of shifts, because those days are either much longer or much shorter.

Mine were always longer, so on the first day I had breakfast at breakfast time, lunch at lunchtime, dinner at dinner time, lunch again (or call it early midnight snack) at 10pm and dinner again at 3.30am and collapsed into slumber at just after 7am. My last night duty featured breakfast when I awoke at about 2.30pm, lunch at 7.30pm, dinner at 3am, breakfast when I knocked off at 8am, lunch at lunchtime and dinner at dinnertime before crawling into bed at 8pm for a well-deserved rest.

~

Moving to my main theme, at long last, some might say, unkindly, brandishing pointy-fingers with considerable irritation at four-and-a-half pages of preambling throat clearance, we focus upon the so-called **Last Supper**. I get the impression this was more of a high tea or dinner by any working definition. Having said that, it was at a low table, which was standard in those days and was effectively a kebab with wine, described in John 13:2 with the words 'the evening meal'.

Judging by all the stuff that happened after this gathering, it must have been over reasonably early, since Judas seems to have recruited a detachment of soldiers and some officials to arrest Jesus. They took him to the high priest immediately, without any mention of having to wake anyone. In the middle east, the people of those days would go to sleep at about 8pm, a couple of hours after darkness fell.

Now, we can see that there are four chapters of chat (well, three of discourse and one of prayer) between the start of the meal and the move to the olive grove. How long does it take to get through four chapters? A lot depends on how quickly people speak and how much we can rely on this being a verbatim transcript. Might John have beefed it up a little for dramatic effect? I doubt it. Or could this be merely the edited highlights of a much longer lecture? Hard to tell.

So, let's take it at face value and allow at least an hour for all this to be said. Does it matter if this is tea, dinner, or supper? Not really.

Recently, I've been thinking a lot about communion.

> *...the Lord Jesus, on the night he was betrayed, took bread, and when he had given thanks, he broke it and said, 'This is my body, which is for you; do this in remembrance of me.' In the same way, after supper he took the cup, saying, 'This cup is the new covenant in my blood; do this, whenever you drink it, in remembrance of me.'* 1 Corinthians 11:23-25

I wonder how you celebrate communion in your church setting? Different churches have a range of different styles, all respecting the scriptures and in obedience to the command of the Lord Jesus.

Bread first then wine; body broken, blood shed – sounds right. I notice, however, that in each scripture where this incident is noted, all of them refer to 'the cup'. Of this, more later, but check Mark 14:22-25 and Luke 22:14-20 and you'll notice that the elements were distributed in the context of a meal, contrasting strongly with the practice of most churches, where communion is either a central or additional part of a meeting for worship, prayer and preaching, not for feasting and certainly not for reclining or prophesies of betrayal.

And I have to say, close examination of the text of the Luke passage shows that Jesus took the cup first, then the bread, then had supper and then took the cup a second time. I've never been in any communion celebration where there's been multiple servings of the cup, despite having experienced the traditions of many different denominations - Church of England, Methodists, Baptists, Evangelical Free Church, Lutherans, Pentecostals and independent charismatics.

Let's talk briefly about the bread and wine.

Jesus was using items readily available at the meal symbolically, to represent his body and his blood. I understand why he chose the bread, since bread (or a similar staple food) would be on every table at every meal. The nature of it is that it can be 'broken' and it is one loaf which can be shared; thus the symbology works on many levels. Similarly, with the cup, we may assume Jesus takes red wine, a potent symbol of his blood.

However, we conveniently assume he takes a red liquid to symbolically represent a red liquid (not too much interpretation there).

And he's sitting at a table on which there's the Passover lamb, so when he's looking around for something to represent flesh, why does he select the bread? Especially since he's been called 'the Lamb of God' ever since John 1:29?

Well, Brian, that's a very complicated question and I have no straightforward answer.

Neatly sidestepping that, here's another contentious issue: alcohol. There, I said it. Some people say that Jesus had no interest in drinking alcohol, so the wine at the Last Supper was non-alcoholic. They might even claim (with not a scrap of evidence) that the wine he produced at the wedding at Cana was a sort of fruits-of-the-forest cordial.

My view is that they have missed three important factors.

Firstly, **having wine** with a meal in the Middle East in those days was **perfectly normal**; let's face it, there wasn't the choice we have nowadays. Coke, Pepsi, J2O, Cream Soda, Lucozade, Lilt, Mountain Dew, Appletise, R Whites Lemonade, Orangina and Dandelion & Burdock were not available. Neither were Perrier, Volvic or Highland Spring; nor mocktails nor fruit squashes nor cordials nor Britvic nor no-added-sugar variations, including Ribena Toothkind; and there was no hint of hot chocolate, grande skinny two-shot mocha hazelnut americano half foam cinnamon two hermesetas with sprinkle to go, nor even PG Tips.

So, the options were reduced to wine, potentially unhealthy water, or thirstiness. Every family drank wine, even giving it to children. Domestic meal-time wine was watered-down (with boiled water gone cold) and not the quaffable cheese-accompaniment of today.

Secondly, just because it is **wrong to over-indulge**, this doesn't put a blanket ban on something. For example, a small portion of a rich food like ice cream (or cheesecake or chocolate brownie or spotted dick or treacle tart or plum duff or sticky toffee pudding or rhubarb crumble with my mum's custard) is fine, although triple-helpings may be less than satisfactory, especially later and certainly when they become a habit.

Starting the day with an espresso is normal (some say necessary), but mainlining caffeine for hour after hour makes one reckless and unsocial. Obviously, consumption of coffee or dairy treats calls for moderation, but they do not lead to the problem which is the direct result and exclusive purpose of taking on board excess alcohol: becoming drunk.

In the New Testament drunkenness is included in six powerful lists of unacceptable behaviour (along with rage, dishonouring parents, sexual immorality and occult practices), which seems to rate it pretty much a Bad Thing To Do. In modern society it is against the law to be disorderly in public and clearly too much alcohol leads to morally or socially unacceptable expression; loss of inhibition, or violence; indeed, the purchase of alcohol is limited to adults and even though parents are free to give booze to their children, wise ones set a strict limit.

We should never condone excessive alcohol consumption. Check the key passage in 1 Corinthians again and you'll see that using communion as an excuse for getting drunk on the church's wine has another effect: leaving others unable to get a look in. But it's firm evidence that communion wine isn't merely a fruit cordial (unless you're prepared to argue that the characters mentioned are quaffing soft drinks and yet are still getting squiffy, which is pushing the text too far). Many churches who welcome all at the Lord's table provide a tee-total alternative, for those recovering from alcoholism. They understand it would be a shame to provide an opportunity for the ex-drinker to get a fresh taste for the stuff.

And thirdly, I have absolutely no axe to grind or criticism of those who choose not to have a drink at any time and prefer to keep communion free of alcohol too. But such folk can seem sometimes to want this rule to apply to everyone. They may claim it's a matter of conscience to avoid alcohol and to have wine at communion at all would undermine their celebration.

My view is that they are **trying to be more righteous than Jesus**, which is always going to end in tears since he's not only an example of sinless perfection, he's also the motive these dear brothers and sisters have for wanting to be holy.

Yet Jesus not only drank wine, he miraculously created six dirty great big twenty-gallon jars (more than seven hundred bottles) of the best wine at that wedding. Furthermore, Jesus referred to himself using the term *the vine* (John 15) – the very plant that produces the grapes that make the wine.

And, let's face it, he explicitly promised he'd be drinking wine in heaven.

> *'Truly I tell you, I will not drink again from the fruit of the vine until that day when I drink it anew in the kingdom of God.'* Mark 14:25

Thus, I'm concluding that since Jesus is the author of the fruit of the Spirit called kindness, gentleness and self-control, he knows that having a tiny sip of wine at communion is completely neutral, when compared with vast over-indulgence, ending up in a state of drunkenness, uninhibitedly embracing associated sins of wild living and debauchery.

On the other hand, the theme of Romans 14 is to instruct us to give respectful honour to those who have what we might consider to be a weaker position than ours. What do I mean? I mean we may have a robust understanding that *not too much* isn't code for *none at all*. Others may feel it's safer to steer clear of any risk by complete avoidance. They are entitled to their view, which is sincerely held. Are they entitled to impose their view on the rest of us? No, but mocking them or provoking them to tears or rage isn't particularly godly behaviour, either. So, let's be nicer than that.

Right, while I'm already in considerable danger of appearing to be deliberately upsetting other Christians (honestly not my intent), let's get our attention once again on the way we practice the celebration of communion itself. In other words, prepare yourself for some thoughts which may cut across your established preferences. Examine them and then reject or embrace or adapt them. But I feel they are worthy of consideration, at least.

Jesus has a good understanding of the very nature of a symbol; when one thing is used to represent another. For example, when Jesus is called the lamb, we do not picture him gambolling in a meadow, being corralled by a black and white dog and a chap shouting 'come by'; rather the symbolic name represents sacrifice and shed blood bringing salvation (Exodus 12:3-13 refers). When the Holy Spirit takes the form of a dove (Luke 3:22) or tongues of fire (Acts 2:3-4) the implications are of purity and light-bringing power and don't focus on practicalities such as feathers or ash. In the case in point, the bread represents the body of Christ broken and the cup his shed blood.

Which brings me to what some might call a sacrilegious question: is it necessary for us to use bread and a red liquid in order to celebrate communion? NB we assume 'the cup' held red wine; but the term 'fruit of the vine' may include verjuice, white wine or the traditional watered-down grape-flavoured acidic drink (see Mark 15:36) of the day.

I think you'll know my style well enough by now to know how I feel about assumptions when it comes to interpretation of scripture. Taking (as an aside) examples from the nativity: Jesus was born in 0BC, in a stable; and the three wise men arrived a few minutes after the shepherds, the same evening. None of these traditional elements of the nativity scene may be accurate but all are based on extra-biblical assumptions.

Anyway, returning to symbols; let's explore what freedoms we might have when we know what the symbols are representing and have a deep desire to retain reverence for the death of the Lord on our behalf.

I've often wondered why we take his command to share the bread and the cup and turn it into a deathly solemn, sombre, religious event. Let's face it, communion is often pretty miserable. I know it is important to consider with great seriousness the death of the Lord in our place. We dwell on his broken body and shed blood, which, of course, are central.

But Jesus didn't die and stay dead. He won our salvation and was raised to life on the third day! There's cause for rejoicing here, people!

Now, maintaining the importance of the cross and all it means, I humbly reflect on what Jesus said when he first shared the bread and the cup with the disciples.

'Do this in remembrance of me.' 1 Corinthians 11:24

Not 'in remembrance only of my death.' He hadn't yet died, so how could they be expected to remember that? *Remembrance of me* surely has a much greater breadth and indeed depth. The disciples would be able to recall his many miracles, the lengthy and amazing discourses, the parables he told, the way he called each of them to follow him; his kindness towards those who were hostile to him; his approach to the sick, the poor, the children, the religious, the soldiers…

Another context in which the word *remembrance* is used is on November 11th, when we give respect to those who died in battle, fighting to preserve freedom for democracy. Whatever your opinion of the rights and wrongs of war, this grateful remembrance does not focus exclusively on the deaths of the soldiers, airmen and sailors. We'd mostly have to use imagination to picture the exact circumstances of their dying moments, yet with Jesus we have several chapters of detail. Rather, we also reflect on the lives, bravery, selflessness and, most importantly, the deeper significance and achievement of military sacrifice. Where might we be if not for their efforts on our behalf?

My point is that *remembrance* is much broader than just the moment of passing, no matter how momentous that death may be. I am convinced

Jesus intended the regular celebration of communion to include remembering his life and ministry and all it achieved. We recall the depth and breadth of his relationships and the amazing fulfilment of ancient prophesies, in addition to his death and resurrection.

In the same way, *a chapel [or garden] of remembrance* is a place where those left behind can go deliberately to recall those who have died and to think about their lives and loves, shared experiences, happy memories and so much more. Of course, this is an appropriate context for sadness, too, since we miss having them around; although in Jesus' case, he didn't stay dead; so sombre, solemn mourning reflects only part of the glorious, wonderful, joyous celebration.

So, what are you getting at, then? you may well ask. This: when we have communion, let's not only dwell on the death of Jesus (this is central and of first importance), but let's also take the time to think about the life of Jesus too, remembering him in his wholeness, his compassion, his identity.

Which is your favourite healing miracle? In what ways does Jesus serve the poor, or the children? How does he treat women, or soldiers, or the wealthy? Make an assessment of how far he was willing to walk to take his message throughout the Holy Land. Put yourself in the shoes of the man who owned the house where the friends destroyed the roof in order to lower the crippled man in front of Jesus. What does he think of Jesus? Consider some of the Old Testament prophesies about the Messiah and reflect on Jesus' fulfilment of them. Isn't it also appropriate to consider some of the scriptural promises of God which are yet to come to fruit?

And another thing: why do we call our celebration of the last supper *communion,* which is a word rooted in the idea of togetherness; yet spend nearly all of the time in isolated silence, deliberately not communing with those around us, blocking out the distraction of the other people? We may say we're communing with God in prayer and that is true.

But then, why is it not common practice for Christians to celebrate the last supper when alone? We wait until we can take the communion corporately, right? Jesus shared the bread and cup around the table with a dozen of his friends.

My vote is for us to commune, to share the bread and cup with each other (gasp!), not necessarily relying on professionals to dispense them (stone the heretic!), talking about our memories of a life lived with Jesus (prepare the ducking stool!) or praying for one another to encounter the living Lord (nobody expects the Spanish Inquisition!)

Now I'm inviting bile upon me, let's quickly suggest that we could celebrate communion (an attitude of the heart) even if we don't have the 'right' stuff to be the emblems. If the bread and the cup are symbolic of important spiritual things, then by definition, the symbols can be pretty much anything, right? I feel there's a limit, but during one term in our church small group we experimented by sharing communion in a different way each week; with bread and wine, granary roll and blackcurrant cordial, naan and cranberry juice, brioche and OJ, poppadum and lager, Digestive biscuits and tea, Jacob's crackers and plain water. And nothing at all, except prayerful imagination and reverence. On the last week, we returned to bread and wine, just to remind ourselves of how Jesus first did this.

Because, of course, when our Lord originally instituted the breaking of bread, he used a slice of Asda's crusty tiger loaf and half a glass of Cabernet Sauvignon, didn't he?

24 Let us ascend

our place in Christ

The scriptures use a wide range of metaphors and symbols to help us grasp the many facets of our relationship with God. I have found it helpful to consider them in a sort of upwardly-escalating order; there is an utterly breathtaking progression.

Hostile

Formerly, we were **objects of wrath**, subject to God's judgment.

> *All of us also lived among them at one time, gratifying the cravings of our sinful nature and following its desires and thoughts. Like the rest, we were by nature objects of wrath.* Ephesians 2:3

We deserved the righteous judgement of God, since we had been dismissive of him or outwardly rebellious towards him; yet he has wooed us, won us, drawn us, called us and saved us. We were running away from him; but in his deep love he revealed himself to us, encouraged us to turn around and run towards him (repentance) and he has welcomed us, restored us and healed our brokenness.

Indeed, he has changed our hearts so that instead of resisting him, we yield to him.

From our former state, we have been raised from one degree of glory to another. On account of the fall we were born in sin. We had hearts of stone that he turned to flesh; we were cold and hostile, yet he wooed and warmed us, drawing us gently to himself, like a mother hen gathering her chicks.

We are no longer enemies of God; Christ has given us a better status!

From mud to magnificent

We are the **clay** and God is the **Potter**. Adam started out as dust; at least we are one step beyond that. However, we are little more than a clod of earth; perhaps we are distinctive in colour and texture and have some potential, but we are without much glory or use.

But God has a creative plan!

> *So I went down to the potter's house, and I saw him working at the wheel. But the pot he was shaping*

from the clay was marred in his hands;
so the potter formed it into another pot, shaping it
as seemed best to him. Then the word of the LORD came to me:
'O house of Israel, can I not do with you as this potter does?'
declares the Lord. 'Like clay in the hand of the potter,
so are you in my hand, O house of Israel.' Jeremiah 18:3-6

God's loving, creative hands shape us, mould us, form something beautiful and worthwhile from an otherwise unpromising lump.

He puts form and character into our random rawness. The kiln-firing process purifies us and we end up becoming vessels into which he will joyfully pour his Spirit, to the point of overflowing and will continue to do so. He even chooses to glaze or decorate what he has made, adding extravagant glory. And from within this vessel of clay come streams of living water, an outflowing of refreshing for the world.

Flock around the Shepherd

Moving up a notch, we should notice that we are the **sheep** and he is the **Shepherd**. This suggests we are occupying a slightly better position up the food chain, but it's hardly flattering; sheep don't have a reputation for being the most graceful or intelligent creatures in the world, after all.

The LORD is my shepherd, I shall not be in want.
He makes me lie down in green pastures,
he leads me beside quiet waters, he restores my soul.
He guides me in paths of righteousness for his name's sake. Psalm 23:1-3

However, it has to be said that sheep work well in a team, know how to follow their master and provide valuable contributions for society in terms of wool for clothing and blankets, employment for shepherds, plus milk on a regular basis and later, meat for roast lunch, chops, hot pot, kebabs, bhuna, etc. Plus, there's a helpful lawnmowing service thrown in, too.

God cares for us, watches over us, counts us out of the fold and back in again. He knows us each by name. He will protect us from enemies like thieves and wolves. He will lay down his life for us.

He will even seek us out and retrieve us when we go astray, bringing us home with great rejoicing, counting one lost sheep hugely important and worth the effort of search and rescue.

Happy to help

The next rung on this ladder shows we are the **servants of the Master,** which at least lets us into the house, even if we have to behave ourselves, watch our manners and not talk too much.

When he had finished washing their feet,
he put on his clothes and returned to his place.
'Do you understand what I have done for you?' he asked them.
'You call me Teacher and Lord, and rightly so, for that is what I am.
Now that I, your Lord and Teacher, have washed your feet,
you also should wash one another's feet.
I have set you an example that you should do as I have done for you.
I tell you the truth, no servant is greater than his master,
nor is a messenger greater than the one who sent him.' John 13:14-16

We have the security of belonging to the household, the dignity of work and the pleasure of serving a just and honest Master.

Our tasks may be somewhat lowly, but we know the Master is concerned to keep us healthy; he does not beat us into submission; rather, he deserves our respect by his faithfulness to us.

Are you content to be a servant? It's great to be humble and to be willing to… oh, hang on, though, since the ladder of metaphors is about to make a swift ascent.

Family members

God also calls us his **children** and calls himself our **heavenly Father.**

Yet to all who received him, to those who believed
in his name, he gave the right to become children of God –
children born not of natural descent, nor of human decision
or a husband's will, but born of God. John 1:12-13

Now we have the privileged possibility of real emotional closeness, which is the kind of love never bestowed upon a drinking vessel or chamber pot. The craftsman may take care and show appropriate pride in his work, but the love described by John is rather more than that.

By the same token, neither does a sheep truly know the heart of the shepherd, though she may enjoy the fruits of his kindness. And a servant may be granted access to the home, but a child truly belongs.

A child is a treasured part of the family, has a place at the table, is given the family name, is protected, nurtured, fully known, fully loved to the uttermost. A Father (a perfect, heavenly Father) loves and trains and seeks the best for his children; a Father gives good gifts, comforts, teaches and disciplines his little ones. He gathers them around him and tells them his secrets and shares family life with them, communicating to them that they belong and are valuable. So precious.

He protects them from harm and always wants to best for them, working hard to provide for them and jealously guarding and keeping them. He would shed his blood for his own. And he provides an inheritance of more riches than they can imagine.

Still, there is something better than even the best parent-child relationship.

Two-way flow

Yet further, levelling the playing field in a way family never can, at least not until the kids have grown up and perhaps not until they have attained adulthood themselves – is **friendship**. It is great to know you belong, to be protected as part of the family and to gain all the benefits of belonging; but to be called a friend is yet more precious. This speaks of something deliberate, intentional; not merely granted by birth, but given by choice.

> *My command is this: Love each other as I have loved you.*
> *Greater love has no one than this, that he lay down his life*
> *for his friends. You are my friends if you do what I command.*
> *I no longer call you servants, because a servant*
> *does not know his master's business. Instead, I have called you friends,*
> *for everything that I learned from my Father I have made known to you.*
> John 15:12-15

Friendship opens a level of communion that a five-year-old can't know with his parents. Friendship speaks of two-way flow, mutual trust and support, honour and esteem. There may still be elements of discipleship and there will certainly be a pooling of strengths and weaknesses, with one providing assistance to the other.

In our friendship with the Almighty, support and help always flows from God, but he esteems us. We are called friends and are granted the honour of that title. We were once enemies of God, rebelling or careless about him; now we are friends. He shares his life with us, desires our company, seeks our best interests, puts up with or grows to love our funny ways or quirky eccentricities, gently correcting us, drawing us closer to his heart and making us more like his perfect, flawless Son when we devote time and attention to his presence and sheltering under his wings.

Do you rejoice in being a friend of God? This is completely amazing, but there is an even higher and deeper level of intimacy and partnership awaiting us at the top of this metaphorical ascent.

Intimacy

Oh, my soul, rejoice! We are nothing less than **lovers**.

The courtship began in the Garden. It deteriorated rapidly into unfaithfulness for a long time but was wonderfully restored at the cross and will conclude in the spectacular wedding feast of the Lamb. We are called the bride of Christ.

I will take delight in you; as a bridegroom
rejoices over his bride, so will I rejoice over you. Isaiah 62:5

I am my beloved's and his desire is for me;
his banner over me is love. Song of Solomon 7:10

The ultimate level of closeness and intimacy (considering I used to be an enemy of God) is reflected in this title. Let us not undervalue the word by associating it only with romantic lovey-dovey sweet-nothing chocolates-and-flowers soppiness or even only with physicality.

Rather, let's rejoice greatly that we are to be comforted, caressed, longed-for, protected, loved, esteemed, honoured, welcomed, enjoyed, sought after and nurtured.

We are treated simultaneously like a sweetheart with her beau, like a fiancée with her betrothed, like a bride with her groom, like a wife with her husband and like a dear devoted Joan with her lifelong faithful Darby. How glorious is that?!

Are there secrets you only share with God? Do you tell him the deepest feelings of your heart or share dreams with him? Perhaps there are dark corners in your soul into which only God sheds light?

My guess is that we all have secrets; those of us with a perfect divine lover can dare to expose them; he won't despise our openness or belittle the trust we are expressing. Even better, he will soothe our pain, forgive our sin and heal our wounds. And he'll strengthen our resolve, reassure us of his perfect love for us and remind us of his constant companionship.

God won't ever be seeking a divorce from his Bride, or even be wanting to take time out, be on a break or to stay away for a season. He's always ready to listen, to keep you company, to hold you close, to spend time with you and to just hang out with you for the sake of being together. He knows what you love and loves the sound of your voice.

He is always perfectly patient, kind, respectful, honouring, calm, forgiving, delighting in the truth, protecting, trusting, confidently believing and persevering (from 1 Corinthians 13:4-7). He constantly, consistently finds ways to show you his love and responds warmly to your efforts to do the same.

He'll never betray you or be unfaithful or expose you or tire of you or stop rejoicing over you. His love is eternal.

His love endures forever. [26 times] Psalm 136

25 I've got my eye on you!

another lesson or two from the work environment

I've maximised variety when it comes to the work I've done.

Now, that may sound like a slippery way of saying I had and lost a lot of different jobs, but that's not really what I mean. Part of the freedom of being self-employed has given me the opportunity to try my hand at a wide range of tasks. I think there are several which turned out to be things I did not excel at; there is a limit to my skill base – hard to imagine, I know. But some tasks I'd have liked to have done more.

For example, I've been paid to design adverts for a magazine about teddy bears; to be an actor in an educational film for children; to proof-read a number of books prior to publication; to write scripts for storytelling television shows; to create and host quiz nights and a Murder Mystery evening; to consult on and write the blurb (back-cover wording) for a best-selling self-help book; to create content for a 75-page church website; to be a voice-over artist for several short films; to deliver training sessions on youth and children's work for dozens of different church groups; and much more. I greatly enjoyed researching, writing and presenting a documentary about a well-known Christian worship band; I loved my brief spell providing fundraising submissions for a local charity; and I am always very happy working on my own projects in between, developing a number of different books, some of which only recently saw the light of day.

However, my heart would leap in celebration when I was called by one particular client, who regularly invited me to be part of his team researching various organisations through the dynamic medium of Mystery Shopping.

This work was very exciting indeed, since it required me to maximise my professionalism: keeping good records, thinking on my feet, being able to maintain my poise even when under pressure or running a risk of being discovered, and developing new skills, plus having my opinion sought and considered by my client.

Rather than being focused on retail outlets, which the name suggests, we worked within the public sector. We were required to explore the quality of customer service provided by several different organisations. For example, I was sent to a youth sports centre to ask about how suitable it might be for my special needs ten-year-old; to a swimming pool to see if I could organise a children's birthday party there; and, most memorably, to a General Enquiries desk for clarity on how changes in my complicated home circumstances might affect my ability to pay the rent (more of that in a moment).

As you can probably tell, I was required to inhabit the role of someone with a genuine enquiry, to see what help I was given or offered or where I was redirected and then to write a brief report on the encounter. Not a difficult duty, I agree, but I had the occasional crisis of conscience until I reminded myself that this was an acting job and that I wasn't telling lies, just playing a part with considerable improvisation.

I was paid by the research agency, but the task was funded by the organisation who had commissioned the work. The object of the exercise was to check that staff were not only giving correct answers to these pretty straightforward enquiries but were doing so in a polite manner and wearing the appropriate uniform or name badge or lanyard or whatever. If the office was clean and the queues short, then so much the better.

In fact, it was substantially an operation to give staff an opportunity to be caught doing something right. After all, if the answer they gave was incorrect or incomplete, or their manner surly or dismissive, then this would reflect poorly on the recruiting procedure and/or training provided, not only on the individual.

Now, this task would be interesting enough if it were a simple matter of attending the correct office, making the enquiry, noting what was said in response and then leaving to write the report. But add to the mix the essential aspect of covert (secret) filming and the whole thing moves up another level of epic!

On different occasions I was kitted out with a tie with a miniature camera in it, or asked to carry a man-bag with a camera secreted in the side, or issued with a backpack with a camera in the shoulder strap. This was my preferred equipment. It added exponentially to the excitement of the adventure when I had to hide around the corner, activate the recording device and then proceed to the office or desk or whatever and complete the encounter, before returning to my hiding place and deactivating the recorder.

Of course, all this secrecy was governed by a strict Code of Practice; we were not snooping, stalking or behaving illegally in any way at all, since we were acting with the full permission of the employer. Indeed, all the staff had been informed that at some time between these particular dates Mystery Shoppers were going to be employed to record and report on the quality of the customer service provided. So, it was all above-board and the digital footage was all returned to the boss of the training department for disposal. We were also instructed that it was specifically stated in the aforementioned Code of Practice governing this sort of covert activity that no staff member would be disciplined as a result of any report we issued (you know, a written warning on their record or things of that ilk) for any errors they may make.

Let's reflect on this; all staff should always represent their employer with professionalism and efficiency anyway, so to check up on them shouldn't be a threat at all.

However, one of the encounters has stayed fresh in my memory even though it took place a decade or so ago. I was briefed to explain to the chap at the enquiry desk that I lived in a flat with my girlfriend, but that things hadn't been going well between us, so she had decided to leave and was going to move out next weekend. I asked how that might affect my benefit entitlement, since I knew I would not be able to afford to rent the place if she wasn't contributing. This interesting scenario demanded slightly more realism in my performance, relating to both an emotional situation and a practical, factual answer.

I made sure the camera in the strap of my backpack was activated and recording. Following a brief wait in the queue (I took a number as instructed and then went forward when the sign indicated that it was my turn), I sat down and explained this conundrum to the bloke. I didn't want to have to move out of the flat but was there any advice he could give me about having the rent reduced or my benefit increased (both rather unlikely, I agree)? The chap took pity on me but had to tell the truth; that there was little hope of either financial solution.

'Have I answered your enquiry to your satisfaction, sir?'

'Well, it's not what I wanted to hear, but I suppose it helps to know for certain that this is drawing the line under me having the flat.'

'Well, I am sorry.'

I began to get up when he motioned for me to stay.

'On a personal basis,' he said quietly, 'Can I make one suggestion?'

'Go on...'

He spoke conspiratorially. 'Jewellery.'

'What?' I was surprised by this new direction for our conversation. I gripped my backpack strap even more tightly, because I sensed there might be something about to happen that would be well worth capturing on film.

'Jewellery. They can't resist it.'

I think I just stared at him.

He continued. 'Maybe a nice necklace or a bracelet or something. Bit of gold, right? It might cost you a few sovs, but she'll think twice about moving out if you win her over. You know, bottle of wine, bit of chat, then spring some surprise bling on her. You're guaranteed to warm her up. Can't miss.'

I was half convinced, wondering if this might be a good idea.

He wasn't finished. 'I think… yeah, here, I'll write down the address of the place where I got my girl a bit of gold.' He took an official company compliments slip and jotted down the name of a jewellery store not far away. It crossed my mind that she might decide to stay if I could scrape together enough cash to… And then I remembered there was no girl, no relationship (broken or otherwise), no flat, no shortfall in rent, no impending disaster. His total belief in my scenario had fooled me momentarily that it was real. I gratefully took the note, thanked him for his kindness and made my escape.

On reviewing the film footage, I was pleased to see that I'd got him perfectly in frame and added subtitles to make up for both the background noise and the decreased volume with which he spoke. My client agreed with me that this was an interesting encounter to have captured. Both the Head of Recruiting and the Director of Training were complimentary about the way I had conducted myself.

The star of my film had given me accurate information and then gone the extra mile, doing his best to bypass the problems I had outlined. If I could fix the relationship, then the rent problems melted away!

There were several other times when unsuspecting staff provided watchable footage and only one occasion on which they began to think my story wasn't watertight. I should have closed the conversation and made a getaway but waited too long.

We were able to draw conclusions about the places where there were insufficient staff and the desk where there were more than were needed; my client advised the Head of Customer Services about queue management and distribution of labour. The work was exciting, great fun, purposeful and technically exacting. I learned how to edit out all the tedious minutes spent waiting in queues (I had to start the recorder before entering the premises, of course, but it was really only the encounter itself that was of interest). I learned how to add captions to the muffled bits. And I earned rather well during that season, since the job was handsomely rewarded. This was definitely one of those jobs which was a win-win!

Some might call it karma (I don't think I would, but you'll see what I mean in a minute) but for a couple of unpleasant years, the boot was definitely on the other foot.

I got a part-time job working in the office for an electrical firm. Neither of the bosses (unhelpfully, both called Tommy) was willing to give up being an active electrician, so they were always keen to work on-site, charging out of the office, making connections, plugging away. Neither of them was down-to-earth, both wanted to keep their current business live and yet were often negative. See what I did there?

I was hired to complete administrative tasks including staff deployment, payroll, expenses reimbursement, banking, sorting the post, manning the phone and signing for deliveries. Stock was ordered for the warehouse, supplied, placed on the shelves, and used on various jobs; but it was essential that we didn't run out of cable or light switches, for example, so someone had to keep records. You guessed.

In addition, I was frequently called upon to achieve monumental admin tasks unreasonably rapidly. Oh, stop moaning, you may say. But one famous morning I was called upon to find bed and breakfast accommodation for a team of six men, requiring single or twin rooms (not doubles), near a restaurant, within a couple of miles of the remote farm where they were fixing solar panels on the roof of a barn. Of course, this installation was already underway, so the rooms had to be available from tonight.

It took me more than two hours' hard work, matching accommodation websites to online maps, calling B&Bs, finding they were busy or had only one double room... I thought it was a fair achievement when I eventually had it sorted.

I paid the deposit requested and sent the details to the boss, who was on-site. He immediately rang me to complain that it was a nuisance to split his team between two different houses. Furthermore, they were further away than he'd like, and neither of them was near any sort of restaurant. What was I playing at? When he heard I'd had to pay the deposit to secure their beds, he was annoyed that I had not been able to negotiate the tariff down to his preferred price of about 38p per bed per night.

So, I didn't mention the distance from where they were working to the nearest place to eat ('what? Not everyone likes curry. And no-one wants curry two nights' running! And it'll cost me a fortune! Can't you do any better than that?')

I genuinely believe he expected me to be able to conjure up a small *Premier Inn* next door to a *Happy Eater* in the grounds of the farm, because that would save on petrol expenses. Now, I'm good, but I'm not that good.

I felt undervalued and dumped upon, which isn't ideal when you're the person representing the firm to the outside world.

Added to this attitude, the company had installed security cameras inside their warehouse and offices, since they sold and installed such equipment. It would be effective, they reasoned, to be able to show a potential customer a remote-access multi-camera security system by logging in from a smartphone. 'You can set it up to alert you, for example, when there's unexpected movement on your courtyard. And then, from your beach lounger in Malibu or wherever you are in the world, you can see your premises and decide what action to take.'

Probably not a bad idea, but it meant that whenever I was in the office, either of the bosses could log in to the system and watch whatever I was doing. That would normally be dull viewing, because I'd be sitting at my desk, answering the phone, reconciling the banking; i.e. doing the things I was being paid to do.

Eventually, I stopped worrying what they might see, realising there were very few security-camera customers who needed to be shown a preview.

But of course, there was the one and only time when I'd forgotten I might be on show and I'd been in the office on my own for most days for several weeks. Perhaps a red mist descended on me; perhaps a need for exercise; but naturally it was on that occasion that one of the Tommys spent time extolling the virtues of his multi-camera security system to a potential customer.

He brandished his smartphone and logged in. Was I typing at my computer or speaking on the phone? No. In the warehouse, logging stock or signing for a delivery? Not so. Standing in the kitchen, waiting for the kettle to boil? Not on this occasion. No, today was the one day ever when, having noticed that our stock of a particular form was running low, I decided to photocopy a few and was inspired to dance to the rhythm of the photocopier.

Tommy and his customer found this endlessly entertaining, because I was blissfully ignorant of their eyes on me – just like the chap at the enquiry desk who tried to persuade me to buy jewellery.

I have never before (nor since) been noted for busting any moves, but Tommy was delighted to pull my leg without mercy the next time he was in the office and the photocopier was running.

And it didn't result in the purchase of a security system, either.

~

I wonder, would you act differently if you knew you were being observed? Why might that be? Is it because you're usually a bit sloppy or careless, or maybe you're not quite up-to-date with the latest information that you are expected to be able to recall at a moments' notice? Are you taking your responsibilities seriously and conducting yourself in an appropriate manner? Or are you using office equipment for entertainment or as a musical accompaniment? Are you trying to recruit customers for your mate's jewellers' shop? Are you attempting to be an untrained, unregulated relationship counsellor on the side?

I refer the honourable gentleman to the Psalm most beloved of my grandmother. NB I fear she may not have quite grasped the subtlety of its meaning, since she usually read the Psalm in the Authorised Version, where it starts *I lift up mine eyes to the hills; from whence cometh my help* and she spoke with vast positivity about the hills close to the back of her house, so I think she thought it was the hills that provided her help, somehow. Anyway:

I lift up my eyes to the hills – where does my help come from?
My help comes from the Lord, the Maker of heaven and earth.
He will not let your foot slip – he who watches you will not slumber;
indeed, he who watches over Israel will neither slumber nor sleep.
The LORD watches over you – the LORD is your shade at your right hand;
the sun will not harm you by day, nor the moon by night.
The LORD will keep you from all harm – he will watch over your life;
the LORD will watch over your coming and going
both now and forevermore. Psalm 121

God is a little bit like those covert cameras; he watches over you, keeping you in sight, always noticing what you're doing, checking out your circumstances and environs, spotting dangers and hostiles, keeping his gaze firmly fixed.

But he's always watching to catch you doing the right things. He loves it when you excel, when you honour him, when you walk in righteousness, when you make Godly decisions, when you resist the devil, when you give him praise and when you remember to pray.

Yes, okay, he's also watching when you mess up and when you are disobedient and when you reject his love. But his affection for you is so perfect that he sends his Holy Spirit to convict (never to condemn) and graciously provides forgiveness and reconciliation.

He's the lover of your soul, remember, like the shepherd who made sure the ninety-nine sheep were safe and went off to seek the lost one. I suppose he watched the sheep getting lost, knowing he'd soon be back to rescue it. I am sure of that, because that's exactly what happened with the non-compliant son in the next story (my favourite parable). He was allowed to go off in rebellion, but then God met him at his lowest ebb and convinced him to get up and go home. The father publicly forgave him and celebrate his return. That's how Father God feels about you when you turn away from sin and ask for forgiveness.

He's got his eye on you and on me all the time, which makes me feel very safe and very loved. I'm very happy that he catches me doing something right, quite often. And not only when I'm dancing on my own to the intoxicating rhythms of the photocopier.

26 The ministry of moist; or more?

considering baptism

Mark 16:16

Baptism is often portrayed as a traditional way of recognising a newborn has entered the family. It's a matter of crowding around the font, hoping the Vicar will correctly pronounce the names you've chosen, inviting certain friends to declare that not only will they educate the child in godliness, but also that they have renounced the Devil (steady on, that's implying something a tad strong, isn't it?) and then providing a slap-up tea in a local bar.

Or perhaps, for those who are taking it a bit more spiritually, it's an opportunity to note the inclusion of a new soul under the Abrahamic covenant, with promises to prepare them for some later date, when they will complete their confirmation classes with a hands-on blessing from a senior church professional.

Both of these events are decided upon and chosen by the child's parents, naturally and are an exercise in either rubber-stamping a birth certificate, or in faith in a distant future. Thus, baptising a baby is seen as a way of welcoming the child into the church family, legitimised by reference to the ancient practice of circumcision. Boys know they belong; girls are made to feel just as welcome by allowing them to have a much more comfortable second week of life.

Moving towards a minority experience now, adult baptism is undertaken as a decision to obey the example set by the Lord Jesus and the commands in the New Testament, to signify a transformation that has already occurred in the heavenly places. It's a public statement about conversion to newness of life. For good reason, this is called believer's baptism.

> *Jesus said… 'whoever believes and is baptised will be saved,*
> *but whoever does not believe will be condemned.'* Mark 16:16

Not believing leaves the individual responsible for their own sin, without a saviour. Believing and being baptised is important. Jesus doesn't mention 'baptising and believing' because that's not the correct order. Believing alone isn't recommended, but is surely sufficient…

> *Do not let your hearts be troubled; you believe in God;*
> *believe also in me.* John 14:1

Being baptised without believing isn't ever mentioned; probably because baptism is taken to be an outward sign of an inward change, whether it's one which has already taken place, or one assumed by faith for when the child reaches an age when they can call upon the Lord for themselves.

Sadly, many babies grow up to reject God and live (and may well die) without repentance and faith. In such cases, have the teaspoonful of water, the fervency of the vicar and the promises of the godparents achieved an eternal transaction, appropriating the blood of Christ to the lost soul and altering an eternal destiny? Why would anyone imagine that, except as wishful thinking, based on no Bible verses at all?

You have already spotted that my view is fairly firm; it's also reasonably orthodox.

There is one body and one Spirit – just as you
were called to one hope when you were called – one Lord,
one faith, one baptism, one God and Father of all, who is over all
and through all and in all. Ephesians 4:4-6

One baptism? Well, I suppose that if someone was christened as a newborn, this is a promise of future faith, so when they find faith later, adult baptism is a valid statement. I also have a friend who was baptised as a child, came to faith as an adult and celebrated it with an adult baptism, but later decided this wasn't valid for some reason (to which I was not privy), so she persuaded her church leader to baptise her yet again. One faith, one Lord, three baptisms, I suppose.

I've only once been a participant in an Anglican baptism service, which was a quite extraordinary spectacle. A teenager to whom I was related had been dedicated in a non-conformist church as a baby; now he was going for adult baptism. This was completed by the vicar in front of the font. I was one of the godparents, promising to train and educate the lad in the ways of the Lord. Nothing terribly remarkable, you might imagine, except in this case, once another teenager was also baptised as an adult, a senior church professional was seated in front of the altar and seventeen confirmation candidates were lined up in front of him, including these two, their foreheads still damp from their earlier anointing. Following some promise-making and a couple of prayers, the candidates processed past the gentleman officiating, who waved his hands in a mildly religious manner, blessing each one. I'd been a godparent for less than seven minutes, start to finish and I reckon I did okay, because for the entirety of the time my godson was my godson, he was in a church meeting. Not many people have that quality of track record!

Perhaps I should have taken this ceremony more seriously, but I can't say I was convinced by the theological calibre of the vicar, his line manager or their rigid commitment to the observances.

Anyway, having belonged to several small churches, I became accustomed in my early years to baptism services in which one or at the most two people were fully immersed in front of the congregation.

Indeed, my own baptism in 1972 was a two-hander, featuring me and my testimony and an older man who gave vent to his enthusiastic desire to preach. His passion far outstripped ability or wisdom, which left many of my friends, who had attended especially, troubled and surprised.

On reflection, I doubt the minister had properly prepared this chap for the event, assisting him in writing a brief, clear testimony with two Bible quotations. My dad had been very helpful to me in editing verbiage and reminding me to mention 'forgiveness of sins' and that I'd erred on the inclusion of verses by a factor of 50%.

Moving to a much larger church introduced me to the concept of a group baptism service. The biggest one I ever attended had sixteen people going under the water during the course of the morning. I think they were processed in batches of two fives and a six, with songs in between, which gave the congregation a bit of a breather. Another of the procedural arrangements was that the candidates had to read their testimony from the pool. My guess is that this was a wise strategy devised by church leaders – once the candidates were up to their waists in cold water, they were more likely to be brief. But what a thrill to hear story after story, giving honour to God, recognising sin, speaking of forgiveness through the death of Christ and rejoicing in newness of life! We should give more time more often to hearing conversion testimonies, for our encouragement and to honour this glorious miracle. Just a thought.

I was even invited to participate in baptising some members of the youth group, who had made profession of faith and asked the Ethiopian Eunuch's excellent question.

> *As they were traveling down the road, the man said, 'Look, here's a pool of water. Why don't I get baptized right now?' Philip said, 'If you*

believe with all your heart, you may.' The eunuch answered, 'I believe that Jesus Christ is the Son of God.' Acts 8:36,37

I don't suppose anyone was actively opposed to the idea, but it took a couple of terms for the church leaders to agree that youngsters could be baptised. Probably, there was a question of consistency that should be observed in these teenagers. They passed the scrutiny. Notwithstanding, it was a true joy to join a church leader in the tank, whatever the temperature or pre-used nature of the water, ask the candidates the official questions and then make the glorious announcement.

On confession of your faith, we are pleased to baptise you in the name of the Father, and of the Son, and of the Holy Spirit.

There was a standard manhandling procedure which ensured that the candidate went right under the water and that neither of us doing the baptising strained our backs in the process of pulling the sopping wet person to their feet. They were quickly ushered to the side while the next candidate climbed in, and then the wet one climbed out, as we got on with ensuring no time was wasted. Changes of the dipping personnel were achieved with similar dexterity.

It was a properly choreographed event— indeed, just like a wedding service, it was subject to a rehearsal.

Speaking of wedding rehearsals, it's sad, but true that ritual sometimes takes precedence over the significance. Ensuring that we're all doing what needs to be done in the right way and at the right time and in the right place can be given top priority, when the reason for including each the various elements either gets forgotten or is given secondary importance.

I attended a jolly wedding rehearsal several years ago. I was doing my utmost to concentrate as the minister went over what to me were very familiar moments. I knew what was required of me, and I was familiar with the moment in the service when I was required. Plain sailing. Even the timing of the bride's entrance down the aisle from the door to the front of the sanctuary, arm in arm with her father, went to plan and everyone was content.

The last piece of action left to rehearse was the transition from the prayer of blessing to the procession of the newlywed couple from the front to the back, which required the appropriate music. So, the minister said he would take the opportunity to pray a genuine prayer over the couple and conclude with the words that were the CD-operator's cue; fair enough.

Unfortunately, his heartfelt prayer was intruded upon by the loud ringtones of the father of the bride's mobile phone. His part in the practice session was long finished, he reckoned, so he answered the business call – 'I need to take this' – and conversed for at least two minutes with a member of his staff. Not being a church-going fellow, I suppose he didn't recognise the sanctity of addressing the almighty and the minister had to carry on while the conversation did the same.

Fortunately, the bride saw the funny side of her dad's lack of deference to the minister, so the groom and I and nearly everyone else greeted the rest of the prayer with undisguised merriment. The minister gave up, said a loud 'Amen', the music played, the couple made their exit and the practice session was over.

At the actual wedding, the mother of the bride took charge of her husband's phone and switched it off. And you'll be glad to hear that the minister's prayer was heard in heaven despite the intrusion and Verity Grace was born after a couple of years or so.

Getting back to baptisms, the most recent one at our church was taking place in the autumn of 2021, when meetings were allowed (subject to some mask rules and various singing restrictions). Since we meet in a school hall, our practice has formerly been to rent the school's swimming pool for baptisms. Unfortunately, the pool was not available and yet there were six people ready to be baptised.

The church leaders asked the school if they could bring in a tank and fill it with water, but the school didn't want to risk their nice newly-polished floor with several hundred gallons of water, in case of accidents. So, the decision was taken to use a large inflatable paddling pool in the car park. It was filled during the course of the morning from a tap conveniently situated nearby (probably for use by the grounds-man for gardening and/or washing the headteacher's Bentley).

This water was decidedly cold, like the weather, so someone thoughtfully boiled a kettle, adding the contents to the pool and repeating this act of mercy as often as they could, albeit with mininal effect. It wasn't exactly steaming.

The baptism candidates were warned and given the option to withdraw or postpone, but five of them bravely decided to go ahead, saying that obeying the Lord's command took precedence over the risk of pneumonia.

The other one wisely suggested that she should be baptised in the spring (by which she meant a few months later, not the outpouring of an aquafer, cartesian well or geyser) and that the swimming pool should be booked well in advance. Sensible woman.

The hardy souls were given opportunity to share their testimonies indoors during the meeting. They stepped forward in t-shirts and shorts, shivering in the severely cold wind and sat in the pool, which was not large enough or deep enough for any other posture. Our church leader kept his remarks to a minimum, helped them under and heaved them up again. They trotted off, sopping wet, to a makeshift changing area indoors. Meanwhile, the congregation cheered and applauded, partly to celebrate the dramatic statement to the principalities and powers that these souls were saved and following Christ, partly to keep warm and partly out of straightforward admiration for their bravery!

You may already be furious about my attitude to celebrating communion, so I'm not going to invite torch-bearing villagers to crowd around my door chanting 'death to the heretic!'

I'm just going to mention that even the word *immersion*, a foundational distinctive in my churchmanship, does not always mean going right under the water. It may mean merely dipping the head into the water; that's why some churches use the expression *full immersion* or *total immersion*, to clarify their intention.

The word *baptise* is rooted in the concept of washing or bathing and does not necessarily imply going right under. It seems that in some cultures, where the river was the source of water, the candidate stands up to the waist and the minister uses a jug or bowl to pour water from above, thus providing the state of wet-all-over, without the (to my mind) essential dramatic element. This is called affusion. Where water is scarce or the commitment to the drama even more tenuous, mere sprinkling (aspersion) could be the preferred method.

My conclusion is that complete wetness isn't the main point of what's happening here; it's the symbolic aspect of being laid down and raised again to newness of life. And let's not forget the significance of washing, either.

By the way, scholars refer to practices which are no longer universally followed, including the wearing of baptismal garments (usually white robes for modesty's sake, but not everyday clothes) and formerly to the symbolism of entirely discarding garments – being naked, as Jesus was naked on the cross, being fully immersed as he was in the grave and then being raised afterwards.

What's your view on baptism? Something for newborn babies, or for adults? Teaspoon or the contents of a tank, a pool, a river or the sea? Is spiritual significance measured by the quantity of towelling required in the aftermath? Is the ceremony a meaningful consecration, or a public demonstration? For other people to witness, or for principalities and powers to observe, and to tremble?

A lesson has been learned from my need to adjust my attitude to what is a sacred moment and what is a symbol. For example, the quantity of water, the dilution of salt or of chlorine and the general temperature all seem to be reasonably flexible.

What won't do is the fearsome accident that took place some years ago (if memory serves, unless of course, this is urban myth – although the Baptist church is not famous for the provision of entertaining or cautionary stories) in which a baptist minister was using the pool built into the stage at the front of his church sanctuary. This architectural forethought provided a good view for the congregation. Once the cover was removed, steps down on one side into the pool were revealed; they led to a level part and further steps on the other side, giving access to the vestry for the purposes of changing.

The chief shortcoming was that the plumbing only extended to the provision of a cold water tap. So, like many in churches with similar pools, the standard practice was to fill it a day or so before the event was due to take place and insert an upright heating element (not unlike that sort you might find in a kettle or urn) to increase the ambient temperature of the water.

Now, doubtless you're already ahead of me and you've guessed that on this occasion no-one had remembered to switch off the electricity before the meeting started. I suppose this is only fair, since this would not have been a three-times-a-week procedure; more like once every few months, so the correct order of activities may be forgotten. Anyway, the minister had used the time available during the previous hymn to get into his ceremonial rubber waders, which were galoshes with trouser legs attached to a bib-and-braces dungaree/overall affair and he descended the steps into the mildly tepid waist-high water. He wore this get-up, because immediately after the baptisms, he was going to preach. He didn't wish to attempt to give his sermon while sopping wet and shivering. Having got into the right position, he turned and invited the first candidate (a young man who was barefoot, wearing suitable shorts and a t-shirt) to join him in the baptistry.

But as he stepped down into the pool, he was immediately electrocuted and fell forward, unconscious. Pandemonium! The minister was unable to lift the inert body; meanwhile the poor young man was continuing to be shocked. No-one could step forward and render assistance, since the danger of electrocution was still present.

At last, some wise soul disconnected the heating element from the power and the candidate was pulled out of the water. He was put into the recovery position and subsequently, an ambulance. Had his heart stopped? Had he drowned? Was he dead? I don't know. The minister's rubberware had insulated him from the voltage.

I have to conclude that while this was undoubtedly a powerful meeting, it wasn't a great demonstration of being raised to newness of life. Makes you think a teaspoonful might be a safer option.

27 Ways to bridge the gap

friendship evangelism

How, you may well ask, can we communicate the gospel to a perishing world? As the decades have progressed, I've participated in many stratagems for introducing folk to the good news and witnessed (see what I did there?) many more.

When I was a boy, I was introduced to some enthusiastic evangelists who wore the uniform of the *Open Air Campaigners*. The OAC badge on their shoulders meant they were often taken, in error, to be airline pilots, as the *British & Overseas Airline Corporation* was not yet defunct (merged with *British & European Airways* in 1971 to form *British Airways*). These creative chaps had two remarkable techniques for spreading the gospel.

One was a ventriloquist, who 'discussed' issues such as sin and selfishness with his schoolboy dummy, which was a lot more entertaining than it sounds. Alongside this, all the staff were skilled in performing a range of routines featuring a sketch board and pots of paint, sharing Bible truth by building up a picture and block capitals, which gathered a crowd and engaged enquirers in conversation. The headings were formed by painting boxes, dividing them into the required number of letters and then adding the negative space in paint, leaving the capital letters in white. I doubt it was unique, or invented by any of the people I met, but it certainly drew attention.

You may have already come across the *Crusaders*, which was an evangelistic boys' club/Bible class. It was so good I was comfortable to invite friends to attend. Through superb games, memorable outings and a deep commitment to bivouac, many boys were attracted from all sorts of backgrounds and the gospel was preached.

I believe there was a girls' version, but I have never met anyone who ever attended. I doubt their games were as good. In those days, remember, gender segregation wasn't an issue, as most of us experienced this at school as well, so we never got to meet anyone of the opposite sex until sixth form, by which time our fascination was at fever pitch!

Anyway, the big plus about *Crusaders*, to my mind at the time, was that it wasn't *Boys' Brigade*, which has the twin drawbacks of being a uniform organisation and expected everyone to be a talented musician, wanting to march.

Once I'd got into secondary school, anther evangelistic feature was the *Festival of Light*, which was marginally associated with the *National Viewers' and Listeners' Association*, led by Mary Whitehouse. Have you noticed how so many of these groups chose names that required accurate use of inverted commas? The *FoL* amounted to, as far as I could tell, a single called *Light Up the Fire* (featuring someone who much later was smart enough to give me a job) and a big rally in London where Christians spoke of the need to clean up the media from sex and violence, as well as presenting the gospel message. I suspect that the main reason I didn't hear more was because many of the senior figures in the organisation were from varieties of churchmanship of which my father did not approve, since they were Anglicans and Baptists. Some were even charismatics.

In the autumn of 1973, I met influential figures named John Talbot and Mike Sprenger. They were part of *Campus Crusade for Christ* (later known as *Agapé*) and were keen to assist my school's Christian Union in being more effective in witnessing. They established *College Life*, a youth meeting with a mixture of Bible Study and entertainment.

One memorable event featured three chaps from my school who were highly motivated to form a gospel folk band and had each bought a guitar, but hadn't had any time to learn how to play. So, they found a suitable song with three chords and performed it the next day by one of them holding down a G chord, another a C and the third a D; each playing when it was their turn. It wasn't a success.

Meanwhile, I was introduced to the CCC main literature, the booklet entitled *Have You Heard of the Four Spiritual Laws?* And of course, instead of using it to help other encounter Jesus, I wasted a lot of time discussing the finer points of the theology implied by the simple language. Chatter was easy, as long as we were discussing issues with other Christians; talking *about* evangelism, rather than doing it! What does the Bible say?

Preach the word – be prepared
in season and out of season. 2 Timothy 4:2

And beginning with Moses and the prophets, he [Jesus] explained to them
what was said in all the scriptures concerning himself. Luke 24:27

My attention was on the letter of the law when it should have been on the lost souls all around me. But once the critique dust settled, I finally realised that here was a way of telling the good news to people with whom I had a relationship. At last, the gospel was something we were supposed to talk about ourselves and not just leave to the professionals with their dummies, paints, glittering stage shows, minor theological inexactitudes and liberal approach to churchmanship.

I found this very worthwhile and, as you may know, joined the staff of CCC once I'd finished my A-level exams. Fortunately, the literature had evolved into the British version (this time, with *Saviour* correctly spelled) called *Knowing God Personally* - this was much more acceptable. No longer were we directed by laws, but well-worded information.

Approving of this new version, I spent a year in London being trained. This included lots of Bible teaching, prayer meetings, scripture memory homework and mostly spending time meeting students in their halls of residence, sharing the good news wherever I could. I met Graham in my first week, started a meaningful conversation with him, showed him how Jesus was the answer to the need he felt for forgiveness and peace in his life. I was not used to getting such an instant response and was quite alarmed when he began openly to weep in front of me, confessing his sin and eagerly receiving Christ as his saviour. What a privilege to a part of this transformation! It was truly a divine appointment for us both, as Graham had his soul saved and I was massively encouraged as I embarked on my mission to take the good news to University College, student by student, door by door.

Graham accompanied me as I continued to work my way around the halls, sharing his testimony of a changed life through his faith. I confess that were some days when I wasn't in the mood for meeting strangers, so I went direct to Graham's door and we went to get a drink or go to see a film. It occurs to me now that he probably had studies to do (after all, he was there to learn how to become a doctor) but I'm glad he was willing to take pity on me from time to time!

After the training centre, I then served for two years in Cardiff and three more back home in Brighton – presenting the good news in schools via lessons in *Personal & Social Education* or as part of the *Religious Studies* course. Finally, I was not just being one of the crowd at evangelistic events; I was standing up for Jesus in front of (sometimes) hostile crowds and declaring life-transforming Bible truth. Quite a development!

As part of the CCC team, I was also able to serve administratively in promoting *Life Anew 82*, the slightly twee name given to a Gospel

Crusade featuring the evangelist Don Double over ten nights at the Brighton Dome. I took responsibility for a youth event and was to blame for setting off all the fire alarms. In addition, we sifted through several thousand requests for tickets to a *Cliff Richard Gospel Tour* concert in the Brighton Centre. I was invited to a meal for those of us who had served, during which I sat at the same table as Cliff (a long trestle-style table for twenty-four and he was at the far end).

I'd been to *Greenbelt*, the Christian Music Festival a couple of times, and developed an interest in Christian Rock music. I knew my band *Matt Black and the Emulsions* could never compete, but then it wasn't a competition – it was a way of expressing gospel truth in a way that might appeal to unchurched young people. Once again, there I was, increasingly finding myself in the crowd and observing others sharing the gospel, rather than taking any personal responsibility.

By 1985, I'd joined Clarendon Church, and for the first time, I learned about the role of evangelist, not just as a professional preacher of the gospel, but as one who served the fellowship in training and encouragement in witness.

> *So Christ himself gave the apostles, the prophets, the evangelists, the pastors and teachers, to equip his people for works of service, so that the body of Christ may be built up.* Ephesians 4:11,12

I learned a great deal under the teaching of Holy Spirit-anointed church-based evangelists.

Not long afterwards, the *Alpha* course had begun to take off and was embraced widely as a tool for explaining the faith in the context of a meal and a chance to ask questions. Following some training, I learned when to give an answer (rarely), when to share a testimony (occasionally) and when to listen (all of the rest of the time). I found that when I'd truly heard what someone was saying, I could pray for them more effectively and make more apt comments. Spouting doctrine was less effective than showing care and concern.

My opinion of *Alpha* developed as I saw, close-up, on several occasions the impact of a Bible talk, some well-designed discussion questions and all the Christians on each table remaining silent as our guests opened up.

News was reaching us of what sounded like revival in Florida, with great crowds queueing every evening to get into church buildings, not only for gospel preaching, but for miracles of healing and other signs following. It was wonderful! Our church was visited by leaders who were experiencing this revival; some friends went to Pensacola to see for themselves. They returned with glorious testimonies and personal anointing, which was contagious.

Ministry times frequently followed the preaching of the gospel and as we got involved, we not only saw healings and other supernatural goings-on, but also realised that people were receiving revelation. The greater miracle of conversion was taking place.

What had changed from the way evangelism had been done before? I think I concluded that it mattered less what was said from the front because relationships made all the difference. Mass evangelism with big-name speakers was all very well, but making friends and giving them time was effective, too.

Going beyond friendship evangelism was a strategy which involved having a shared interest with someone. Spending time fishing or cycling or watching football or trainspotting or doing any number of worldly/neutral activities was reckoned to be a valuable form of outreach. No longer were we considering people as 'contacts', but as friends – another person who also liked to collect stamps or go jogging or drive to a country pub or take a wander around Ikea…

Let's get down to brass tacks and make this personal. Many of you will remember that I have an outstanding friend known as HD – yes, the chap with the beach hut, the wet car, an impressive understanding of physics and no appreciation at all of the Portuguese tongue.

We recognised that there was a significant lack in our circles of acquaintance, and while we desired to witness for Christ, first of all we needed to develop some friendships with people who had not yet had a life-changing encounter with Jesus.

Both of us were committed to our church, and both of us were employed by different but entirely Christian businesses. HD worked for a printing house, overseeing the presses and their operators. By this time I was working for Frontier Publishing, providing articles and sub-editing skills to productions serving *New Frontiers International*, working in an open-plan office with several desks.

This meant that most of our workmates were Christians; a fact which brought untold benefits. HD speaks with great warmth and respect toward his employer, who treated him with great kindness – almost fatherly affection – and taught him many skills, too. He showed him how to get the best out of the printing press and to maximise its effectiveness beyond the expectation of the manufacturer; and also ways to encourage the staff and get the best out of them, which served the customers and helped profitability for the company. Christian principles provided direction for the firm in many ways – in deciding which customers to take work from; in setting a fair price; in making promises about delivery of work that could be kept rather than broken and which didn't take advantage of the staff in the meanwhile; paying bills promptly; having a high standard of customer service; and so on.

At the same time, my office was filled with highly-respected Christians, some of whom are best described as 'spiritual giants' and 'pure as the driven snow', while the rest of us were doing our best to follow the Lord with a whole heart, despite having a bit more of a sense of humour. But I found working in an environment where there was a unity in our commitment, almost no shouting, swearing or bloodshed, and regular staff prayer meetings a great pleasure as well as a considerable challenge.

HD and I met for lunch on Mondays and Thursdays, sometimes going to the local café where the lady we had nicknamed *The Disco Queen* (on account of a few involuntary dance moves she once made when the radio was playing Michael Jackson's hit *Bad*) used a creative form of shorthand when taking our order. If either of us selected the all-day breakfast with chips, she wrote 1 x 1 extra, which meant, we supposed, *one serving of menu item one plus the most often-requested addition*. Why this amused us so much is hard to recall.

Anyway, during one of our lunch appointments, we discussed our concern that we didn't have much meaningful contact with people who were not part of the church. Our desire was to establish friendships with people and tell them the good news. We weren't looking for 'contacts' or to make converts; rather, we were genuinely trying to find a way to explain the gospel to people who might not otherwise hear it.

We shared an interest in playing bridge and while HD was vastly more experienced, we both wanted to progress. We knew there were bridge clubs in the area and reckoned that if we improved our game, we might join a club, make friends with other players and have opportunities to talk about faith with them. Yes, we were playing the long game, but we decided to give some attention to learning and enhancing our skills, so that we might be taken seriously by the folk in the community centre. I did some research and purchased a series of three teach yourself books – one on *Bidding* (communicating your cards' combined strength), another on *Playing as Declarer* (when you win the contract) and the third on *Playing as Defender* (when you don't). Yes, it was technical stuff and highly detailed.

We decided to sacrifice one of our eating-out lunchtimes each week and to give the time to study these books together, helping one another to understand the complications and keep one another encouraged and accountable. It was much more convenient (and quiet) for us to meet in my office, since the presses were often continually running throughout lunchtime, fulfilling a print deadline which required that the printer work on through and go home early in recompense, leaving the printed matter to dry. That made me the host, so at one o'clock on Thursday I would boil the kettle and make two coffees, by which time HD had sauntered down the road to join me.

There wasn't time for lengthy chatter, since these books required concentration. Over the course of a couple of years, we improved our understanding of the technicalities. We developed a healthy level of skill, such that we were eventually ready to take on the beginners' table at the community centre.

It didn't occur to us at the time, but the purposefulness and regularity of our lunchtime studies were noticed by my very righteous and 'believing the best' colleagues in the office. They saw the concentration we were putting in, along with the animated discussions we often had about such topics as *hearts, giving a lead, sacrifice, honour, weak or strong* and *being vulnerable* (maybe even *the last trump*) and they understandably concluded we were studying the Bible together. Their assumption earned me a good deal of not-deserved respect, although what theological interpretations they made of such terms as *flat hand, length and strength* or *escalating Gerber* is hard to imagine.

Perhaps they decided we were discussing deep theology.

Meanwhile, the time and effort we put into our studies began to pay off in the ways we'd hoped. We met Peter and Joan, both enthusiastic players at the local drop-in games club and had a deal-up there most Friday evenings (usually after a donor kebab and a game of pool).

It felt successful to have a way of engaging with unchurched folk, becoming genuine friends with them, able to be what were referred to as 'nice, polite young men'. Neither HD nor I waded in with gospel tracts, but we made it clear that we went to church, were more bothered about friendship than winning every possible rubber and took a genuine interest in these delightful local people.

In addition, we chanced upon Sally, a lady in the church who played club bridge with her husband Don, who wasn't a person of faith. I'd met him at a community group barbeque the summer before. They were very excited to welcome us to their home (one evening a month) for several hands of bridge, interrupted by the most magnificent home-baked brownies, sponges or flapjacks. We often chatted about our faith, as Don was interested to hear our views.

I feel certain our humble, friendly and cake-appreciating style contributed to the day when he finally laid down his objections and asked Jesus to save his soul.

We learned a great deal about playing techniques, although Don's assessment of our watertight point-bidding system, which always meant we avoided getting in too deep, was *I pity you*. His approach was much more adventurous, which used to annoy Sally, but won them shedloads of points, often through gamesmanship and intimidation. He had a long way to go to become a good Christian card player.

Developing our bridge playing also gave us an opportunity to learn from complete strangers.

We were chatting about being *we* or *they* during one of the intervals in the *Ken Dodd Laughter Show* at the London Palladium. The ladies in front of us heard us, recognised the terms we were using and turned to introduce themselves - they were players and had spent the morning at a Bridge Club off Oxford Street. They told us about a convention they'd learned – a way of communicating technical questions and answers between partners, entirely within the rules, but by using standard bids. The signal they told us about is for use when where one player opens the bidding with one no-trump and their partner responds two clubs. This is the *Stayman Convention*, they explained, a way for the responder to indicate that they don't have a flat hand (which would be preferable for proceeding in no-trump) but instead have at least four cards in one of the major suits – hearts or spades. This inexpensively invites the opening-bidder to rebid two hearts or two spades if they also have four cards in either suit (they'd bid two hearts if they have four cards in both majors since partner can, if they wish, raise it, economically, by one more step up the bidding ladder to two spades) or deny it with two diamonds. We reckoned this might come in handy.

We thanked the ladies but then we were all distracted by the great drum of Knotty Ash, *how ticked I am* jokes and the hilarious *what is my name, Aziz?* ventriloquism act. On the train home, HD & I discussed the usefulness of the convention, but neither of us could remember the name of it, so from then on it became known between us as *The Ken Dodd Bid*.

When we begin a rubber, we declare at the start that we play a weak no-trump, *Ken Dodd* and the Picard manoeuvre, so our opponents are fully informed. This ensures we are not accused of having secret codes or tricky signals to indicate which cards we've been dealt – rather we have transparent indicators. Opponents are entitled to ask what each convention signifies, so we explain: twelve-to-fourteen points, *Stayman* and voids count as a fifth ace in Gerber, so there's no confusion. Yes, it's up to *we* to know what's happening and up to *they* to notice as well.

Both HD and I thoroughly enjoyed becoming more proficient at bridge and rejoiced greatly that through playing, we'd made friends and been able to provide a measure of influence for the sake of the gospel.

Some highly-righteous Christian colleagues of mine never found out that far than studying the scriptures, we were learning to play cards.

28 Best man again and again

silver medal place Revelation 19:6,7; 21:1-7

I have been powerfully privileged to be a best man more than once.

First time was a fierce learning curve for me, coming to grips with the many duties and administrative demands; foolishly, I thought it was mostly about the stag night and speech.

Tony (all names have been disguised to avoid GDPR issues) was in my class at Infant School; we were four years old. We weren't especially friends from the off, but we became accustomed to each other as we progressed through the education system.

By the time we were eleven or twelve, we had clicked and both became Christians within a couple of years. Tony was already attending the parish church and was a key part of the Young People's Fellowship when I made the move from going to church with my parents.

Within a little while, Tony dated a girl named Hannah, who had also been in our class at the Infants school. A short time after they stopped seeing each other, I tried my luck with her for a few weeks. I was so keen, that I denied my musical taste and bought her a copy of the Donny Osmond single *Puppy Love*. She was very pleased, but severe musical differences do not a suitable foundation for a relationship make, so she dumped me soon afterwards.

I remained friends with Tony and together we formed a band with our pals Rory and RH. Our goal was to perform songs with gospel content and we were busy playing live gigs for three years while we completed secondary school. Tony and Rory went on to university; RH & I continued as a duo.

I visited Tony in his halls of residence in London and discovered that student life was filled with intense study, which made me feel a lot better about not being a student myself. Deep into his second year, Tony began to go out with Valerie and he proposed at Christmas. For reasons which escape me now, he didn't ask me to be his best man until three weeks before the wedding. On reflection, since all the admin was done and the stag do already organised, I suspect there may have been someone else in post before and I was just a sub. But I didn't think about it at the time. There were no shenanigans at the stag do and I turned up on the day with my suit and my speech.

All went according to plan. I behaved myself throughout, being unbelievably polite to his parents and hers; I was on the top table, of course, positioned between her mother and his great aunt, which wasn't a barrel of laughs.

My speech was a hit; I was given lots of brownie points for having been a childhood friend. The normal things ensued – cake-cutting, ensuring the band were all set-up in time and then the disco (this was 1978, remember).

Moving forward five years: Martin, one of my best friends from the church YPF, who had been in the school year below me, returned from his studies by the Thames at half term and took me out for a pint. He told me he'd met Selena and he wanted to marry her, although she didn't know this yet. I was even more pleased when, not long afterwards, she was included in the secret and had given her enthusiastic assent. It seemed suitable to Martin to ask me to be his best man and I readily agreed. This time around, I saw the full picture and was roped in for several of the admin jobs.

Once again, the day went according to well-laid plans. I behaved myself, being exceptionally polite to his parents and extremely civil with hers. I made no secret of my fascination with the chief bridesmaid, but of course did nothing about it. The speech went well and the afterparty was as good as such things ever are.

By 1993 I was part of the youth group leadership team. Miriam was fourteen when she was appointed as editor of the youth magazine. I worked alongside her, helping to write articles and select contributions, as well as providing graphic design flair. Several years passed and Miriam began to date Isaac, a member of the youth team. They became betrothed. It was great to have been friends with each of them independently and then very joyous to be asked to be Isaac's best man. I agreed, of course and we worked well as a team, drawing together the hundreds of threads required to create a wedding-day tapestry.

On the day, most of the event was seamless, although the timing went a bit awry, since every element took several minutes longer than expected. The service over-ran and then the photos took forever. Getting everyone sat down at the reception dragged endlessly and then Cousin Stanley took his place at the piano and worked his way through a pretty extensive repertoire of *songs from the shows*, which was not what I had expected and added almost an hour to the time allowed for the meal, as the caterers had been told (in error) not to clear the starter crockery while Stan was singing. So, they waited (in the other sense of the word) and the timetable slipped out of control.

Once we'd eaten, there were about twenty-five minutes before the 'evening only' guests were due to arrive. I thought to myself, *well, if we get the speeches out of the way in about fifteen mins, then cut the cake, we'll be about right.* Oh, but I was young and foolish.

The father of the bride got to his feet, unfurled the two dozen or so pages of his speech and made a start. He didn't hurry and he made no attempt to edit on the fly. In fact, after twenty minutes of heartfelt remarks about Miriam, he signalled to his co-conspirator, who switched on the projector, cueing in a further quarter of an hour of baby pictures, holiday snaps and random family photos (all of which required, in his opinion, extensive explanation). The lengthy speech from her highly emotional dad sparked emotions in the crowd; mostly rage and frustration.

Eventually he concluded and was about to propose a toast. Most people had finished their drinks long before, so the waiting staff were called upon to serve everybody. Since many of the evening only guests had already arrived, they were also served drinks so they could join in the toasting. There was nowhere for them to sit, so they crowded between the tables, hampering the progress of the waiters. It was bit of a shambles, frankly. The groom's speech wasn't long, but by this time we'd over-run rather dramatically.

And it was now my turn. What to do? Cut the speech I'd spent many creative hours composing, with bible verses, anecdotes, clever quips and heartfelt warmth? I was reluctant. Could I rush it? Cut the gags? Leave out the Christian bit, which was the part I'd been specifically asked to include by both the groom and the bride's father?

In the end, I gabbled my way through most of it, but by this time the crowd were not only restless but becoming ugly. So, I cut my losses, raised a glass and wound it up.

The afterparty featured a quality band and I had the loveliest of dancing partners; this was a very good conclusion to a trying day.

Six years passed, and my top friend Jeff Lambrayne announced that he and Nancy were engaged to be married. He asked both HD and I to be his best men and we divided up the responsibilities.

The happy couple needed some persuasion not to rewrite the rulebook. Their initial plan was to wipe the slate clean and put all the elements of a wedding day into a different order. Fortunately, the vicar (and the law of the land) forced them into some conformity, but they were still keen to start the reception with cake-cutting, then have the speeches and finally bring out the dinner. I calmly painted a word-picture of crying babies, complaining children and frustrated parents antagonised by the extensive delay this would cause. I agreed it would certainly ensure a novel and memorable occasion, but I felt under pressure that it'd be the speechmakers who would have to exercise extraordinary crowd control as lunch got pushed back towards 4pm. They relented, eventually.

We all attended the rehearsal, which was in a rural church, the coldest building I've ever been in. Not only was it sub-zero (January wedding), the building lacked a toilet. Tomorrow, one hundred and forty guests would be crowding in, with nothing on their invitations to warn them that this village church was entirely looless. *H'mm*, I thought, *potential issues here?*

And then the organist had brought the wrong sheet music. At least it wasn't that famous mistake where the couple asked for *Everything I Do, I Do It For You*, the romantic theme song from the 1991 film *Robin Hood, Prince of Thieves* and got instead the jaunty theme song from the 1950s tv show – *Robin Hood, Robin Hood, Riding Through the Glen*. But it upset the groom more than a little, because he had been very careful to be specific about which tune he wanted.

However, the stag do was a quiet evening with the groom and the best men in a restaurant. We ordered our food and had pleasant conversation, trying to keep the mood light, so that Jeff remained calm and relaxed. When our food arrived, we tucked in with characteristic gusto.

'How's your steak?' HD asked me.

'Just how I like it,' I replied, through a mouthful of medium rare beef. 'Your lamb chops?'

'Beautiful,' he replied. 'What about your fish, Jeff?'

'Well,' Jeff replied, 'it seems okay, but I've never had monkfish before, so I don't know what it's supposed to taste like.'

Fear gripped his best men's hearts. He'd chosen a food that may or may not agree with him the night before his wedding in a building without a toilet. The *what if?* scenarios rushed through my mind; many of them far too horrendously unpleasant to contemplate, especially while trying to eat. Jeff didn't seem too bothered when we expressed our concerns, but I think that was mainly due to an overdose of adrenaline in his system. Fortunately, the way things turned out was just fine, but playing with fire seemed to be the wrong way to behave.

The event itself went well (the churchwarden had mercifully put the heating on and the organist had been forcibly supplied with the right sheet music), although when guests began to emerge from the building, many of the gentlemen and boys availed themselves of a hedge alongside the road, from which a mysterious golden stream began to flow. What the ladies did, I shudder to imagine.

It did mean the crowd dispersed quickly, since folk took off at some speed to get to the reception, although there was a long queue of ladies for the ladies' inside the shop at the first petrol station on the journey.

The reception itself was a triumph, with celebrations, good food, two best man speeches and a guest appearance of HD's Commander Worf full-size cut-out.

The bride and groom's getaway was supposed to be in HD & Jeff's Bedford Motorhome Dormobile Debonair named Jolly. We'd tied the traditional tins to the back bumper, but the departure was thwarted by the caterer, who was eagerly (some say strongly) asking for his money before the groom disappeared from sight. I think there was a misunderstanding, as of course the groom intended to pay, but he had been expecting to receive an invoice about a week afterwards. The caterer wanted to be paid on the spot, since he'd been burned (not his delicious food, thankfully) in the past and so was being slightly menacing. Naturally, Jeff didn't have lots of twenty pound notes stuffed into his hired wedding suit. Fortunately, I had my credit card with me (in case of a wedding vehicle petrol tank emptiness issue, for example), so I stepped up, which calmed everything down and Jeff settled with me when they returned from Crete or Cyprus or wherever it was they had been.

After my move to Birmingham, I befriended a teacher named Jacob, who was keen to get involved with the youth work. We got on straightaway and enjoyed many hours in productive theological discussion as well as education system banter. After a couple of years of being fast-tracked into senior positions, he was headhunted to take up a teaching post in Dubai. I was privileged to pay a visit to this astonishing city and be shown the many sights, which ranged from wild camels to an unfinished motorway which abruptly stops in the middle of the desert; to world-famous skyscrapers; an extraordinary shopping mall with a vast fish tank in the middle; another, with a snow-covered ski-resort in the middle; a beautiful metro system; and a superb highway, across which Jake drove us on a magnificent eleven-lane drift from the far right of the on-ramp over to the fast lane.

When he returned to the UK for the summer, Jake met and fell in love with Gabrielle, another teacher. By Easter, they were engaged and Jake caught me by surprise when he asked me to be his best man. I was genuinely expecting him to prefer one of his college mates, or a work colleague. But he chose me. This was the first and last time I've wept in his presence.

Plans were made, fortunes spent and complicated schedules organised and eventually the parents, the bridesmaids, the ushers and I were each given a sixteen-page A4 book with highly detailed lists of who was to do what where, including the collection of suits, transport arrangements, hotel bookings and the order of activities through the day. There were many more supplementary duties including collecting the groom's wedding suit from their first-night honeymoon hotel. Anyone else would get changed at the end of the reception (ref *going-away clothes*) but Jacob managed to find a far more complicated way to achieve this.

The reception went well (especially my very funny speech, naturally) except for the announcement of the readiness of the spit-roast pork during the evening. I was informed by the caterer that this was ready, so I announced it. Guests went to collect their food but found it wasn't ready, by quite some margin. That was, of course, my fault. I was very gracious, calm and almost overflowing with forbearance, especially toward the irritatingly dozy member of the catering team who had dropped me in the Clarks from such a great height by his stupidity, carelessness, misjudgement of preparation, cooking and presentation times and his general over-enthusiasm. But I wasn't judgmental in the slightest. Not remotely. And I'm certainly not still cross about it. Well, hardly at all.

Now in the interests of transparency, I should declare that two of these five marriages have not survived; Tony and Valerie parted company and Isaac and Miriam have also divorced. This is very sad, of course. Miriam has since remarried, which is happier; Tony re-established his relationship with Hannah and they have married – childhood sweethearts indeed.

Now, you are asking, very probably: how did you manage to be the best man four and a half times and never the groom?

I should say it's not for want of trying, nor for want of desiring. It simply never happened for me. I got within a few weeks of a wedding on one occasion but didn't make it across the winning line. The (previously mentioned) lovely woman in question got married a couple of years later, to my homegroup leader. A bit awks.

Yet the question on my lips is a different one: how come I'm so good at being great friends with blokes yet seem unable to adapt this when it comes to womenfolk?

Nothing is certain, except that people will let you down, me included. What's less sure is how we deal with disappointment, how determined we are to forgive one another and the meaning of true love.

I've been around several couples whose marriages have broken down to the point of divorce. It is tough to watch. Marriage is clearly hard work and requires deep commitment and determination on both sides, all of the time. I observe partnership and fun times; I don't observe the best of times, of course; and I have sometimes had to witness painful times when each is hurting the other, repeatedly breaking the 'for better, for worse' promise. I am saddened by it. I hope I'm not judging it, because the truth is I expect I've been preserved from marriage because I wouldn't be particularly good at it; I'm too selfish. I doubt I could cope with being a disappointment to the woman I claim to love, or with the careless way I'd failed to love her. I think I'm perhaps a bit afraid of making such all-encompassing promises to someone, even if I had every intention of keeping them. There would have to be bucketloads of trust, forgiveness and grace on both sides…

Nevertheless, I wouldn't want this admission of humanness to put anyone off from the prospect of becoming my wife, should she be considering her options. The position remains wide open and the rewards persist in being far more fabulous than she – whoever she may be – can ever imagine, while also being nothing less than the woman with such glorious good fortune deserves.

You may find this strange (I know I do) but there's another wedding to which I've been invited and in which I shall play a central role. This time, it's not administrative or supervisory. I won't have to arrange flowers, suits, hotels or getting wedding presents from the reception to the couple's new home; I shan't be called upon to look after and then produce a ring or to announce transport back to the wedding breakfast or to make a leg-pulling-but-ultimately-respectful speech. No, this time I won't be the best man, not by any stretch of the imagination.

This time, I'll be a miniscule, but significant part of the bride. This time, the groom is utterly perfect and the bride is indisputably beautiful, pure and preserved for her husband, by the power of her husband. The choir will be of flawless quality. There's no need for an MC in robes; nobody to read a poem while the register is signed; no mother weeping; no photographer; no fascinator-vs-hat wars among the fashionistas; no 'evening only' guests; no catering personnel; no awkward hymn-singing; no waiting in case someone will 'speak now, or forever hold their peace'; no small boys in ill-fitting suits; no ludicrous kilt-wearing; no drunk uncles making fools of themselves; no intensely-rehearsed first dance exhibition…

This time, there'll be the true love and sacrificial devotion that earthly marriages are supposed to symbolise. This time, it's for keeps, without doubt. This time, the assurances are eternal. The new home is more spectacular and desirable than you've ever imagined. The Father of the groom will draw us closer, assign us to mansions, receive praise and glory far beyond telegrams or shiny wrapped boxes.

Then I saw 'a new heaven and a new earth,' for the first heaven
and the first earth had passed away, and there was no longer any sea.
I saw the Holy City, the new Jerusalem, coming down out of heaven
from God, prepared as a bride beautifully dressed for her husband.
And I heard a loud voice from the throne saying, 'Look!
God's dwelling-place is now among the people, and he will dwell with them.
They will be his people, and God himself will be with them
and be their God. He will wipe every tear from their eyes.
There will be no more death or mourning or crying or pain,
for the old order of things has passed away. Revelation 21:1-4

This deserves a bit more than raising a glass of warm Lambrusco or Schloer as we chant together 'To the bride and groom.' This deserves the loudest, longest, loudest, most heartfelt and grateful 'Hallelujah!'

Then I heard what sounded like a great multitude, like the roar of rushing waters and like loud peals of thunder, shouting: 'Hallelujah! For our Lord God Almighty reigns. Let us rejoice and be glad and give him glory! For the wedding of the Lamb has come, and his bride has made herself ready.
Revelation 19:6,7

29 We need to talk about Jesus

keeping Christ central John 1:3

Here is a series of Bible studies aimed at encountering Jesus through his life, our response and times of worship

This has been motivated by a growing desire to ensure our focus wasn't only on God the Father and the Holy Spirit, but also actively concentrating on the glorious, beautiful, wonderful Son of God, saviour, redeemer, advocate with the Father, King of the Jews, good shepherd, true vine, image of the invisible God, lion, lamb, way, truth and life, our Lord Jesus Christ.

I'm not pretending that the topics covered here are necessarily the most important ones, although Christ's death and resurrection are essential, as are the studies about his identity, his mission, his way of dealing with people, his teaching and his purposeful storytelling. What I'm getting at is that I could have selected other miracles, other teaching topics and other parables.

I was keen to establish a style where we examined the scripture, checked parallel passages where possible, asked questions of the text and didn't settle for sharing our ignorance or merely expressing our well- or ill-informed opinion, but made sure Jesus was the central focus and the Word of God our source material. Respecting contributions is vital, I agree, but elevating scriptures above them is necessary, too.

That's why each study or meditation suggests verses to read; some of these are parallel passages to the one under specific scrutiny; and asks questions without necessarily giving a complete answer, or, in some cases, even any answer at all.

Study themes: two kinds of baptism; three defeats for the enemy; two key teaching topics; two mighty miracles; two wonderful stories; and three 'Great's.

Just a note on style: it can be more helpful to all if the leader poses questions, welcomes on-topic answers, asks others to comment and allows free-flowing discussion. Bold leaders ask a question and invite more than one answer. Very bold leaders refrain from declaring the 'correct' answer, as this practice discourages further conversation.

The object of the exercise is for us all to spend time with Jesus, not just for us to learn something or listen to the leader. There may be a suitable time for that; this isn't it.

1 Baptism of Jesus

To read: Matthew 3:13-17; Mark 1:9-11; Luke 3:21,22; John 1:29-34)

Please notice very similar phrases used by the voice from heaven each time the baptism is described: *this is my Son, whom I love/you are my Son, whom I love; with him I am well pleased/ with you I am well pleased.*

Why do we have three almost identical passages? There's only one account of the wedding at Cana and yet we believe that. Only one healing at the pool of Bethesda, one raising of Lazarus, only one upper room discourse… Is baptism more important?

In the Matthew passage, John the Baptist tries to deter Jesus on the grounds of his own unworthiness – he showed proper humility, yet Jesus invited him to continue. This suggests we can impart spiritually without being perfect first. A man with crippled legs can pray for healing for others, as it's not a part of himself he's giving away - it's the power of the living Lord at work through his servant.

Consider the Holy Spirit symbols of a dove and fire. Interpret the symbols. What about airborne purity and consuming power?

v17 Why did God speak audibly on this occasion? Probably he's identifying his son, making a public statement of his love, using the recognised *I am* expression, affirming that *being* is very much more significant than *doing*. Anything else?

Yahweh *or* YHWH *is God's proper name in Hebrew. The importance of it can be seen in the sheer frequency of its use. It occurs 6,828 times in the OT. That's more than three times as often as the simple word for 'God' (Elohim – 2,600; El – 238).*

What this fact shows is that God aims to be known not as a generic deity, but as a specific person with a name that carries his unique character and mission.

John Piper, *Bible-daily.org,* Exodus 3

The I AM expression contains a number of implications: God exists, he is singular, he is eternal, he remains in the present tense. This reflects his 'secret' name, not to be spoken aloud, sometimes expressed as *Jehovah.*

What's the point of baptism? Check Mark 16:16, Matthew 28:18-20 We can be pretty sure that Jesus believes, so why does he submit to baptism. The devil knows who he is (see Matthew 4:1-11), so Jesus doesn't need to declare it to the principalities and powers, does he? Think about consecration (being set aside) and identifying with the Messiah Kingdom, which was John's baptism. What's the value of baptism as far as we are concerned? Have we all been baptised in water? Is christening the same? (see chapter 26 for further discussion on this topic)

Take a while to worship the loved son.

2 Temptation of Jesus

To read: Matthew 4:1-11; Mark 1:12,13; Luke 4:1-13

Matthew 4:2 mentions a forty day fast – consider how this might be a very good thing. Is it necessary? Is Jesus setting a good example, or being a very holy consecrated prophet? Do you know anyone who has been on an extended fast of any kind? How did they get on? Did they survive?

v2 Is it wrong to be hungry? Why is this a temptation?

v3 How does Jesus counter the bread temptation? Why does he quote from Deuteronomy?

v5-6 Is it wrong to be confident in your identity? Why is this a temptation?

v7 How does Jesus counter the 'are you really the Son of God, even though God has just declared it' temptation? In what ways would jumping off the temple roof prove his identity? Jesus sees right through it and uses another quotation from Deuteronomy.

v8,9 Is it wrong to appreciate scenery? Is this the temptation?

10,11 How does Jesus counter the 'all this I will give you' temptation? Jesus knows who deserves worship, quoting from the same book for a third time. Meanwhile, are you starting to think you should become more familiar with Deuteronomy?

Deep question for the sturdy of heart: was it possible for Jesus to have given in to temptation? Check Hebrews 4:15. Jesus was 100% pure God and 100% unfallen man. His temptations were only from outside himself, as he had no fallen nature. Thus, Jesus could be tempted to sin by his righteous ambition to minister to many… So, if Jesus had no sin nature, was his refusal to yield to temptation somehow easier for him? Jesus was tempted in every way that we are and many more ways besides, such as being tempted to take up his glory again. Is comparing our sinfulness to Jesus' purity a worthwhile exercise?

What was the 'opportune time' for which the Devil went to wait? Suggestion: see Luke 22:39-46. Compare the parallel passage in Luke 4:1-12. Why are the temptations in a different order? Does it matter?

Check 1 Corinthians 10:13. What can we conclude if God says we will not face a temptation beyond what we can bear? How does this inform you about the temptations you suffer? Clue: are you strong enough to bear them?

Pray for strength to resist temptation. Matthew 6:13 may be a worthwhile starting point.

3 Healing the leper

To read: Luke 5:12-16; Matthew 8:1-4; Mark 1:40-45

Focus on Luke 5:12. What is leprosy and why is it such a big deal? What does falling on your face signify? *Lord, if you are willing, you can make me clean.* This is a statement, not a question. It's not begging.

What makes the leper think Jesus might heal him? How does he know Jesus has the power to heal him? Why does he call Jesus 'Lord'? How has he heard of Jesus, or has he discerned Christ's identity spiritually? Why might Jesus be unwilling to heal him?

v13 Jesus reached out and touched the man. Why, do you suppose, this is mentioned? What's the significance of the laying on of hands? Is this a 'prescribed method'? Jesus commands the man to 'Be clean!' In what way is the man obedient to this command? To whom/what is Jesus speaking? Should we talk to diseases? Why or why not? How many months later did the doctor conclude that the course of medicine had been successful?

v14 Why is Jesus apparently keen to keep this secret? Discuss the merits of showing yourself to the priest and making sacrifices. Which members of the community will see what's happening and ask the right questions? Consider the downside.

v15 Why do crowds gather? What are they eager to spectate?

v16 Why does Jesus withdraw, since he only has three years to get his mission done? Why does he have no apparent marketing strategy?

Does the disease of leprosy have a deeper significance as something Jesus can heal? *Infectious, destructive, social implications, fearful, untreatable, needs a miracle – like sin.*

Check John 14:12-14. Does this mean we can heal people? Physical sickness or spiritual disorders? Both? What does 'greater' mean in this quotation?

Ministry: pray for healing, if the Holy Spirit gives you boldness (see 2 Corinthians 3:12).

4 Giving

To read: Matthew 6:1-4 see also 1 Corinthians 9:13,14; 1 Corinthians 16:2; and 2 Corinthians 8:12-15

v1 What acts of righteousness can we keep entirely secret? Jesus' words are about motive - being kind in order to be seen being kind. But isn't being kind a good thing anyway? Does God reward kindness given with a mixed motive? Let's talk about doing good deeds in order to be rewarded. Has there been a time when you did a good deed or act of kindness without looking for a reward?

v2 'Announce with trumpets' - What can this mean? A Salvation Army brass band to herald your offering bowl? It probably refers to the large horn-shaped collectors into which visitors to the Temple could throw their coins. This made an impressive sound as they rattled against the brass and found their way into the box below. The smaller the coins, the more noise, so exchanging cash into small-denomination temple coinage was a popular approach. This is where the money-changers came in; not only did they swindle the worshippers with short measure, but they also helped them to announce their generosity with great pride. Small wonder Jesus called them 'thieves' as he turned their tables over!

Why are those who give alms or offerings called 'hypocrites'?

v3 Describe a time when you did the left-hand/right-hand shuffle. What are the kinds of reward your Father gives?

Look at 1 Corinthians 9:14. Is Paul justifying taking up an offering before he addresses the unbelievers? Where does Christian Aid fit in? How can the gospel provide a living? Does your church leader take a salary?

Now check 1 Corinthians 16:2 What are the differences between passing a plate and standing order giving? Consider advantages as well as disadvantages. Is either method a form of disobedience? Find texts to support your argument. Look at 2 Corinthians 8:12. This appears to offer validation for giving only when you are in the black. Discuss. 8:13 is solid ground for socialist politics — for the many, not the few. True?

8:15 Define *too much.*

Application: Where are you with your giving? Guilty reaction when the plate is passed? Hilarious generosity? Long-forgotten regular painless technology-automated deposit? Cash-machine intentionality? Secret distribution?

Worship the Lord who has given so freely.

5 Parable of the Sower

To read: Matthew 13:3-8 & 18-23, Mark 4:3-8, Luke 8:5-8 & 11-15

Luke 8:5,12 What's unhelpful about the path? Why is it an unfruitful place for the seed? What is wrong with the sower or the seed that results in the message failing to get established?

v6,13 What did the seed on rocky soil lack? Give examples of 'times of testing'. What is meant by 'fall away'? Can we have assurance of our salvation? Can we be confident? What 'proof' is there?

v7,14 What do the thorns represent? Is there anything the farmer can do about thorny ground? Is it good soil which has received poor seed? In what ways can we check our maturity? Since maturity is an absolute, that means all Christians are in danger of being choked by life's worries, riches and pleasures, right?

8,15 What does the 'good soil' do with the seed of the word? Consider such words as hear, harken, listen, pay attention to, concentrate on... How can we more effectively retain the word? Bible study, meditation, memorisation, worshipping with Bible verses set to music (a good habit of former generations, but sadly not so much recently), read the word in many translations... What are the characteristics of endurance?

What does the seed represent - at first and latterly?

Why does Jesus focus on the seed, the ground on which it lands and on the context in which the young shoots are growing? He might well consider the spiritual qualities of the sower and the lostness of the lost.

Discussion question: should we pray primarily for the people hearing the gospel preaching, or for the preacher and the preaching of the word?

It may help to personalise each of the four soils. The path is represented by *Luke Warm*, where the seed lands, but is not welcomed or nurtured. Then the rocky soil provides only shallow places for the roots to grow, so progress is impeded. This is *Mark Time*. Thirdly, the place where the thorns grow in competition with the plants causes them to be choked, stifled and to *Peter Out*. Lastly, thank the Lord, the good soil of *Percy Vere* demonstrates how to welcome the seed of the word, allow it to develop deep roots and provide nutrition.

Application: In what ways can we tend the soil of our heart to be good soil? Can we add metaphorical fertiliser, do some ploughing, invite God to water it and weed out the distractions of life? Is this entirely a solo activity or can we serve one another in this?

Worship.

6 Prayer

To read: Matthew 6:5-13, Luke 11:1-4, Luke 18:1

Matthew 6:5 Why would anyone pray standing in the synagogue or on the street corner? What reward have these hypocrites received? Is this applicable to our society in any way?

v6 What if you don't have a room? What is the principle here? What time of day does Jesus recommend? Is Jesus opposed to prayer meetings or prayer in church? What reward does the man who prays in secret receive (careful, or you might step into v5!)?

v7 What is pagan babbling? 'True prayer is lifting up the soul and pouring out the heart.' Vain repetitions of stock phrases seems not to be acceptable. Where does this leave the Book of Common Prayer? Or reciting the Lord's prayer? Or songs such as *Good Good Father*? Are there some instances when repetition is valuable?

Consider Matthew 26:44 – is this the same fault? Does Luke 6:12 conflict with this verse? Prayer is not to inform God about stuff, or to show off our pastoral care or wise consideration of possibilities. Prayer is humble submission to the Lord of all, making requests, not demands. It can also be an appointment to worshipfully pour out our hearts.

v8 Why should we pray, then, if God's already on the case? In what ways are we acknowledging God's in charge?

v9 So here's a structured, definitive prayer worth learning and repeating, right?

Our Father - not merely my Father, which is brilliant, but ours! And he's not merely the creator, judge, glorious King, sovereign Lord and eternal sustainer, he's abba (daddy) as well! *In heaven* - not my father on earth (less than perfect, actively a bad person, abusive, absent or non-existent) but instead glorious, wonderful, without fault, consistent, caring, present, available, eternal.

Hallowed be your name Not meaning your name is 'hallowed', but your name is respected, honoured, treated as holy. If even the name is holy, then this reflects holiness of character.

v10 *your kingdom come* We pray for the establishment of the kingdom of God, setting his rule and dominion is a fallen world. *Your will be done* Praying as Christ prayed in his passion (check Luke 22:42). We obey God and pray that others obey him too.

On earth Right here in this fallen world - calling on God for the rule of his kingdom and will. *As it is in heaven* Our goal is extravagant, calling for heaven on earth.

v11 *Give us* We acknowledge that even our staple food comes from God and is not something we earn or deserve, but a gift. *Today* This strongly suggests that we should pray frequently, not asking to stock up, but for perishable goods, so we need to pray again tomorrow. *Our daily bread* Not a request for grouse, venison, caviar or Rolls Royces, but humble portions.

v12 *Forgive us our sins* So we've honoured God, expressed our humility and now recognise our weakness and failure. This is a polite request to be forgiven. Do you think we should try to name our sins specifically? Perhaps this would show our regret and determination to turn from them (repentance). On what basis is this prayer answered? *As we forgive those who trespass against us* What if God forgave us in the same measure, with the same reluctance, slowness, half-heartedness and resentment. What a terrible state we would be in if it meant this! This is a daily reminder that we can and should pass on the grace we have received.

So, if this doesn't mean *forgive us in the same way*, what does it mean? Are we requesting a sort of tit-for-tat forgiveness?

v13 *And lead us not into temptation* This means, surely 'do not let us be led into temptation'. Is it sinful to be tempted? Check out Luke 4:1-13 again. Is it dangerous to be tempted? *But deliver us from the evil one* - save us, spare us from a meeting with Satan. Does Satan tempt you? Do you have occultic encounters? Is your daily experience a negative supernatural one?

Application: This is called the Lord's Prayer - rightly or wrongly? Scripture memorisation is good, yes? Does Jesus intend us to recite this prayer from memory? Perhaps this a structure for prayer, showing us to start with Godward worship, to agree with his intentions, to ask for what we need, to confess our sin and to agree we are weak and require his strength to walk in his way.

Pray. Let's not merely talk about it, not just discuss the intricacies of it, avoid simply admiring examples of it; but let's actually get down to it and talk to the all-powerful, loving creator!

7 Parable of the Prodigal Son

To read: Luke 15:11-23 see also Acts 2:38,39

How does a parable differ from an allegory? Into which category does this story fit? Justify your conclusion.

v12 The son's request (demand) implies his entitlement to the share. Do you agree? What are some of the attitude issues associated with a sense of entitlement? For what reasons did the father agree to the suggestion? Can we legitimately presume that in this story, the father represents God? Why, or why not?

v13 Why, do you suppose, did the son go to a distant country? What does *squandered* imply? What is wild living? Why, do you suppose, doesn't Jesus give us details about the sins of this wayward lad?

v14 The narrative introduces issues of personal responsibility as well as external circumstances; both create need in the boy. Consider: count up the poor choices the boy has made so far: asking for his inheritance early; taking it; leaving; wasting his wealth; spending everything he had…

v15 Consider the intense pressure on the boy – enough to inspire him to deny his heritage, to humble himself and to serve a local owner of livestock.

v16 Add to the social deprivations the boy is dealing with – now he's actively longing to eat pigswill. Describe the quality of food offered to pigs in the middle of a famine. Consider the depth of hunger reached to desire to eat such produce.

v17 What is meant by the phrase *he came to his senses*? Is this divine revelation, or merely getting his thinking straight, having considered his options, or something else? Gone is the sense of entitlement; now he's comparing his state unfavourably with his father's hired men.

v18,19 Describe his plan. What assumptions is he making? Would you describe his approach as blind hope, confident trust, last chance saloon, or in other terms? Check Psalm 51:4 *Against you, you only have I sinned* Jesus' listeners would have noticed the similarity. In what sense had King David sinned solely against God? NB Bathsheba is pregnant and widowed, Uriah is murdered, Joab is implicated… The prodigal takes a wider view than David. Which is accurate? Consider the difference in status between a son and a hired man.

v20 Plan formulated, he starts the return journey. Consider how the father could have seen his son still a long way off. What might Jesus' listeners have expected to be the reaction of the father? Rage? *Get off my land!*? Eager, welcoming forgiveness and celebration? Further squandering of his assets? To run is an undignified display – why would the father be willing to show such enthusiasm?

v21 Note: the son only got part-way through his planned speech.

v22 Consider the significance of a new robe, a ring and fresh sandals. Perhaps the father was embarrassed by his son's appearance in a pig-swill stained coat, with worn-out footwear from his long journey. And lack of jewellery (perhaps he'd pawned or sold his rings when his cash ran out…). Could this be the explanation?

v23 Discuss the value of a fatted calf. When was it due for slaughter? When will this father come to his senses and stop squandering yet more on the waster lad?

v24 The expression *was dead and is alive again* reflects the death and resurrection of Jesus… so should we infer that the son represents Jesus? Why or why not?

v25-27 It appears that the older son hadn't been included in the invitations to the celebrations. Why might this be?

v28 What is the older brother angry about?

v29-30 His complaints appear justifiable. Why do they fall on deaf ears? In what ways might he have partied with a goat? Who does the older son represent? If he has stayed at home all this time and not yet realise his brother has returned, why does he assume the inheritance share has been spent on prostitutes?

v31-32 Which of his sons does the father prefer? Or is that unclear?

In what ways does this parable teach us about; repentance; confession; forgiveness; restitution; Jesus intention to bring clarity through the medium of narrative theology?

8 Feeding 5000

To read: Matthew 14:15-21, Mark 6:35-44, Luke 9:10-17, John 6:5-13

Luke 9:11 Consider four ways in which Jesus was kind to the crowd: he welcomed them, he taught them, he healed them and he cared for their physical needs.

v12 The disciples were being considerate of the needs of the people; is there a role for administering the preachers? Helping them by pointing out practical considerations, such as suggesting better use of or investment in PA equipment, for example.

v13 Is Jesus being unrealistic? Substantiate the amount of food - breadsticks & bloater paste. Great business for the bakeries in Bethsaida snatched from them. What does Jesus think about bakeries?

v14 How many people in the crowd? About 5000 men, many of whom, perhaps, were skiving from their jobs in order to hear Jesus. I suppose some of them went alone, leaving their wives and kids at home; other took their whole family. By the same token, I suppose there were lots of unaccompanied women & children…

So, the true size of the crowd (allowing an average of two kids per family, which is probably not enough for Middle Eastern families of NT times) could be reaching 20,000, quite easily. And let's face it, the picnic was so tiny, it was a child's portion. So, an inaccurately-named miracle, I guess, if we include women and children when counting.

Anyway, why does Jesus sit the crowd down in groups of fifty – is this significant? Why had they been standing to listen?

v15 The disciples act in obedience to Jesus. Did Israelites traditionally have picnics? Did they used to sit down to eat? Is there anything about this that goes against Jewish laws? Where were the places for ceremonial washing before handling food?

v16 Why does Jesus look up? 'Broke them and gave thanks' is reflected where else? Who distributed the loaves and fish? So, in whose hands did the miracle of multiplication take place?

v17 One bite would not have been satisfying. What can we say about the multiplication factor? How many baskets would the original lunch fill? The disciples collected the leftovers when all were satisfied. Does this speak into our approach to giving and to charity? NB first 10% is what we owe, leftover basketfuls are what we give… Twelve baskets of leftovers; twelve disciples. Consider the size of leftover pieces, given the open weave of a wicker basket. Reflect on the bounty of God's kindness. The extravagant generosity here is truly remarkable.

Application: Pray that we'd all be willing to participate in the miraculous. Ask God to give you generosity with your surplus.

Worship the abundant Lord Jesus.

9 The Great Exchange: Death of Jesus

To read: Matthew 20:17-19, Mark 10:32-34, Luke 18:31-34

Luke 18:31 Define the term *Son of Man.* Check John 5:27, Mark 10:35, John 1:49-51… Sometimes it signifies nothing more than 'yours truly', while different interpretations suggest it compares and contrasts *Son of Man* with *Son of God*. Scholars undecided. What did the prophets write about the Son of Man (about the messiah)? NB the yuletide Festival of Nine Lessons and Carols refers…Check Isaiah 7:14 (*a virgin will bear a son*); Isaiah 9:6,7 (*unto us a child*); Micah 5:2 (*you, Bethlehem Ephrathah*).

v32 *handed over to the Gentiles* What does this mean? Jesus clearly knew the mistreatment that was about to happen. Check Genesis 39:20,21; Psalm 23:4

v33 *rise again* Perhaps we have become rather too accustomed to this surprising, extraordinary, wonderful miracle!

Mark 10:45 does the Son of Man deserve to be served? Check Philippians 2:6,7. In what ways does Jesus serve a) his disciples b) us? *And to give* compare and contrast John 3:16. Was Jesus' life taken from him, or given by him? John 10:17,18 What does this teach us about suicide? Consider the term *ransom*. Who pays? Who demands? What outcome? Think also about the words *exchange, substitute, swap. Ransom for many* How does the great exchange take place? Why is God willing to swap his son for me? What does this say about my value?

This would be a good time to celebrate communion and to give worship to the lamb of God, sacrificed for me.

10 The Great Escape: Resurrection Morning

To read: Matthew 28:5-10, Mark 16:9-14, Luke 24:28-35, John 20:10-17

Key witnesses to the resurrection of Jesus were Mary Magdalen, the other Mary and Salome, who went to anoint the corpse after the sabbath day was over; and Cleopas and his companion, disciples who were on the road to Emmaus.

Jesus' body had been removed from the cross and quickly made ready for burial within a short time. Why was there a bit of a rush? See Mark 15:34, 37, 42, 46. Job half complete, the Passover was about to begin, so they left it, planning to return on the Sunday morning. Why is it significant that the stone was rolled away? How substantial was the stone? NB this is more likely to be a disc than a boulder. Was there anything else preventing access to the tomb? See Matthew 27:66.

On a scale of one to ten, where one is *not at all* and ten is *certainty*, were the disciples and the women expecting Jesus to be raised from the dead? Surely, he had said he would (see Luke 9:22), so why didn't they believe him? Why did Jesus appear first to the women?

John 20:24 Why do you imagine Thomas was not present when Jesus first appeared in the upper room?

v28 Why was Jesus content for Thomas to declare *my Lord and my God* when he saw the nail-wounds in Christ's hands? Blasphemy oaths such as this weren't common in those days; perhaps he meant it?

Luke 24:15 Consider what might have been the topics of conversation as the disciples walked.

v16 Why didn't they recognise Jesus at first?

vv17-20 Imagine how hard it must have been for Jesus to keep a straight face during this explanation.

v21 Examine these words and seek out any faint references to promises Jesus had made, or claims about his identity.

vv22-24 Once again, the faithfulness of the women is honoured.

vv25-27 Try to mention some of the highlights that Jesus might have chosen as he interpreted the scripture for these men.

vv28-31 Consider how much more amazing this incident was compared with the way we celebrate communion. What did Jesus do that gave them cause to recognise him? Or did they just put two and two together?

vv32,33 It was evening (see v29) before they left the house and returned the seven miles to ensure the rest of the disciples heard their news.

Reflect on the example of eagerness, enthusiasm, determination and zeal that they showed. Do we share the good news of the resurrected Christ with similar resolve and excitement? Take a while to give thanks to God the Father for raising the Son and for revealing him to us by his Spirit.

11 **The Great Commission**

To read: Matthew 28:16-20

Matthew 28:16 Why are there only eleven disciples? Why do they go to Galilee? At which mountain do they assemble? (possibly the Mount of Transfiguration).

v17 The disciples see Jesus but express little surprise, because they have seen him since the resurrection already. Which of them worshipped and which of them doubted, do you suppose? Check out 1 Corinthians 15:6, as this may apply here.

v18 *Jesus came to them* NB this is all Matthew says about the resurrection. Take a moment to ask why. Matthew is writing to Jews, who are familiar with the prophecies about the Messiah, after all. Maybe Matthew is, in a way, taking the resurrection for granted, as an expected response to the rejection, torture and death of Christ – he shows his authority by appearing, alive again.

What does he mean by 'all authority'? Final authority? Non-delegated authority? How does this fit with Ephesians 2:2? Or 1 John 5:19? Check 1 John 4:4. Who has the right to give authority? Hebrews 2:7-9

v19 *Therefore* On account of Jesus having all authority, *go*. How does this fit with Matthew 16:18 (I will build my church), which suggests he will stay and experience the power of unity? What does 'go' mean? Check Acts 1:8. What does 'make disciples' mean? Fishermen & tax accountants who follow Jesus until the going gets tough? How can we 'make' disciples? Are you a disciple? Are you contributing to others, so that they develop as disciples?

Who appoints disciples? Check 1 Kings 19:19-21 (Elijah/Elisha); Matthew 4:18-22 (Jesus calls Simon, Andrew, James, John); Acts 9:27,28 and Acts 11:25,26 (Barnabas mentors Paul). Is it okay to request 'please disciple me'? Is it arrogant to ask 'let me disciple you/come follow me'? Can we disciple by stealth?

v19 *disciples of all nations* Is this implying multi-cultural, multi-ethnic disciple quotas should be met? Or is it more of an emphasis on Jews and Gentiles? *baptising them* Again there's an emphasis on water baptism. *in the name of the Father and of the Son and of the Holy Spirit* trinitarian baptism signifies what?

One name, three persons. Covenant declaration of faith to the world and the spiritual realm.

Father: creator, preserver, benefactor.

Son: Jesus is God's son, you are the Christ (Matthew 16:16), prophet, priest & king.

Holy Spirit: to empower us, provide gifts, inspire worship, assist our conduct

v20 *teaching* Is this part of the disciple role, or the role of the Ephesians 4:11 pastor/teacher? By what methods can we be taught? What are the topics of our curriculum? Obedience, knowledge of Jesus's commands, respect for Jesus's role as commander. Mention some of the commands of Jesus. How can we *teach* obedience? Merely by modelling it? Ends with a reassuring promise. Not the best translation here: have a guess at what the original says. *I am with you always* (implication). NB I AM with you, not against you or merely leading you, but sometimes carrying you.

Enduring: How long is always? What limitations or exceptions are mentioned? Conclusion: go, make disciples, baptise them, teach them; Jesus is with you. Can we be confident Jesus is with us? Discuss *'Jesus' parting words show that the Christian life is all about what we do'* Consider ways in which you may put this commission into practice in your life.

Are you going? Are you making disciples? Are you being a disciple? Have you been baptised? Are you encouraging those who have not, to be baptised? Are you provoking the elders to set aside baptism meetings, and to advertise them strongly, even though there may not be any obvious candidates yet?

Are we thoroughly trinitarian? Are we aware of what Jesus commands us to do and to be? Are we obedient to his commands? Let's be praying that we remain obedient, following him, looking to him for leadership, example and fellowship.

12 **Baptism in the Holy Spirit**

To read: Acts 1:5,8, John 20:22, John 7:37,38, Acts 2:1-8; Acts 19:6

Acts 2:1 The name pentecost means fiftieth. It's a Jewish harvest festival, fifty days after Passover. What conclusions may we draw from *they were all together in one place*?

v2,3 Consider the significance of the sound of *a violent wind* filling the whole house and *what seemed to be tongues of fire* resting on each of them. Can we conclude that these are symbols of the Holy Spirit? Why, do you suppose, does Luke take such pains to use terms as *sound of* and *what appeared to be*?

v4 What did each disciple do or say or believe or sign or pay or earn or achieve or inherit or swap or swallow or overcome or recall to qualify for baptism in the Holy Spirit? What can we conclude from this? What evidence is provided to assure us of this internal spiritual activity? How does this incident tie in with John 20:22. Discuss any difference between *receiving* and *being filled.* At which point does regeneration take place? Or has that already happened? NB among commentators, there is some difference of opinion about this…

What experience have you of speaking in tongues? How would you define it? A prayer language? A praise language? A language you've never learned? Ecstatic utterance?

v5-8 It seems the gift the disciples were using meant they were understood by people who recognised the words they were saying. Should we describe this as *interpretation of tongues*?

See 1 Corinthians 12:7-10, where a list of spiritual gifts is provided: word of wisdom; word of knowledge; faith; healing; miracles;

prophecy; discernment of spirits; speaking in tongues; interpretation of tongues.

Check Acts 19:1-6. In this incident, it seems Paul encounters Ephesian believers who have only been told a part of the good news. They've put their trust in Jesus for salvation but have not heard anything about how to live the Christian life. They've been justified but have no understanding of how to be sanctified. They have never even heard of the Holy Spirit! So, they are Christians, but not trinitarian. How can this be?

v3,4 What is John's baptism? How do you suppose people as far away as Ephesus, on the west coast of Turkey, more than three hours' flight (if you could get a direct flight, which you can't) away from where John emerged from the desert for his very short local tour got to hear even this truncated message about repentance and dedication?

v5 Compare this verse with Matthew 28:19. Paul appears to be bypassing his trinitarian values once again.

v6 What is the special significance of the laying on of hands part of this ceremony? Does this impart anything in particular? What evidence is there that these Ephesians were baptised in the Holy Spirit? This time there's no sound of a rushing wind or what appeared to be tongues of fire. Why not?

But the Ephesian twelve immediately speak in tongues and prophecy. What does this tell us about the distinction between these two gifts? One is directed to God (like a prayer), while the other is directed from God, speaking to his people or to unbelievers.

Check out 1 Corinthians 14:1-3. In what ways should we welcome such gifts into our meetings?

30 Assessing Aslan

Narnias Univers

John 1:3

I think I've mentioned somewhere that I had the vast privilege to make friends with some heroes of the faith who live and minister in Denmark.

Jantzen and Leila seemed to take to me for some reason and even invited me to their country to speak to groups of pastors and children's workers about our vision for children's ministry which goes beyond Sunday morning childminding or merely storytelling. I was asked to speak about drawing children into each Biblical topic; helping them not only hear the story, but to try to put themselves in the narrative; asking questions to explore more deeply and to assist comprehension; and then, most importantly, how we can apply today's lesson to our lives.

The tour was great fun. I learned a lot about bread rolls, coffee and theology students as well as a smattering of the language.

The following year, I returned to Denmark for their first-ever children's ministry conference, where several hundred church folk gathered to be inspired, encouraged and challenged. Among the topics to which I was asked to bring enlightenment was entitled *Løven, Heksen Klædeskabet og Bibelen**, which caused me some concern, to say the least.

At first, I was baffled (remember, I was only fully confident with thanking God when the soft drinks arrive – *Hallelujah, Coca-Cola* – as that's the same in every language) but fortunately Leila brought clarity by use of the expression *Narnias Univers*. Not a typeface (and neither is *Mordors Helvetica*) but a reference to the world and legends associated with CS Lewis's fabulous novels. This was a chance to talk about teaching children gospel truth through the Narnia narrative. What a brief! I was very excited to do my research and to prepare a seminar with video clips (the 2005 film had just been released), an all-singing, all-dancing powerpoint show and some theologically-inspired caution.

Re-reading the book was a joy, especially as I found passages which struck me as fresh, since I'd not studied the text for several decades. Re-watching the film was less of a thrill, since it was just as disappointingly superficial as I'd remembered, although when the computer-animated character voiced by Liam Neeson makes his entrance, it was spine-tinglingly impressive.

---

* *The Lion, the Witch, the Wardrobe and the Bible*

I happened to be present when someone from my church used the film clips when speaking to our Sunday School kids and I listened with growing concern as they explained that this story was an easy-to-understand, child's version of the gospel of Luke, starring the Pevensie children as the disciples, the witch as the devil and of course, Aslan as an exact copy of Jesus.

You will doubtless be surprised at my claim that I kept silent throughout, despite growing in temperature below the neckline. It's possible that I may have pulled a few faces during this discourse, but I tried not to distract the speaker or frighten the children. But, as you might guess, my disappointment was at fever pitch.

Exhibit one: in his 1966 book *Of Other Worlds*, CS Lewis clarified his position, correcting what today might be called urban myths.

Some people seem to think that I began by asking myself
how I could say something about Christianity to children;
then fixed on the fairy tale as an instrument, then collected information
about child psychology and decided what age group I'd write for;
then drew up a list of basic Christian truths and hammered out
'allegories' to embody them. This is all pure moonshine.
I couldn't write in that way. It all began with images;
a faun carrying an umbrella, a queen on a sledge, a magnificent lion.
At first there wasn't anything Christian about them;
that element pushed itself in of its own accord.

Lewis was an acclaimed expert on the subject of allegory yet he maintained that the books did not fit that description and preferred to call the Christian aspects of them *suppositional*. This is similar to what we would now call fictional parallel universes, such as Rose Tyler's story in *Doctor Who*; the entire MCU; or the fantasy of *Middle-earth*.

From the horse's mouth, the *Chronicles of Narnia* is a made-up story in which Aslan is a Christ-*like* figure - although even Lewis would admit that the tone and detail in the final novel *The Last Battle* has a strong aroma of Revelation about it.

In passing, I am happy to mention that some people feel that there is a 'right order' in which to read the books, since *The Magician's Nephew* (published sixth) and *The Horse and His Boy* (published fifth) clearly provide backstory relating to a time before the setting of *The Lion the Witch and the Wardrobe*. But I'm sufficiently sophisticated to cope with Lewis' literary erudition and his 'filling in the gaps' intent.

Now then, *Aslan* is the Turkish for *lion* (so is Aslan a delight? Perhaps he's the true honey-flavoured delicious sweetmeat, the positive, long-lasting version of the passing, faded sugar and starch powder-sprinkled cubes the witch offers Edmund?) Probably this amounts to taking it too far… This is the allegorical problem, because, by definition, every part of an allegory is a hidden representation of something more significant. Let's consider where Jesus says

I am the true vine, and my Father is the gardener…
I am the vine; you are the branches. *John 15:1,5*

Yes, at last, a Bible verse! Jesus isn't claiming to be a chardonnay liana; he's using the meaningful literary device of allegory to emphasise identifying with his followers and their complete dependence upon him, just as branches are part of, integral to and dependent upon the vine. Together, we produce fruit, or suffer the consequences.

It's not a parable; it's not merely picture-language.

The Parables of Christ are not allegory, but simply expressions of deeper spiritual truth by means of tales and characters to whom we can relate. *The Good Samaritan* isn't about Samaritans, donkeys or hotels; it's about expectation, religious correctness, but mostly mercy. We'd be wrong to explore too deeply into the psyche of the typical Samaritan; Jesus is actively helping us see that's discriminatory! No, he's showing us the hollow, superficial nature of religious observance as contrasted with a deeper righteousness, where the bloke does the right thing and shows mercy. We should be merciful and God is merciful to us.

One example of allegory is George Orwell's *Animal Farm* (1945); the Russian revolution played out using pigs, sheep, a horse and hens. They rebel against the farmer but end up worse off. They represent historical characters – Tsar Nicholas II, Stalin, Marx, Trotsky etc.

Another very well-known and much-respected allegory is John Bunyan's *The Pilgrim's Progress* (1678), where the journey of faith is represented by an everyman's encounters with a range of obstacles.

Returning to LW^2, we encounter within its pages

Between the lamp post and Cair Paravel on the Western Sea lies Narnia,
a mystical land where animals hold the power of speech …
woodland fauns conspire with men … dark forces, bent on conquest,
gather at the world's rim to wage war against the realm's rightful king …

and the Great Lion Aslan is the only hope. Into this enchanted world comes a group of unlikely travellers. These ordinary boys and girls, when faced with peril, learn extraordinary lessons in courage, self-sacrifice, friendship and honour. Focus on the Family's TW^2 radio series (1998): Intro

Many heated discussions have centred around not only CS Lewis' intent, but also pointing out that he wrote these books during the fifties and that he was in tune with his own era, including some of the attitudes of the day which may not translate well into our times.

He was, for example, British; he incorporates what some may call Victorian values; to our eyes he often seems politically incorrect. Surely the same accusations can be made of Charles Dickens or Thomas Hardy, yet our respect for them as authors eclipses these apparent errors. Indeed, JRR Tolkien is immensely popular despite similar so-called weaknesses: he includes very few female characters (although all of his women pass the *Bechdel* test - none are mere pretty/screaming victims or servant girls); he also fails when it comes to diversity... Of course he does, as he was writing in 1954-55. At that time Oxford wasn't exactly a hotbed of multi-racial communities and his subject matter was a fantasy universe populated by orcs, elves, dwarves, hobbits, a wizard and a stoor hobbit called Sméagol, so he can be forgiven for not having included a positive figure of African or Asian descent.

Yes, I realise that I should try harder to stay on topic. So, back to LW^2.

There are, as I see it, several issues which need to be explained in some detail to children before we provide blanket praise for this book.

For example, we should note that in the world modern children inhabit, fur coats are symbols of animal-rights-denying wealth, not merely protection from the cold, as CSL intended. We need to be wise when we see that the evil character is female (is this discriminatory, sexist, too close to the baddie in Oz or in Cinderella?).

Please be aware that melting ice is reckoned these days to be a Bad Thing, so careful explanation of the Pevensie children's joy when it happens in Narnia is required. Modern readers may become concerned about the relationship between the children and the professor - no need for worry, but it starts a train of thought which may be problematical.

Lucy goes off with Mr Tumnus and everyone should be shouting *stranger danger* with some justification; and many of the animals are disrespected, to say the least. CSL decided to use familiar creatures (except for the fawn) and assigns somewhat two-dimensional characteristics to them, giving them archetypical narrowness – the beavers build a dam, the dogs bark and pull a sleigh, the eagles fly majestically, the stags look great silhouetted on the ridge of the hill and the unicorns are suitably mysterious. The lion, refreshingly, has a nuanced character and considerable backstory. We'll consider this further, starting towards the foot of the next page.

We should be asking the text several questions. Firstly, is the Wardrobe the doorway to spirituality? Let's compare LW2's famous portal with biblical truth.

Wardrobe	**Spirituality**
Wooden	x
In a room in an old house	x
Intermittent effectiveness	x
Contains fur coats	x
Experience can be or corporate	√
Requires faith	√
x	Linked to repentance
x	Joyful
x	Willing heart, not a secret hiding place/runaway

Enough about furniture, at least for now. Let's consider the White Witch, also called Jadis, a creation of George MacDonald in his 1895 masterwork *Lilith.* Is she an accurate representation of Satan?

Witch	**Satan**
Ruler of the present age	√
Spoils	√
Uses persuasive words	√
Unfulfilled promise	√
Temptation	√
Passing pleasure	√
Encourages selfishness	√
Treats followers harshly	√
Proud	√
Liar	√
Believes in her personal invincibility	√
Sees death of Saviour as victory	√

Ultimately defeated	√
Female	x
Focussed on Turkish Delight	x
Powerless immediately after resurrection of Saviour	x

Please be wise in giving too much focus on the Witch or on the enemy of souls. Let's reflect on the cautionary words of 'Jack' Lewis himself.

> *There are two equal and opposite errors into which our race can fall about the devils. One is to disbelieve in their existence. The other is to believe, and to feel an excessive and unhealthy interest in them. They themselves are equally pleased by both errors...*
> CS Lewis *The Screwtape Letters* (1942), preface

Does the expression 'white witch' soften her wickedness - some speak of 'white lies'. What if she were called the Black Witch? Is that racist? Or more evil? Is there a danger of sowing the seeds of confusion?

> *'Come now, let us settle the matter,' says the* LORD.
> *'Though your sins are like scarlet, they shall be as white as snow; though they are red as crimson, they shall be like wool.'* Isaiah 1:18

We need to tread carefully when helping children find the truth through this tale. At last, we've got to the central issue: is Aslan Jesus?

Aslan	**Jesus**
Mysterious & frightening	√
Human characteristics	√
Royal	√
Subject of prophecy	√
Tender-hearted	√
Worthy of respect	√
Powerful, yet humble	√
Behaves as a substitute	√
Forgives	√
Bearded	√
Has controlled strength	√
Turns up well over halfway into the book	√
When he arrives, there is newness of life	√
Good & fearsome simultaneously	√

Provides followers with weapons	√
Speaks of a longed-for, faraway place	√
Does a restoring work	√
Honours a higher authority	√
Sheds his blood	√
Keeps his promises	√
Loves the company of his followers	√
Submits to humiliation: taunted, mocked, jeered at	√
Could have stopped his torture & execution anytime	√
Observed by followers	√
Dies & alive again soon afterwards	√
Discovered alive with the dawn	√
Different appearance afterwards	√
Dead are raised	√
Battle is fought	√
Gives followers royal status	√
Once saved (i.e. made a Prince), always saved	√
Will return, some day	√

Yes, that's a lot of ticks and a lot of similarities. However, there are also some vastly important differences which it is wise to consider when tempted to make dramatically incorrect statements like 'Aslan is Jesus'.

Vital distinctions

Aslan	**Jesus**
Shines with the sunrise	Found in likeness as a man
Arrives with great fanfare	Humble, lowly arrival
Mysterious, secretive discipleship	Openly followed
Powerless if physically absent	Heals at nine miles range
Emotionally distant	Loves disciples; loved by them
Content that characters swear by his name	Obeys commandments about oaths and blasphemy
Keeps his impending death a secret	Tells his disciples he will die
Helped greatly by a sheep-dog	Relies on his Father
Destroys the enemy straight away after returning to life	Satan's eventual destruction promised
Restores the sinner to his previous state	Makes us new creations, redeemed, empowered

Wanders off at the end; we know not where	Ascends to the right hand of the Father
Has 'other things to do'	'It is accomplished/finished'
x	Performs many miracles
x	Gives lots of time for teaching
x	Lots of time for storytelling
x	Salvation through repentance
x	Raised to life by Father
x	Reveals a higher authority
x	Death is in prophetic heritage
x	Different, resurrection body
x	Is supernatural
x	Is the creator

It does occur to me that we may encounter a slight confusion when considering lions in scripture.

The Old Testament is packed with references to lions - sometimes these emphasise the fearsome roar and bite of the king of beasts, while at other times, the stateliness, nobility and stalking skills of the lion are held up for admiration. Leo gets a bad press in the book of Daniel, of course, but God keeps his servant safe.

Amos describes the unluckiest chap in Scripture, who runs from a lion only to meet a bear and when he gets away, he rests his hand on a wall and is bitten by a snake.

In the New Testament, the apostle Paul describes how he was delivered from the mouth of a lion (2 Timothy 4:17); and the apostle Peter warns us that the devil is prowling like a roaring lion (1 Peter 5:8). But these negative images are countered by the Revelation 5:5 description of Jesus as the Lion of Judah. An angel roars like a lion and the beast (of 666 fame) has a lion's mouth.

So, what to conclude? The Bible isn't coming down very firmly on either side: a lion may be an image representing evil, or it may be an image representing good. My feeling is that we should be careful; we should not communicate to children that lions always symbolise the Messiah, because they don't.

And God said 'Let there be light' and there was light. Genesis 1:3

The Mighty One, God, the LORD, *speaks and summons the earth from the rising of the sun to where it sets.* Psalm 50:1

Through him all things were made; without him nothing was made that has been made. John 1:3

Surprisingly, (well, it caught me out), there isn't even any acknowledgment of God in LW[2], only of an impersonal Deep Magic; I'm honour bound to speak of the Almighty, the maker, the LORD, the righteous one, the majestic king of heaven. Aslan appears to be subject to the Lore of Deep Magic, while the Lord Jesus reigns supreme, subject to no higher authority, because he is the highest authority! Jesus spoke a word and galaxies came into existence.

I sense some may be growing weary of my determination to pick out every minor error or weakness; I shall relent momentarily, but wish to remind you of the need for wise caution when drawing comparisons or using allegory/poetry/fiction to communicate theology, especially to children. Not to mention

'If anyone causes one of these little ones – those who believe in me – to stumble, it would be better for them to have a large millstone hung round their neck and to be drowned in the depths of the sea.' Matthew 18:6

Stern, or what? Well worth bearing in mind, at least.

Are your Sunday School teachers trained? Help them avoid a watery doom and protect the children in your church! (Okay, so maybe you don't have the authority to call a training session, but it's a suggestion…)

Another thing not to mention are the websites which claim all kinds of hateful, uncharitable things about Lewis; drinker, smoker, sexually immoral; his salvation apparently came through intellectualism, not revelation; lack of 'born again' testimony; wholesale embracing of ecumenicalism, teaching in *Mere Christianity* about your own path; lack of condemnation of Roman Catholic theology re Purgatory; the unbiblical premise of *The Great Divorce*; connection of the Pevensie Royals to the holy bloodline of the Priory of Sion…

So, I'll avoid mentioning any of them, even in passing.

Perhaps most important of all, Aslan's death is not linked with the remission of sin. Yes, Aslan forgives Edmund's selfishness, unkindness and disloyalty, but it's not clear by what authority or justice.

In Jesus, however, there's no doubt that redemption is won for us by his death on the cross in our place.

Without the shedding of blood there is no forgiveness of sins.
Hebrews 9:22 RSV

Substitutionary atonement tells that tale.

Final question: can children distinguish between fantasy and truth? I suspect that they can, somehow. But we need to be wise in emphasising that the Bible story is the truth, or they may lump such spectacularly unlikely and apparently far-fetched tales as the parting of the Red Sea, the battle of Jericho, the healing of Naaman, the virgin birth and the resurrection of Jesus together with stories about fairies, pixies, talking animals, Harry Potter, My Little Pony, Hans Christian Andersen, Mary Poppins, Thomas the Tank Engine etc.

What a shame if they remain unaware that the Good News of Christ is life-changing stuff!

31 Stop 2 C what it's there 4

glancing @ 2 Corinthians

The Bible is a substantial volume. It's a physically thick book and that can be intimidating. Furthermore, we approach it with some trepidation, knowing it's meaningful, yet sometimes feeling that we might not understand, let alone agree with all its statements and claims.

I checked, and this is a work of more than 720,000 words (some versions are considerably longer: NIV 727,969, authorised 788,280). To provide a comparison, a substantial novel will be perhaps 100,000 or so words long; one of my favourite novels, *Catcher in the Rye* is just 73,404 words; a long novel can be nearly three times that (eg *Harry Potter and the Deathly Hallows* contains 198,227). Famed for its size, *War & Peace* contains 587,287 words.

The famous concordance by *Cruden* (published 1773), based on the Bible's authorised version, contains more than 225,000 entries – each one itemising a different word used in the Bible.

Some words appear many times: we might expect such words as Lord, sin, forgiveness, Jesus, cross etc to be repeated. But you may be surprised to learn that the word *therefore* appears 442 times in the Bible. For a book known to be full of narrative, praise to God, wise words and prophetic statements, one might not suppose there would be such an emphasis on systematic argument or logic. But that's exactly the style employed by, for example Jeremiah and Ezekiel in their works: they account for 116 occurrences.

The apostle Paul seems to be equally committed to reasoning: his letters clock up another 77. The word *therefore* indicates that a conclusion is about to be drawn: *this is true, and so is this; therefore, conclude this, or behave like that.*

An essential practice when you're reading the Bible: when you see a *therefore*, stop to look what it's there for.

I checked out the *therefore* passages in 2 Corinthians for a Bible series I was preparing. These six examples may be of spiritual help.

Firstly, we shall consider the ministry of the Holy Spirit, with which we have been entrusted. (My emphasis in quotations throughout).

> ***Therefore***, *since we have such a hope, we are very bold.*
> 2 Corinthians 3:12

When Moses came down from Mount Sinai with the two tablets of the covenant law in his hands, he was not aware that his face was radiant because he had spoken with the Lord. Exodus 34:29

Paul spends the earlier part of 2 Corinthians 3 reasoning that the ministry of the Holy Spirit is even more glorious than anything previously encountered. The presence of God on the mountain was very glorious and the law Moses delivered to his people was equally glorious, as it showed them how to live. But the good news about Jesus is far, far more spectacularly glorious beyond that.

You very quickly run out of descriptive words, because most things in this world are very far from glorious, I suppose.

After a while, Moses began to lose the radiance from his face. He initially wore a veil so people would not be dazzled; later, it was helpful in obscuring the reality that his countenance wasn't shining so much anymore. The glory had begun to fade.

But for us, the presence of the Holy Spirit is an even more spectacular glory; one that does not diminish but one which grows and strengthens! God has transformed us from death to life and filled us with Holy Spirit power, to enable us to walk in freedom and demonstrate God's might. Speaking of those who believe, Paul uses the wonderful expression *being changed from one degree of glory to another* (v18 ESV).

How marvellous!

Not stopping at justification of our souls, God is flooding us with sanctification as well! God declares that we certainly have the hope of ever-increasing glory and that this gives us good reason, as well as the power, to be very bold. We can be courageous in evangelism, reaching out to people with spiritual gifts, rejoicing in lives set free from legalism and all sorts of other ways.

Surely, we should not be surprised when we find ourselves eagerly stepping forward to explain the good news, or to offer to pray for healing, or to declare God's truth, or to pray in languages we have never learned, or actively escaping from temptations which may previously have trapped us.

The Holy Spirit provides power to live as a Christian, walking in victory, unashamedly standing up for Christ!

Carrying on from where we've just reached, Paul immediately launches into another aspect of the new life in which we have been born and he uses another *therefore*.

Therefore, *since through God's mercy we have this ministry, we do not lose heart.* 2 Corinthians 4:1

Once again, Paul develops an argument that raises our excitement and leads to an inescapable conclusion. As a direct result of this glory with which we have been endowed, we are strengthened not only with boldness to be active for the sake of the Lord, but we also receive inner courage to help us persevere.

We are given the fortitude to continue in the work (*we do not lose heart*). We don't collapse under the burden of the ministry because God gives us strength; we faithfully endeavour and persist, empowered by the same Spirit. We have this ministry of the Holy Spirit despite our unworthiness; God has shown us mercy and kindness. This results in a determination within us to keep on keeping on in holiness, honesty and accurate exposition.

Why does God choose us? How far does His mercy extend? Will He just overlook our sin? How can we ensure our lives are holy, honest and in line with scripture? Moses' glory faded, eventually. How can we be sure ours won't?

Now the one who has fashioned us for this very purpose is God, who has given us the Spirit as a deposit, guaranteeing what is to come. ***Therefore*** *we are always confident and know that as long as we are at home in the body we are away from the Lord.* 2 Corinthians 5:5,6

This time, the conversation has turned to the theme of home. Now we are saved, our citizenship is in heaven. We eagerly await the time we shall be clothed with our heavenly dwelling, even while we remain here on earth. The contrast between the eternal and the mortal is stark, but we can be fully confident, he says.

When you pay a deposit, this signals your firm commitment to pay the balance. That's why most deposits are *non-refundable*, to triple underline the certainty that whatever you're paying for is yours and that you'll stump up the remainder of the price. Paul says the Holy Spirit indwelling every believer is God's deposit; God can always be utterly relied upon to do what he says he will do, yet he's kind enough, overabundant enough and generously gracious enough to add yet more security. Also, a guarantee is an undertaking to keep his word.

It's absolutely certain, with crossed oak leaves and a brass nameplate. And yet God dollops on his Spirit with a trowel. I think he means it!

Paul's in the groove now and we're quickly upon yet another *therefore.*

For we must all appear before the judgment seat of Christ,
so that each one may receive what is due for what he has done in the body,
whether good or evil. ***Therefore****, knowing the fear of the Lord,*
we persuade others. But what we are is known to God, and I hope
it is known also to your conscience. 2 Corinthians 5:10,11 ESV

We love and respect the Lord, obeying him and working hard to do as he has commanded. We don't need to try to please him because he's already delighted in us. But we respond to his love with effort and unflagging labour for his glory, empowered by his Holy Spirit.

Each Christian will be rewarded for our faithful service of the Lord, no matter how humble. Perhaps we exercised self-control or prayed sometimes; maybe we put chairs out for a church meeting or resisted temptation to yawn loudly during a sermon; the Lord will also know when you were teaching Godly principles to children or sharing the good news with a friend.

These verses also warn that those who are not believers will need to face God and receive justice for their wicked ways. On account of our awareness of the judgement seat, we work hard to inform, teach and testify about the goodness of God and persuade others to consider him for themselves.

The fear of the Lord is an interesting expression, capable of more than one interpretation.

Sometimes, *fear* is about being frightened, anxious or alarmed. This kind of fear can be helpful, keeping us from dangerous activities, like snowboarding or jumping from a moving bus.

I've only done one of these and I'm too smart to throw myself off a mountain. However, in the days of open-platform buses (I was eight) I was coming home from school one day and as we approached my stop, I stood on the open platform, waiting for the conductor to ring the bell to tell the driver I wished to alight at the request stop. I knew it was morally correct for me to alight here, as I'd only paid enough fare (1½d) to get me here and no further.

But the conductor was upstairs, collecting fares. Receiving no instruction to the contrary, the driver accelerated, assuming there weren't any passengers who had requested this stop and he could proceed to the next one. Meanwhile I considered my options, but not sufficiently well. As the bus roared past the *request stop* sign, I timed my fearless leap almost perfectly, but with little consideration of how I was going to decelerate in time for a safe landing. Unfortunately, I took no account of the concrete post to which the *request stop* sign was attached. I coincided with extreme accuracy and considerable force; everything went suddenly dark.

I found out later that kind passengers who had observed this madness rang the bell, even though this was not permitted; the bus stopped; one of my teachers was also on the bus and ran to fetch my mother. I was taken to hospital to have my head examined. Several days (see what I did there?) later, the doctors let me go home since I had not done myself permanent damage.

In this case, an appropriate amount of the *scared* type of fear might have helped me protect my skull from catastrophic impact, although I'd have been facing a longer walk home from the next bus stop and a mother concerned that I was late.

Getting back to my point, then, this type of fear can keep us from embarking upon adventure or make us shrink back when we ought to step up. Giving in to anxiety does not sound much like faith… There's a scripture which says

> *There is no fear in love, but perfect love casts out fear.* 1 John 4:18

How can this be? The love of God (which is perfect) is directly opposed to fear; yet we're called to know the fear of the Lord. Surely there is some confusion here. Ah, then this must be the other sort, the *fear* that means deep respect, honour, reverent awe.

> *The fear of the Lord is the beginning of wisdom.* Proverbs 9:10

We do not shrink back, scared of our father God – at least, not now that we have received his love and forgiveness through Christ. No, on the contrary, we run gleefully into his presence and welcome his affection. But we're still respectful, acknowledging his majesty and might, honouring his purity and holiness.

This is the fear which isn't primarily emotional but is mostly the appropriate response to our understanding of God's greatness and authority. A very different *fear*, right? Our love and devotion for God motivates us in witnessing. Christ died for us, so we are prepared to live for Him and speak up when opportunities arise. What is the message we have? How can we communicate it more effectively to our friends? Are there any ways we have not tried?

Paul's not finished.

> ***Therefore****, since we have these promises, dear friends,*
> *let us purify ourselves from everything that contaminates body and spirit,*
> *perfecting holiness out of reverence for God* 2 Corinthians 7:1

The promises to which Paul refers concern fatherhood, God walking with us and causing us to be his people. Since God has promised to be our Father, out of respect for him and his name, we make every effort to keep away from contamination, hindrance, sin and distraction.

What difference does it make if God is our Father? What is the true role of a Father? How can we keep ourselves pure without becoming monks or nuns?

Later in this letter, Paul refers to a *thorn in his flesh*. This is taken by many scholars to signify some medical condition which affected his eyesight; they offer as evidence verses which emphasise Paul's consistent use of scribes and one occasion when he points out the clumsiness of his own handwriting (check out Galatians 6:11).

> *Three times I pleaded with the Lord to take it away from me.*
> *But he said to me, 'My grace is sufficient for you,*
> *for my power is made perfect in weakness.'*
> ***Therefore*** *I will boast all the more gladly about my weaknesses,*
> *so that Christ's power may rest on me.* 2 Corinthians 12:7-10

It is clear he had hoped God would heal him, but apparently this did not happen. Evidently, God had other plans; healing may not be the only way God can demonstrate his power. Of course, some Christians have been healed and God is glorified in their wholeness. But consider, on the other hand, the testimony of some who have lived with disabilities or injuries and have not been miraculously restored. They retain their *thorn in the flesh* and set great examples of forbearance, perseverance and spiritual depth.

Indeed, I know a young man whose disability causes him pain in walking, yet he is so grateful that he can. Maybe one day, he won't be able to walk independently anymore, he says, so he thanks God for the mobility he currently has. I am filled with respect for this excellent attitude. He is truly boasting about his weaknesses; not to glorify the disease, or himself, but to express gratitude to God. Christ's power is resting upon him.

32 Good Friday?

vigil gathering

Psalm 22

For many years, our church has hired a school hall for Sunday meetings and rented some office space for administration and pastoral meetings. But eventually a suitable building became available to buy and we took possession late in 2017. It was ideal for offices, small meeting rooms, a youth lounge, prayer meetings and worship evenings. We continue to use the school halls for Sundays, because they were spread around the city and could accommodate much larger crowds.

But now we had our own space, I began to develop a vision for a way to use it for a Good Friday event. I spoke to the lead elder, who encouraged me to run with this idea. He wisely advised me to focus on the evening (I had originally considered an all-day drop-in extended meeting), since this would be a fresh approach for many of our church people. I trimmed my expectations and met with the two church leaders delegated to give a lead for this.

We had great planning meetings, encouraging one another, considering scriptures, songs, activities, prayers and other elements that could make up the evening. We were used to a worship-notices-preach format on Sundays, but wanted to break away from this, partly out of a desire to make the evening unpredictable.

We settled on a six-part programme. We agreed from the outset that we would focus exclusively on the events leading up to the death and burial of Jesus. There was no relief from the sadness and mourning for the disciples, so we felt it was the right approach to give the cross full attention, without rushing on to the empty tomb. We would, of course, make great celebration of the resurrection at the Sunday meeting, but meanwhile this was not going to be an event with a happy ending, just to make us feel better.

We advertised the event *as Good Friday? – an interactive evening of reflection*, which was both intriguing and gave us a bit of time to clarify our plans. We emphasised that this would not be a time of celebration, but one of lament. It will be different from our normal meetings! We worked hard to have lots of different people taking part, as well as ensuring that trusted folk were seen to be in charge. That helped those who were nervous of the unusual aspects of the meeting – such as the activities, or the silence – could participate with confidence.

People came in great numbers and packed our meeting room.

'We invite you to participate, not merely spectate. We intend to be deliberately not triumphalist; not even having a proper conclusion.'

We started with the Jesus Culture song *See his love* 'nailed on to a cross/perfect and blameless life/given as sacrifice…' We had no band, no extended solo, just one acoustic guitar and a great deal of passion. Simple but effective.

- Theme 1 **Betrayal**

Reading: Luke 22:54-64, where Simon Peter denies Jesus.

Key verse: *And he went outside and wept bitterly.*

Reflection: silently consider how you might have acted in similar circumstances. Might you have behaved in a similar way? What was he afraid of?

- Theme 2 **Substitution**

Reading: John 18:28-40, focuses on Barabbas

Key verse: *'I find no basis for a charge against him. But it is your custom for me to release one prisoner at the time of the Passover. Do you want me to release "the king of the Jews"?'*

Response: in writing, or with silent prayer, put yourself in the sandals of the man who deserved the punishment. What if Barabbas looked into Jesus' eyes as they stood there before Pilate and the crowd? What did he see in them? What do you see?

Song: *This is amazing grace* 'This is unfailing love/That You would take my place/That You would bear my cross'

Reading: I nervously suggested to the elders a small extract from *substitute,* the novel I'd written about Barabbas and they eagerly agreed this would be a suitable element.

I selected the moment after Jesus has died, when Barabbas has been set free. He is sitting with his wife, reflecting on how his wretched life was exchanged with this Christ-figure.

> 'I was having to make myself ready for death. I didn't know how I would deal with actually dying - you know, the afterlife, judgment, whatever - but, worse than that, I was so scared of the process, particularly the crucifixion process. I knew I wouldn't be tough enough to cope. I feared every part of it - the long walk carrying the wood, the spikes through the hands and feet, the agony of joints and the inability to breathe without torturous

pain... But watching him go through it all on my behalf – in my place – was so much more than I had expected.'

He shook his head and held his peace for a moment, to decide if he preferred to try to eliminate the vile scene from his memory, with all its significance, or to try to recall every detail, lest he forget its significance. extract from *substitute*

- Theme 3 **Injustice**

  Reading: John 19:1-16 Pilate condemns Jesus

  Key verse: *When Jesus came out wearing the crown of thorns and the purple robe, Pilate said to them 'Here is the man!'*

  Reflection: Jesus identifies with us! Let's bring to God those times when we feel mistreated or unfairly judged. Consider the injustices against us and then the injustices of others, both locally and nationally. Write them down.

  Response: Take the paper, get up and put it in the bowl of salt water, to represent the bad taste injustice leaves, bring it to the cross and leave it there.

- Theme 4 **Guilty**

  Reading: Luke 23:32,33,39-43 Jesus is crucified

  Key verse: *When they came to the place called The Skull, there they crucified him, along with criminals – one on his right, the other on his left.*

  Song: *How Deep The Father's Love for Us*, excluding v3

  Response: communion. While we often have communion in small groups, using the pass and sip method, this time we provided chunks of bread and a bowl of 'wine', inviting those who wished to participate to step forward, take a piece of bread, dip it in the 'wine', eat it and return. Meanwhile, a soloist sang *When I survey the wondrous cross.*

- Theme 5 **Darkness**

  Reading: Matthew 27:45-54 Jesus gives up his spirit

  Key verse: *When the centurion and those with him who were guarding Jesus saw the earthquake and all that had happened, they were terrified and exclaimed 'Surely he was the Son of God!'*

  Reflection: The Roman Officer accurately identified Jesus. He saw the sun's response to Christ's death and recognised his supremacy.

  Song *Forever (The moon and stars they wept)* omitting the last verse

  Response: short video clip from a film showing the death of Christ

• Theme 6 **Funeral**

Reading: Luke 23:44-56 Jesus dies

Key verse: *Jesus called out with a loud voice 'Father, into your hands I commit my spirit.' When he had said this, he breathed his last.*

Eulogy: Well, it's certainly a sad, defeated day for all of us. John, Mary, Simon, Matthew, all of us, but I've been asked to make a few comments on this solemn occasion and to reflect on the life of Jesus. I am sure all of us here today who spent time with him, laughed with him, heard the things he said and saw the amazing things he did – all of us would say he was truly remarkable. Those of us who knew him knew they were loved by him. Simple as that. His capacity to love with depth and great care at the deepest level was breath-taking. **But he's not with us anymore. And we will miss him.**

We would agree that he was a great person to be around, a gifted wood-worker, a diligent and faithful son, a true friend and a wonderful man to follow. We have warm memories of him. But now, that's all we have. Memories. **He's not with us anymore. And we will miss him.**

We started calling him *Rabbi* and *Master* but he was so different to the other teachers. He called us *brothers* and *friends* and we were so glad to be friends of him, friends of each other. He taught us about loyalty and devotion; even about affection and brotherly love. And then he shocked us with the phrase 'greater love has no-one than he lay down his life for his friends'. At the time, we thought it over-dramatic or symbolic, but now we have a fresh understanding of what he meant. He was indeed our brother, our friend. **But he's not with us anymore. And we shall miss him.**

We will never see his like again. Never. Oh, yes, I know he said he would rebuild the temple and he said he would return; and he said he would be celebrated as one who defeats death, but I can't imagine – he couldn't have imagined that he would be killed so violently, so cruelly; that he would die in humiliation and shame. So, we know for sure he's gone. We cannot see how it could be possible for him to be restored to us. We have to find a way to carry on without him. We have to. **He's not with us anymore. And we will miss him.**

Right from the start, he was so kind and caring and chose us, didn't he James, when it seemed so unlikely, calling us out from fishing nets and accounting books and political intrigues – a genuine worthy Rabbi, unlike any other – always ready to welcome the outsider – the adulterous woman at that well, that crazy guy with the demons, people not of our race, even lepers… **But he's not with us anymore. And we will miss him.**

You'll remember, Simon, the day the crowds were so great and his talk was so fascinating that they stayed late and had nothing to eat until Jesus blessed the bread and fish and got us to hand it out and we just kept on and on and it didn't run out and everyone was satisfied? **But he's not with us anymore. And we will miss him.**

And even when his time was up, yes, even as he was being executed, his care for you, Mary, making sure you were going to be looked after… **But he's not with us anymore. And we will miss him.**

I will always remember – I doubt I shall ever stop wondering about his peace and calmness, even when being betrayed, treated unjustly, rejected, denied. **But he's not with us anymore. And we will miss him.**

Some other friends will join me in a moment to place flowers here as a mark of love and respect and good memories. Then, once the Passover weekend is done, I'll be returning to my home town of Emmaus. And I shall take with me memories – such happy memories – of Jesus. That's all we have now.

He's not with us anymore. And we will miss him.

Reflection: Think about the sadness and loss the disciples must have felt. Consider the mournful phrase used by the disciples on the road to Emmaus 'we had hoped'. Their expectations were dashed, their beloved rabbi slaughtered, their Messiah gone. It may be helpful to carry those discouraged, defeated feelings for a day or so… But come prepared for Sunday morning, when we shall engage with the impact of what happens as Mary and Peter and John visit the tomb and discover the next part of the story.

My God, my God, why have you forsaken me? Why are you so far from saving me, so far from the words of my groaning? Psalm 22:1

We thought he brought it on himself, that God was punishing him for his own failures. But it was our sins that did that to him, that ripped and tore and crushed him – our sins! He took the punishment, and that made us whole. Through his bruises we get healed. We're all like sheep who've wandered off and gotten lost. We've all done our own thing, gone our own way. And GOD *has piled all our sins, everything we've done wrong, on him, on him. He was beaten, he was tortured, but he didn't say a word. Like a lamb taken to be slaughtered and like a sheep being sheared,*

he took it all in silence. Justice miscarried, and he was led off –
and did anyone really know what was happening? Isaiah 53:4-8 MESSAGE

[Jesus], found in fashion as a man, he humbled himself
and became obedient unto death, even the death of the cross.
Philippians 2:8 Jubilee Bible 2000

...we have complete victory through God, who has shown his love for us.
Yes, I am sure that nothing can separate us from God's love –
not death, life, angels, or ruling spirits. I am sure that nothing now,
nothing in the future, no powers, nothing above us or nothing below us –
nothing in the whole created world – will ever be able to separate us from the
love God has shown us in Christ Jesus our Lord.
Romans 8:37-39 Easy-to-Read Version

33 Musical youth

a serving biography

I'm not going to tell you about the bands I've been in.

No. I won't even mention the name of *Tradd* – a name devised, like *ABBA*, from the initials of our names, although, unlike them, there were six of us and one of us didn't have their initial in the name. So, I may have misremembered this. Also, do you realise that if Benny & Bjorn had been Steve and Dave, their band might have been called *ASDA*?

Anyway, *Tradd* was an entirely acoustic group, very folky and rather serious. Our first gig was also our last. We took part in an evening of 'entertainment' put on by the local Catholic church. Having even to darken the door of the place was a big issue for some of us. Well, me, mostly, for reasons which escape me now. I nearly persuaded one of the other chaps to join me in saying *no* to the gig, but then he became enchanted by the redhead beauty in the band, who wanted to go ahead with the booking and he capitulated. What a lightweight!

Tradd broke up soon after, citing 'musical differences', but truth be told, it was that some of us were honest enough to admit that the presence of girls in the band was a distraction; the girls in question had already concluded that we (the boys) were insufficiently musically skilled. That accusation stung a little, so we committed ourselves to practice, rehearsal and a change of name and direction.

This leads me to say not a single word about *Spinaker* (yes, incorrectly spelled – a simple mistake, yet one which distinguished us from a sail despite the meaningful picture-language). No-one ever muddled us with Portsmouth's tower, nor Netflix's multi-cloud continuous delivery platform, since neither existed at the time. *Spinaker* filled several of my schoolboy years with folk/gospel, featuring Charlie, the double bass composed almost entirely of araldite. This is not the place to go into any detail about Richard, who became a missionary to South America and a headteacher in New Zealand, or about Roger, an around-the-world yacht skipper who performs with his band *The Archangels* even to this day. Nor will I even hint at anyone who developed into Professor Tim PhD, BSc (Hons), the internationally-recognised nerve specialist and lecturer.

Long before the foolish shorthand so beloved of commentators and headline writers, coining the abbreviated names of *FloJo*, *SuBo* or *BoJo*, these dear gentlemen consistently referred to me with the affectionate nickname *AzBaz*, and have continued to do so, despite protestations.

Girls flocked around us, with varying degrees of virtuousness. We regularly resisted attempts to allow more than one brief harmonica solo, 'going electric' (although we discussed it endlessly) or even improve our between-song banter – for example, *this is a Japanese number called Tu-Ning* and *we were going to play you a song by Bob Dylan, but then we thought 'no, he never plays any of ours'*.

We performed a vast number of gigs; in school, many folk clubs, at lots of church events and mini-festivals, in old-folks' homes and in Salvation Army halls – usually to wildly appreciative audiences, despite the increasingly lengthy explanations of the gospel we included at every opportunity, although the Salvation Army officers liked this and joined in with be-ribboned tambourines, which we resented a little.

As A-levels approached, we realised our time as a band was up, so we recorded an album. We did it in one long afternoon and evening session because the stereo microphone around which we gathered was borrowed and we'd promised to return it the next day. Some of the first track on side two was wiped from the master tape before any cassette copies had been recorded, but we continued anyway.

Thus *A Bucketful of Life* became available.

None of us ever twigged that we could have done this earlier and sold merchandise at our gigs. In our naïvety, we didn't even have a logo for the band, let alone mugs or t-shirts adorned with one of the many merry catchphrases borrowed from our top hits, like

NOW IS THE LAST SETTING OF THE SUN
or PETER, JAMES & JOHN, GO AND PUT YOUR SANDALS ON
or NEW WORDS WILL BE WRITTEN
or HE COULDN'T CHEW ALBERT ON T'GUMS
or OH REALITY, YOU'RE SO VILE

I won't mention my very brief spell with *River Nile*. This was mostly massive overconfidence, featuring Mark, who became a very successful software guru and Dec, a lead guitarist who has gone on to fortune and fame and very much greater volume.

History points but momentarily to a scratch band called *Jane's Trousers*, an ill-considered, ill-fated one-performance-only excursion into experimentation with a range of music from funk via lounge jazz to 60's rock 'n' roll. We had agreed to call ourselves *In Transit*, inspired by the legend written down the length of the left leg of the oxford bags sported by one of our singers, but unfortunately between rehearsal and show time she went home for tea, changed her clothes and so we had to review the name of the band.

And a hefty veil should also be drawn over *Frosty & The Snowmen,* jazz-blues with a strong emphasis on my brother's song about an Armadillo. At an open-air music festival on the seafront (near to the venue of Slimboy Phat's so-called triumph) I unwisely wore a figure-hugging costume, enraging the otherwise sympathetic crowd. Enough said.

Ed Banger & The Nosebleeders (hard rock) never got out of the rehearsal room, which is probably an expression of the mercy of God.

And although it wasn't our fault at all, performances by a not-yet-named but particularly gifted band (though I say it myself), drawn together to play worship music for the young teens at the 1992 Stoneleigh Bible Week, were silenced prematurely and spectacularly. We were completing a sound-check prior to the first meeting, obeying the instructions of the man responsible (I use the term loosely) for balancing the sound.

However, he accidentally but catastrophically introduced a whole pint of orange squash to the mixing desk, creating a short-lived range of fascinating noises, a strange aroma, a small quantity of blue smoke and, of course, permanent silence.

We weren't that bad, you know.

However, I am inspired to mention the relative success of *Matt Black & The Emulsions,* because this was the fulfilment of a personal ambition: to write and record my own songs in a recording studio. Oh yes.

At the time, I was working with the School's Ministry (now called *Discovery*) of *Agapé,* an evangelistic agency. Despite some opposition from places I'd expected support, I'd joined the staff with determination to explore my abilities and gifts, reckoning God had called me, but I wasn't sure what I was supposed to do. In the meanwhile, I thought, a bit of evangelism and Bible training would be a good start.

So, I soon found myself living away from home for the first time, in a flat with the other male trainees, assigned to knocking on doors in a hall of residence belonging to University College, London. I was sharing my faith almost every day, studying the Bible and learning about communication. It was a lot to deal with all at once, but my confidence in God was high.

I remember praying 'Lord, I am so glad that you have placed in me a message about your love which I can share with others. Let me be like a relay race runner, passing on the baton to others who will be able to run further and faster than I ever could.'

Now, two important points need to be mentioned. One: these may not have been the exact words; but the relay race image was definitely in there, with the stress on how much more effective the people further down the track would be, provided I played my part adequately.

Second, athletics was not something in which I have ever taken any part (or, indeed, much interest), so for me to think of it was unusual. It's possible I'd been reading, among other verses, Hebrews 12:1,2 and 1 Corinthians 9:24,25. Both of these scriptures are about running the race, but they are primarily about completing the challenge and not so much about the early stages. See also

I have fought the good fight, I have finished the race,
I have kept the faith. 2 Timothy 4:7

So, who knows? But I was grateful I'd been given the 'baton' of truth and was eager to be faithful with it.

As I was saying, in my persona as *Matt Black,* I was commissioned to create a multi-media show featuring a huge screen (purchased from a local cinema when it was upgrading), state-of-the-art slide projectors, a custom-built triggering device and a multi-track cassette tape deck, which was high-tech for the time. These days, I suppose we'd supply bluetoothed Virtual Reality headsets. But it was pretty impressive for 1979 (shortly after Palaeolithic Man discovered flint tools) with analogue equipment and a stripped-down budget. We had the option to display images and lyrics simultaneously, or double- or even triple-screen images, which kept the audience guessing where to look.

I devised the storyboard, selected and directed the actors and worked with a talented team (including HD and Lambrayne) to take the photographs. The biggest challenge was to make the soundtrack match the grand ambition of the visuals.

I wrote five songs and practiced them until I was ready to play them under the expensive time-pressure of a recording studio. I fund-raised to provide the budget required for the project. I borrowed some of the instruments I was going to need. And I recruited a band to perform the musical numbers. One of my friends is the afore-alluded-to talented guitarist with a wife who may or may not have changed her strides. I'll call him Dec Stamm, since he's now an internationally-recognised star, honest. At the time Dec played with a band with the line-up I required: drums, bass, keys and two guitars; they made loud but very tight funk and I was sure they could be all I needed.

I attended a rehearsal and explained the deal to them: they would learn the songs and provide their talent and instruments; they would not be paid; I would direct the music and finance the recording process, thus providing them (free of charge) with vital studio experience; thereby reducing their anticipated costs for an up-coming demo album recording. I pointed out that they'd have a clearer idea of the way things happen in such hallowed and expensive-to-hire premises. I knew full well that I was getting the better end of the deal, but they were accommodating chaps. They agreed.

So, I played them my songs, each of which represented a different musical style (punk, funk, soft-rock ballad, cocktail jazz, heavy rock) and these were quickly learned, arranged, improved upon and extended; we were ready!

The day of the recording was full of learning experiences for us all, lots of laughter and much skilful playing. Chief among the good memories was thrashing my way through the punk-style song and then standing bemused when the studio engineer ran through from the control room to thoroughly detune my guitar before I thrashed again, recording a second track of discordant noise. Another strong memory was the aggression of Dec's 100W guitar amplifier which was turned up to eleventy-stupid to record the rock solo. It was so loud that even with the amp in the drum booth and all the sound-proof doors shut, we could still hear it very clearly in the control room before the mic was activated.

Recording the vocals was my task and it is a matter of some pride that I was able to sing the lyrics in one take, double-track my voice (sing exactly the same again) in one more and provide harmonies similarly smoothly. I discovered that I wasn't too shabby at this particular feat. Of course, this reduced the studio time dramatically. Marvellous!

The joy of a fulfilled ambition was complete when the engineer actually used a razor blade to cut the quarter-inch tape and splice it together with another part of our recording in order to achieve what was required: he extended the final track by an additional verse. I know that these days this is the simple function of two electronic button-presses, but such options were not available at the time, mainly because sabre-toothed tigers and vast behemoths were roaming the untamed savannah as it continued to smoke from the cooling magma generated by tectonic plate-shifting.

The songs featured a punkish rant about 1980s society:

I can't take the pace; this farce makes me puke.
Who wants to win the rat race just to get a nuke (in the ear'ole)?
Oh yeah I just wanna be
Allowed to make my own mind up about what happens to me;
about what happens to me; about what happens to me…

And concluded with a revelation about the church:

But it's right before your eyes; don't need no angel in the skies;
It may come as a surprise – there's no need to criticise.
It's not a pack of ancient lies;
They may be foolish, maybe wise, but they're Jesus in disguise!
(both songs ©1981 Campus Crusade for Christ)

Many years later, I returned to the studio and arranged for the technicians to take the reel-to-reel master tape and digitise it onto a CD. A few years after that, I've now learned how to record the CD onto a hard drive, upload it to i-tunes and save it in The Cloud.

Anyway, the tape-slide show *Breakdown* was seen and heard by many young people. The message of salvation in Christ was preached through loud music, large visuals, powerful lyrics and contemporary artistic merit.

Just after my time with *Agapé*, I became a member of a large charismatic fellowship in Brighton, known at the time as *Clarendon Church*. Since then it's been *Church of Christ the King* (CCK) and is now called *Emmanuel*. I soon joined the team working with young teens, given the name *Dunamis*, a Greek word denoting strength and power, especially the power to preserve; from the word we get others such as *dynamic* and *dynamite*, etc. We began to develop programmes and teaching courses to enhance the wonderful pastoral/evangelistic ministries of the pioneering leaders, Chris and Debbie Jarvis.

The youth group was a vibrant, exciting Saturday evening event, where (at its peak) more than one hundred youngsters would gather to hang out and for sport, cookery or even craft workshops, plus a worship time and a talk, followed by *Mellow Moments* for those in years 10 & 11, when we addressed issues relevant to increasing maturity.

In addition, we often maximised the opportunities of school holidays for special events in our church premises: *24-hour Dunamis, 4444-minute Dunamis* and *99-hour Dunamis,* which were straightforward sleepover parties of increasing length.

Summers featured important trips to Bible Weeks, where I was invited to be a part of the youth work leadership team, developing the teaching programme, activities and direction for the worship band and leaders. Many of my best memories of these meetings involve seeing dozens of young people streaming forward to express their desire to give their lives to Jesus, or to recommit themselves. How wonderful!

Equally exciting were the queues that rapidly formed when we invited those to whom God had been speaking during the worship to share words and pictures. Many of these provided challenge or encouragement, but since young people were involved, we could be sure there would also be a few weird contributions of the 'penguins on a tightrope' sort. We worked hard to exclude these, since they were usually spurious, gave focus to attention-seekers or distracted from the genuine ones.

'What do you think God is trying to say?' was a good way to invite the young person to stop and consider, almost always met with 'I don't know.' I was tempted to reply 'Neither do I' but usually resisted and then reflected on my question. Was it the case that Almighty God was having trouble in his attempt to be clear, or was it we were not great at hearing him or interpreting our impressions, pictures, words, etc?

So, we followed up by 'I think perhaps you should go back to your seat, pray some more and ask God to help you work it out.' Often this was a helpful way of acknowledging that they were probably doing their best to participate, without exposing them to any discouraging laughter from the crowd.

On more than one occasion, however, a person I'd sent back to their seat returned a little later with a thoroughly Biblical explanation of what was represented by the picture he or she was hoping to share and, in one very special case, who it was for.

My bad? Perhaps, but everyone involved was learning and was eventually encouraged by the experience.

However, some of the 'tightrope-penguin' people would return with additional giant red hippos or a message that 'we shouldn't make friends with Muslims' and such desperadoes had to be told 'well, we've probably had enough of those sort of pictures and words for one meeting by now, I'm afraid; come back next time if you feel God has reminded you of the picture, or gives you something else – especially if he gives you an interpretation and even more if it's from the Bible.' I took the task seriously, realising it was a significant privilege to filter these and try to administer the order in which they were shared, weeding out the obvious heresies and deciding when to leave gaps for reflection. In this we were trying to obey the instruction of Paul:

Two or three prophets should speak, and the others should weigh carefully what is said… For God is not a God of disorder but of peace – as in all the congregations of the Lord's people. 1 Corinthians 14:29,33

Mind you, this wasn't in a church meeting, but a youth event at a Bible Week, so after discussion among the team, we agreed it was okay to interpret these instructions fairly loosely by pausing between batches of three and then hearing some more.

Many lives were changed by the inspiring worship, by means of the faithful preaching of the Word and through the demonstration of spiritual gifts in these meetings.

For me, Bible Weeks spanned a fifteen-year period and featured many memorable moments (including the orange squash/mixing desk disaster), some of which were beyond the meetings themselves.

One afternoon I was prevented by a group of security officials from removing my car from the car park, because they considered I was driving it erratically – apparently, they had concluded that they were witnessing a theft. I managed to talk my way out of that by producing evidence from the glove box and my backpack on the rear seat, showing my name and address. I didn't have the car's log book, or the receipt from the garage where I had bought it, but challenged them to check my car's number plate with the address registered for it with the DVLC. Reluctantly, they let me go with a stern warning to drive more smoothly. For goodness' sake.

Another year, I succeeded in keeping my vehicle on the showground (against the rules) for the whole week, parking it in different places each day, collecting several brightly-coloured PLEASE MOVE THIS CAR TO THE CAR PARK stickers (including one which said PLEASE MOVE THIS CAR TO THE CAR PARK, ANDY BACK which was when I knew for sure that they were on to me).

It was a slightly disconcerting experience on the last night of one Bible Week when I was accidentally locked into the on-site shop. It was after many of my friends had already gone home. Since it was before the era of the mobile phone, I had no way of contacting the site office or the shop managers. I sat down to read one of the many Christian books that were on sale and worked out how to persuade the coffee machine to provide something warm and wet. After a couple of hours (or so it seemed), I rifled through the bin to see what sandwiches had been thrown away, still sealed in their triangular plastic sleeves. I was bored and peckish, despite having previously decided that this food was nasty leftovers and had been out of the fridge for slightly too long.

Eventually, I was rescued by a night security volunteer who had spotted movement inside the shop and assumed I was some sort of miscreant up to no good. I was consuming a thrown-away egg and cress sandwich and reading a borrowed copy of *Future Grace* by John Piper, which should have planted a doubt in his suspicious mind. Instead of reconsidering, however, he used his radio to recruit a small hit squad and planned to burst in mob-handed to wrestle me to the ground or beat me into submission with his oversized torch. Fortunately, I caught a glimpse of the assembled high-vis jackets and willingly surrendered, whereupon I was recognised to be a non-thieving, non-vandalising non-ruffian. However, I was strongly chastised for wasting the security team's time and for distracting them from more important tasks. Such as preventing innocent campers from driving their own cars, I suppose. No apology was offered on either side.

And now, at last, for a change, a story with no alleged law-breaking. Being a senior member of the team providing teaching and leadership to 1400 young teens, I was invited to preach at least once each week. However, in the summer of 1993, I was in great agony of soul due to the nasty circumstances I mentioned in chapter seven (p46) and nearly backed out of my appointment. I'm glad I was able to set my personal feelings aside for the evening and call upon God for his grace and mercy to intervene. The Lord was kind to me and I fulfilled my responsibility. I can't remember anything I said, but I do recall what was prayed over me by our team leader, just before the meeting began. He prayed that God would enable this mature soldier of Christ to impart wise advice to these new recruits and trainees. I was both honoured and envisioned by that description. I hope I went some way toward living up to it.

There were many other special times in the gatherings of young people; some where the activity of God in young lives was powerfully evident, with large numbers of them enjoying his manifest presence and life-changing power. These included healing from various illnesses or injuries, deliverance from spiritual forces of oppression (or worse); and supernaturally-revealed issues brought to the surface for confession, prayer, counsel and so forth. In every case, it was essential for us to have a gifted and self-sacrificing team (counsellors, people willing to pray and support workers to manage the queues) labouring alongside those of us with a more visible role.

This is probably not the place to itemise the many God-inspired prophetic insights shared in these youth settings. However, I can clearly point to lives utterly devoted to the Lord, the establishment of specific churches and the destruction of the Berlin Wall. Each of these were mentioned specifically.

God has worked amazing spiritual advances in young hearts through Bible Weeks and of course through the faithful, consistent input provided by faithful youth workers during the rest of the year, living out the Christian life, providing a good example of devoted discipleship, service, humility, quality leadership and lots of fun.

It is my firm belief that encounters with God in these settings have changed the face of Christianity in this country. Wild claim, you may say (and I thought that even while I typed it), but then there is evidence. It is a simple matter of listing the young people into whose lives God spoke in those exciting days.

The game-changers among them are now leading churches, serving as an elder or his wife, developing their worship ministry, running home groups, preaching and prophesying. Many of the rest are caring, serving, faithfully praying, working, supporting and ministering… This is best illustrated not by naming names (my list would be lengthy yet would sadly fail to be comprehensive) but by considering a brief but heartfelt conversation I had with the Lord.

I was at Newday, the national youth teaching and worship event, serving my local church youth group, a couple of years after the Stoneleigh Bible Week had closed. On the first evening I was feeling rather sorry for myself, because (it seemed to me) all those years of experience being a key part of the team providing preaching, leadership, encouragement and service from the front had been passed over. I was now, it seemed, surplus to requirements, because younger fellows were being chosen.

I felt 'put out to grass' and discouraged, so I began to talk to God about this disappointment. 'It's like they don't need me,' I moaned. Then the

Lord, using his kindest and yet most firm voice gently suggested I look carefully in the brochure and check the names of those invited to speak.

'That's not going to help much; it'll just rub it in…' I thought. But I saw names I knew. 'Oh, he's done well to get invited,' I thought. 'And him – oh and him, as well. And she's leading worship!' Suddenly the truth dawned on my self-centred, cement-filled mind. The young man providing overall leadership was a character originally from *Dunamis* (you know, the youth group I helped to run in Brighton). And so were two others, both now church elders, on the preaching team. Another was on the counselling team and a fifth ex-Dunamite was taking a leading role in worship.

'They don't need you,' the Lord said with firmness, but oh! with such warmth, 'because you've done your job and done it well.' I had played my part in developing these mighty warriors! My thoughts turned immediately to the prayer I had prayed when starting out in youth work, all those years before, referencing the Biblical themes of athletics and my interpretation of being in a relay team. Those formerly-young people named in the brochure had taken my meagre baton and were already running faster and achieving far more than I could.

I began to weep as I confessed my self-centredness. Tears flowed abundantly in response to God's reassurance of his continuing love. He had answered my prayer with such kindness, providing a new generation, bringing more significant spiritual impact that I ever imagined.

And the things you have heard me say in the presence of many witnesses, entrust to reliable people who will also be qualified to teach others. 2 Timothy 2:2

Yes, there are verses about honouring fathers and respecting those who are senior and these cheeky boys were momentarily forgetting them; but then there are also verses about God doing a new thing, about fresh wine, how the latter trumps the former, and about change. I had been ignoring the verses about the benefits and glories of youth.*

I felt a sense of fulfilment washing over me. I sat, my face wet, on that deck chair, surrounded by tents and the evening calm, as God provoked me to adopt this new aspect to my serving. Perhaps my days of being on the platform were over, but there was still plenty to do to help those

* Proverbs 16:31, Titus 2:2, Isaiah 43:19, Matthew 9:16-17; 1 Samuel 10:6,7, 1 Timothy 4:12, Psalm 144:12

ministering publicly. I was glad to take a role behind the scenes but directly in front, twice a day, of several blocks of portable toilets and showers needing a cleaning crew.

And in latter years, I have ended up working with the night security team myself. It's been a privilege to work alongside some excellent colleagues, help protect the campers, answer the emergency telephone line and perform many other duties. I have worked to avoid some of the errors of over-enthusiasm and of omission I have already described. I have happily permitted drivers to drive their own vehicles and ensured premises were vacated before locking them up for the night.

However, heavy veils are being drawn, even now, as I fashion these sentences, over some extreme naughtiness I discovered one night.

Say no more, but cans and bottles were confiscated.

On two occasions I had excellent reasons to call out the on-duty-but-fast-asleep fire officer. I was commended for my alertness to potential danger, but got the distinct feeling that their words were code for *next time, wait until there are actual flames engulfing at least half the site before you dare to disturb me, alright pal?* Or perhaps I misunderstood.

A few years ago, when I moved to Birmingham, I shared my vision for youth with the church leader. At the time, we both knew that there were no young teens among the offspring of the members, but that the oldest of the children were fast approaching the stage when they'd be qualifying. So, I recruited a few willing colleagues to serve with me on what became known as the *emerge* team and we prayed for wisdom, love, courage and unity. When we opened our doors for the first time, there were eight adults and four young people. We agreed it was best to avoid overwhelming the youngsters, establishing a small core team and invited the other volunteers to visit regularly on a rota basis. Four young people became five and then four and for a short spell, three, until sufficient time had passed so that we were able to invite the next year group, who were by now old enough to attend.

Several years on, I am thrilled that from shaky beginnings, *emerge* has grown to a group of twenty-five or more young people gathering on a Friday evening. I thank the Lord for the enthusiastic team serving the youth each week. I continue to support them in prayer, even though my time in active service has come to a close.

Nevertheless, I can still be found in my season-ticketed seat in the grandstand, cheering on those who carry the baton to God-appointed places of which I could only dream.

For further thought

1 Try not to slaughter your guests (p9)

Elijah 1 Kings 18:20-40

- Consider the guests at this event. In what ways did Lynette failed to be an excellent hostess? Was Ben's contribution positive or not? Which errors might you point out to them? Would they take notice?
- Do you consider the 'lessons learned' to be the right lessons? Is anything missing? Make a list. How might Steve react if he reads this? Would he be justified?
- What is the attraction of green-eyed blondes (eg Charlize Theron, Scarlett Johansson, Amanda Seyfied, Rachel McAdams, Elizabeth Lail) that so appeals to virile young men?
- What was wrong with being a Baal-worshipper, anyway? How would you have approached the demonstration of God's might on Mount Carmel? How do you differ from Elijah? Are you similar? Are you as confrontational?

2 Ice, noise, grace, chips & spears (p18) *David & Jonathan*

1 Samuel 20:1-42

- In what ways do friends enliven or enrich your life? Consider the friends you love the most: are they perfect people without any annoying habits, weaknesses or inadequacies? How can negatives be overcome? Be specific about why you're friends.
- In how many ways are you a good friend? Perhaps you could discuss this with a friend; you may be surprised how encouraging their answers are!
- List times when you were less than top quality. Don't discuss these but consider expressing thanks to friends who have stood by you.
- What do you make of Kate & Sean and their taste in food, company, music? In which ways has Olly missed the mark in the area of hospitality?
- Explore the questions in the final paragraph and the claim Jesus (Christ, of Nazareth, son of God, not the blind cat) makes about sacrifice.

3 The Waiting Game (p25)

Abraham receives his promise

Genesis 12:1-4; 21:2-5

- Is your experience of the doctor's clinic as bad as described? Or worse? How many life-threatening diseases have you caught from other patients? Does time really bend or is this apparent phenomenon simply a psychological reaction to the severe strain of clinic attendance while feeling under the weather? Give thanks for treatments and medical practitioners whose work has benefited you and your health.
- Score one point for each error you can spot and correct on the various incompetent notices. Answers: p272.
- Do you have patience? Does it make a difference when you're waiting for a promise to be kept? How can we encourage each other to exhibit more patience?

4 **Wither Leviathans?** (p33)

Bible reading

- Have you started, developed, improved, forgotten, abandoned, or started again the hard-work habit of Bible reading?
- Have you fathomed 'wineskins in the smoke'? Commentators suggest that the maturing process for wine included hanging it high above the fire for a while so that the skins absorb the heat and aroma from the smoke. However, good timing is vital; dried-out skins split and spill their contents.
- Why do we all struggle with this important spiritual discipline, when we know it can bring such joy and revelation? Which of the bible study methods and aids suggested have you used — daily notes, studying a single verse, meditation, reading a whole chapter or book at a time? Have you ever attempted memorisation? Which translation(s) do you find the most helpful? Why?
- What errors have snake-handlers made in their interpretation? How can we avoid similar errors?

5 **Yuletide for Raluces** (p39)

Christmas; worldly vs spiritual

- How can we resist the dangers of secular Xmas, while still enjoying spiritual Christmas? Define these oft-mentioned terms: consumerism, gluttony, gift, celebration, tradition, festival.
- What's your opinion of using credit cards? Do you have any experience of getting deeper into debt than you intended? How can we stay 'in the black'?
- Knowing God, whose incarnation we celebrate, makes a difference. Discuss.

6 **Naan can compare** (p42)

currying favour

- In what ways does a couple's life change when a baby comes along?
- Why are lasagne, quiche, stew, casserole and apple crumble so often among the uninspiring meals provided for the new family? Do these choices reflect generosity, keen awareness of the couple's preferences, ease of transport/delivery or something else?
- Why do most of us love a curry? Discuss the rich variety of Indian cuisine.
- Why do most of us find it hard to receive generous gifts? Why are singles so often left off the *make a meal for the new parents* rotas?

7 **Time for a conversation** (p46)

talking and listening to God

- Consider what depths of intimacy can be shown by someone who: knows your present feelings are temporary; is committed; remains fully concerned; is sympathetic and empathetic; is wise and runs deep; is non-judgemental; allows you to exhibit some self-indulgence; loves perfectly?
- Which form of language is most appropriate when talking to God? What impresses him most? What convinces him most? What distracts him most?
- What is your opinion of these anecdotes of mild misbehaviour during prayer meetings? Should we

be serious and formal? Why or why not?

- 'I pray, leaving the results to God.' What's your view of this? How can we measure results? Should this have any impact on how we pray?

8 **The wrong guy?** (p56)

CV: Moses Exodus 2:11–4:17

- Make a list of Moses' character traits & decisions. Do you think your church would appoint him to be a leader? Would your church invite him to preach next Sunday? Or welcome him into the congregation?
- Make similar lists for Gideon & Saul of Tarsus.
- Notice how many times 'What God saw' occurs in the text. What does God see when he looks beyond your weaknesses, poor life-decisions, failings, sins and inadequacies? NB ask these questions of others, to seek their views on your character; you may be surprised or encouraged by their answers!
- Do you dare to pray that you will, by God's grace and mighty power, rise above weaknesses and circumstances and obey him, fulfilling his plan? The implications of getting an answer could be enormous!

9 **Riding the epact cycle** (p60)

Easter

- Consider the various symbols that are used at Easter: chocolate in all its forms, but especially egg-shaped; rabbits; bonnet parades; chicks; hot cross buns; Friday football matches; egg hunting; and some supermarkets and DIY stores closing on Sunday afternoon. Which of these accurately point to any aspect of Easter?
- What do you think to the idea that peanuts could be a worthwhile symbol of new birth and therefore become a suitable Easter gift? Can you suggest anything better?
- In what ways does your family celebrate Easter or even mark the occasion?

10 *a.k.a.* **Entitlement** (p66)

Christian Unity?

- Why do Christians seem to choose 'distinctiveness' over unity? Do you think our denominational differences are important? What if we laid aside our differences? Is this a good idea or first steps on the road to heretical oblivion?
- Work through the list of denominations and try to express what is unique about each one. What separates us — beliefs or practice? Or both? Is that welcome? What does Jesus say in John 17:22-23? Isn't he being a bit idealistic? Isn't he entitled to be idealistic?
- Did the disciples sing from a hymn-book or did they have the words projected on a screen? Is either method right or wrong? Does sitting in a pew make me more Biblical than sitting on a plastic chair or a bean bag? Unplanned, spontaneous (and thus likely to be of variable quality) worship contributions or a well-written Prayer Book? Which do you prefer? And, excuse me, but since when exactly were your preferences the plumbline for how God desires to be worshipped?

11 **Escort to Wales** (p69)

Jonah

• Critically discuss the relative merits of Kate's unexpected, delicious, alfresco sea-side pasta carbonara (chapter 2) and the threat of Nancy's ill-defined casserole, with perhaps a watery gravy, or (worse) lentils, swede and turnips reduced to mush. Factor in any effects of the breakfast. Consider also Lynette's steak (eaten by Ben) and an annoyingly snaffled lamb chop.

• How do the distractions of the journey — detours, delays, frustrations, hold-ups, accidents, weather conditions, 'what-might-have-beens', the need for wisdom, having to live with decisions — illustrate life in all its richness? Where do determination, faith, hope and keeping your eyes fixed on the goal come in?

12 **What, no wwwebsite?** (p74)

mission, identity, legacy of Christ

• Identify and discuss the famous people listed at the start of the article, as some may have set good examples.

• Who are your heroes? This time it's a genuine question. Alive or dead, real or fictional, spiritual or otherwise, male or female — it's your opinion, which is valued. Give reasons for your answers.

• The new version of the article, like the original, is tending to focus on what Jesus didn't do, compared to biographies of celebrities or famous historical figures in politics, the military, the arts, sport, etc. Does this put Jesus in a new light? What positive actions, achievements, honours, victories are missed out? Does the new version (or the original) properly revere Jesus and his ministry?

• Consider this quote 'Christ's life has impact due to his mission, his identity and his legacy — not so much his actions or his (very unsophisticated and frankly quite inadequate) marketing strategy. This exposes the *One Solitary Life* article to be dramatically missing the point.' Do you agree? Discuss.

13 **Words of power** (p77)

from the cross

• Consider what Jesus says about others — his mother, those who are executing him, the repentant thief and a disciple. When every breath comes at such great cost, why expend agony like this? What qualities does he display?

• Some Christians dislike the suggestion that when God the Son was on the cross, God the Father poured out his wrath against sin. How else can we interpret Jesus' agonised cry 'why have you forsaken me?' See Mark 15:34, Luke 23:46, John 19:28-30; and Psalm 22:1, which Jesus is quoting.

• The final three statements provide a helpful summary of Christ's death — he suffered physically, his work is complete and he gave up his spirit. NB these happened 'while we were still sinners' (Romans 5:8). Allow a few minutes' meditation on these truths to lead into a time of worship.

14 Sunny climbs (p83)

God who preserves

- Consider any errors you may have made with language, maps and signs. What caused these complications? How were they resolved? How does this relate to interpreting Bible verses or prophetic pictures?
- Reflect on occasions when God held you safe when you were in danger. Include incidents of spiritual jeopardy and also physical ones. Perhaps, for example, you tend to worry, but God reassured you; or you were being tempted, when a way of escape became clear.
- Take the opportunity to thank God for his amazing faithfulness. See Hebrews 13:5, Matthew 28:18-20 and 2 Peter 3:9.

15 Privet lives (p94)

lost by chance, nature, accident

Luke 15:4-32

- Have you ever been in a similar privet maze or a metaphorical one? How did your experience match mine? Have you ever been lost or start to fear when the solution to a problem eludes you? How can this feeling be overcome?
- How did our hero attempt to dismiss panic?
- What does the wealthy little boy represent?
- In Luke 15, consider the different ways each lost one was returned from a state of lostness. Who or what seeks, discovers and returns that which was lost? Consider character traits of each individual in these parables.

16 Oh yeah? (p101)

miracles

- How can we walk the fine line between believing in amazing miracles and being credulous fools with no appreciation of science? Does God expect us to leave our intellect at the door when we enter church? How can we live with the tension? How can we balance faith and logic?
- What miracles have you witnessed? Should such events surprise us? Look at 1 John 5:14,15.
- Check out Hebrews 12:2. How can we do this and discover fresh truth?

17 Losing the syrup (p104)

the ten commandments

Exodus 20:1-17 Galatians 3:24,25

- What's your view of the Day of Rest laws listed here? Which will bear spiritual fruit? What makes you think that? Which, do you think, matter to God?
- Does your church permit or even encourage conversation before the meeting begins?
- What's your opinion of the short-lived brunch idea, with bacon, sausages, bread, cakes and filter coffee? How might your church attempt this? Or is it so deeply flawed an idea that it should be avoided?
- Do you have an opinion on Sunday bike-riding for boys?
- Is your choice of clothes different on a Sunday? Why or why not? Do you think God cares all that much about how we are dressed? And what about providing hospitality to students? Is this righteousness in action? Or merely providing an

opportunity for them to be gluttonous? And should hospitality ever be gender-specific?

- What's your Sunday routine? In what ways do you rest? Or do you work hard at serving the Lord? How can we find a balance? Or have I missed the point again? And if 'rest' doesn't mean chillaxing, then how can we maximise what God intended?

18 **These three remain** (p111) *lesson learned in lockdown*

- What are important lessons you learned from the season of lockdown?
- Have you had flatmates with ambitious redecorating ideas? Were their attempts successful? Or costly?
- What is your approach to sharing accommodation with people who support teams of which you don't approve, or love styles of music you don't like, or follow a political ethos different to yours? How can we be 'unequally yoked' with Leeds United supporters, for example?
- Share any testimonies of effective bubbles. Describe the adjustments required and the benefits gained. How can the delights of bubbling affect the rest of the week?
- Have you ever 'vagued out' of a sermon to give attention to a passing comment, or to a part of the verse not being focussed upon? What do you suppose preachers think of this practice?

19 **Lost again** (p123) *woolly walkabout* Luke 15: 3-7

- Why is the shepherd in the parable so bothered about his lost one? Isn't his prime responsibility for the ninety-nine?
- In what ways does Jesus give his attention to the lost while ignoring the saved? Is this the message of the story? If not, what is?
- Do you know of any 'righteous people who do not need to repent'? What might this expression mean?
- Consider the kinds of party celebrated in heaven. Is alcohol served? Chocolate cake, peanuts, sausage rolls, caviar on blinis, oysters, fatted calf, pitta bread? What style of music is played? Will there be a smoke machine, DJ, a 'caller' for the cèilidh, postman's knock, smooching?
- Look at the 'what if' questions and conclude which scenarios have spiritual lessons (probably not all).
- Correctly completing the wordsearch reveals the phrase 'great rejoicing', as you might have guessed.

20 **Two ways to make custard** (p134) *25th December*

- What are the Christmas traditions in your house? Are they new and fresh, or old and established? Do any of them help you celebrate the nativity story more effectively? Are some distractions?
- What's your opinion of the idea of helping those less fortunate than yourself on Christmas Day? Or is the family holiday most strongly protected?
- Which elements would you include in the church meeting if you were given the chance to lead on Christmas morning? Select suitable well-known songs (and perhaps a

solo), plan readings (and readers), think about testimonies (name names) or 'vox pop' spontaneity; include perhaps a helpful visual aid or dramatic element, choose a preacher (or prepare a talk yourself – at least find a text). Not so easy, is it?

- Summarise my *but now* sermon from Romans 3:20-24.
- Why did the church leader smile throughout, do you suppose? Was he willing me to succeed, or amused at the thought of my inevitable failure (or keeping score of errors)? Why, oh why, are his talks still so lengthy?

21 **Embrace the love** (p140)

responding to God's warmth

- What's your favourite Christian song (you may have more than one)? Can you identify why – tune, style, quality of lyric, 'worshipful-ness factor', Bible content, capturing an emotion, poetry, a happy memory?
- Examine the carol *Away in a manger*. Which Bible verses are referred to? Note lines which may detract from or add to the account. Draw conclusions.
- Does the 'progression through a worship time' seem familiar? In what ways does the worship band in your church require training? How might that happen?
- Have you ever tried 'treasure hunting'? Why or why not? Do you suppose it is such a success every time? In what ways might using your imagination be risky? Does God ever fill your mind with images or words which might be prophetic? How could these be expressed or shared? What would you say to Julia if she asked you for an explanation?

22 **Fleece of cake** (p148)

guidance

- Do you agree that Gideon's woolly-fleece-tests reflect a concerning lack of faith? Consider why God played along, even though this may not have been the ideal behaviour of someone God calls a 'mighty warrior'.
- In your view, did I show a lack of gratitude when offered a permanent job? Many people move to further their career – do you think this is in some way God's guidance or is it disloyalty to church life? How can we be sure?
- Reflect on the journey Sean took (see what I did there?) to become a split-diff and suspension expert, only to later quit that job to work for the church.
- Assess the pastoral counselling skills of the elder who simply asked me 'What do you want to do?' Is that sufficient? What other questions might you have asked, given the circumstances?
- State your opinion of the multiple bosses pushing me out of the door? Could their decisions be a part of God's guidance? What do you think of the way the CEO treated me? Generous? Expedient? Paying me off?
- List questions to ask when weighing up options for a big change or a move or starting a relationship. Are they sufficient? Navel-gazing? Unanswerable? And how might you

describe the 'feeling of peace'? What characterizes this?

• Why do you think I was so slow to make my decision to move home? What was I waiting for? In what way should we give credibility to those silly co-incidences like the crossword clue? Why do you think that featured so strongly in the way I recognised the leading of God? Where do scriptures fit in? And advice? Or warnings?

• How can seeking guidance lead to appreciation of God's love and power? Note examples from your own life. Reflect on the benefits of humble obedience.

23 The names of the meals (p158)

communion

• Do you agree with the extensive analysis of meals times and names? Can you add any further clarity?

• Compare and contrast the original Passover (Exodus 12-14), the Passover-celebrating meal known as the Last Supper (Matthew 26:26-29) and Paul's instructions for communion. In what ways is the death of Christ reflected through the bread, the cup (and contents), the eating and the attitude? How can we remember Jesus when we share this meal?

• What are the important differences between the Passover meal and communion? Give attention to preparation and cooking of meat; doorposts; footwear; angelic threat; timing; geography; status of participants.

• What's your opinion about the red liquid question? Is there a right answer? Are there scriptures which might shed some light on this? Please let Brian know.

• Is alcohol present when your church celebrates communion? Why or why not? Do you think providing alternative red liquid for recovering alcoholics is a caring idea, or one which exposes or even emphasises their past weaknesses?

• Consider Biblical lists in which drunkenness is one of the prohibited activities. How many other sins (witchcraft, sexual immorality, carousing, idolatry etc) are subject to a 'not too much' rule? Why is consumption of alcohol different? Are we carelessly lacking integrity?

• How does Romans 14 apply when someone with an opinion that differs from yours needs to be considered? List issues for which there are a range of views. Examples: the narrative of Genesis 1-3, infant baptism, same-sex marriage…

• Consider symbols in modern life, like a wedding ring, a bus-pass, the pictogram that warns a garment is dry-clean only, or the gift of a red rose. Why is it essential to distinguish between deep meaning and the mere symbol of it?

• Take time to reflect on the life and ministry of Jesus; his attitude to children, women, the poor, religious leaders; those who opposed or mocked him.

• How could you make communion increasingly corporate or at least less isolating? How do you feel about the status of those who serve the bread and wine? Should this always be the work of 'professionals'?

• What is your opinion of the many non-standard ways to share communion? What about our experiments with symbolic elements? Why are some people so concerned with accurately reflecting New Testament practice (boldly assuming that what happened back then can be known or interpreted)?

24 **Let us ascend** (p170) *our place in Christ*

• Work slowly through each of the descriptions of our relationship with God. How do you benefit from qualifying for them?

• In what ways are we informed or comforted by the imagery of the potter's wheel? Seek out other scriptures referencing clay and hands at work, such as Ephesians 2:10; Job 10:9; Isaiah 45:18.

• Consider foot-washing – a picture of humility, cleanliness, sanctification, dignity, service…

• How do you speak to and treat your friends? Reflect on how this differs when interacting with relative strangers. What are the pleasures of friendship?

• Revel and rejoice in being intimately known and loved by God, using songs with truth and with expressions of love. If you can find songs with both, so much the better.

25 **I've got my eye on you** (p176) *God's watchfulness*

• What is your view of the practice of secretly filming workers to assess their efficiency, politeness and knowledge? Is it intrusive, or unfair, or subject to abuse? Would you be willing to work where the boss could remotely log in to the camera system without you realising it? Does that make him a snooper?

• In what ways would you adjust your behaviour, speed, concentration, photocopying, etc if you knew you might be being watched at any time?

• Check Psalm 119:168. Is the point that the Lord is hoping to catch you doing something right, or carefully ensuring your protection? How do you feel about God constantly observing you – safe and loved, or convicted and ready to repent? Either way, it's good news, right?

26 **The ministry of moist – or more?** (p184) *baptism*

• What is baptism to you? A social gathering to celebrate a new-born? A church-family welcome under the Abrahamic covenant? A fully-clothed and knife-free form of circumcision? A good excuse for the church to hire the swimming pool and have a gala? A witness before heaven and earth of spiritual life? Something more?

• Do you have an opinion of the woman who had three baptisms? Attention-seeker? Letter-of-the-law merchant? Hedging her bets?

• How could anyone be a more efficient godparent? What are the responsibilities and joys of this? Which scriptures describe the role?

• Are you in favour of baptismal candidates being given a chance to speak? Should this be limited to a pre-prepared, mentor-edited testimony? How many scriptures are optimum? In the water or in the pulpit? How could this go wrong?

- What do you think about processing sixteen people in the same meeting? Does this devalue each one's experience? Is it less meaningful? Is it a powerful demonstration to the unchurched guests?
- Which is your preferred method: aspersion (sprinkling), affusion (pouring), or full immersion? What about self-immersion? And what words need to be said? Are you favouring teaspoon, font, baptistry, pool, tank, skip, river or sea? Or doesn't it matter?
- What's your opinion of preachers wearing rubber galoshes/waders/dungarees? 'Squeak to one another with psalms, hymns and spiritual songs' Ephesians 5:19 (amended).

27 **Ways to bridge the gap** (p192) *friendship evangelism*

- What is your view of street-corner preaching? Are some styles better than others? What about Salvation Army bands? What about shouting scriptures about judgement? What about street-drama or illustrated lectures?
- Have you considered the *Four Spiritual Laws*? Is this unacceptably American in style? In what ways does the *Knowing God Personally* version express the truth in a more British way? Is active evangelism of this sort too confrontational? Is the 'wait until they ask' approach ever visible in the New Testament?
- What is your opinion of Graham, the man I met and led to Christ in his hall of residence? Was he 'ripe fruit' or did I manipulate his loneliness? Why was he sometimes willing to accompany me on my efforts to visit his colleagues and ask impertinent questions about their religious beliefs?
- Describe the distinction between para-church evangelistic agencies and church-based evangelists. Where does witnessing fit in?
- What do you make of people who work for Christian companies? Is this 'staying safe' or 'serving the body of Christ' or something else?
- Do you conclude that we intended to impress my righteous work-mates? Or was it a genuine accident, which we then turned to our advantage? Is the Stayman Convention a useful tool? Can you guess why our opponent Don felt pity for us?
- Why do some Christians disapprove of playing cards? Why is gambling considered wrong? Isn't there a dark side to most hobbies, games, sports and pastimes? Even so, how can we befriend those outside the church?

28 **Best man again and again** (p201) *silver medal place*

- Why were Tony's relatives willing to give 'brownie points' for childhood friendship? Do you imagine involvement with Hannah forged a connection?
- What can you read between the lines in the episode concerning Martin & Selina? Is there a hint of 'should he, shouldn't he' about this? Is it right for the Best Man and the Chief

Bridesmaid to interpret wedding-day etiquette as meaningful?

- What caused Isaac and Miriam's wedding day to overrun? Should cousins be permitted to perform? Who has the authority to edit Father of the Bride speeches? If you had been Maitre D', how would you have handled the drinks distribution débacle?
- Do you sympathise with Jeff and Nancy's eagerness to have an unpredictable nuptial feast, changing the order of activities? Can you see why this wasn't a great idea? Doesn't appointing two best men demonstrate a failure to make decisions?
- What's your view of the sixteen-page book of detailed instructions? Is this good planning, failure to trust or micro-management? Should the waiter whose ignorance caused pulledporkgate be given his cards? Why not?
- Why do marriages break down? Do we provide sufficient training/ encouragement?
- List the differences between weddings and the marriage feast of the lamb.

29 We need to talk about Jesus (p209) *keeping Christ central*

- Why have we elevated the importance of sharing opinion over the discipline of studying the scripture?
- What is the significance of the I AM name?
- In what ways does the temptation of Jesus differ from our daily temptations?
- What is the value of looking closely at Jesus' miracles, teaching and stories?
- Why do we consider the cross so central? In what ways does the resurrection demonstrate the identity of Christ?
- Why is our trinitarian belief important?
- When was the last time your church gave time to a session for teaching about baptism in the Holy Spirit? Is that satisfactory, in your view?

30 Assessing Aslan (p225) *Narnias Univers*

- Are the Biblical themes in the *Chronicles of Narnia* accidental?
- Is my analysis of *Animal Farm* sufficient? In what ways does an analogy differ from a parable?
- Do you think it's fair to judge Tolkien and Lewis by modern standards? Consider a similar treatment of *The Merchant of Venice*, *The Miller's Tale* or the *Song of Solomon*. What lessons can be drawn here?
- 'Jadis (the White Witch) is more like Satan than Aslan is like Jesus'. Discuss.
- Examine the distinctions between Aslan and Jesus and find verses to clarify or confirm your conclusions.
- What is Jesus without God? How can anyone mistake an under-authority, mortal creature for the sovereign, eternal creator?
- When does underplaying stories of Santa, the tooth fairy, Harry Potter become a denial of the joy of fantasy

in the hope of enhancing faith in the Ark, David and Goliath, feeding the 5000 and the resurrection of Christ?

31 **Stop 2 c what it's there 4** (p235)

glancing @ 2 Corinthians

- Which is the longest book you've read cover to cover?
- What's the difference between justification and sanctification? Which of them is a work of the Holy Spirit?
- Turn to the person on your left and mention something they've done (or refrained from) which qualifies them for a reward. Will it earn them salvation? Is it an evidence of their sanctification?
- Where is the line between 'in the world' purity and becoming a monk or a nun?

32 **Good Friday?** (p241)

vigil gathering

- Should a so-called 'happy-clappy' church have meeting like this, where both happiness and applause are discouraged? Do songwriters have a point if they complain that the final, resurrection-based verse of their song was omitted?
- Why might this kind of meeting have met with resistance? Identify what we did to avoid this. Try to understand reasons for opposition.
- What was Simon Peter's mistake?
- If you had been in the crowd at the trial of Jesus, do you think you could have stayed silent? What if you were Barabbas? Be realistic.
- Has God ever promised that our lives will be characterised by justice? Why do we feel this so keenly?
- Is guilt the best feeling to bring to communion? Why or why not? Consider insights in chapter 23.
- How did the centurion reach his conclusion? What convinced him?
- In what ways does the Eulogy deny the truth about Jesus? How did Jesus persuade the men on the road to Emmaus, if this is what they were thinking?

33 **Musical Youth** (p247)

serving biography

- List some of the benefits of playing music with others, trusting them to play at the height of their skill, working together to produce a rehearsed sound which cannot be achieved alone.
- Do you approve of enlisting help in an evangelistic project from unbelievers? What are the issues?
- What does the relay race 'baton' represent in the way it is described here? Consider alternative ways of expressing the process encompassed — discipleship, leadership, mentoring. Since pride is a sin, what are better ways to describe a positive, confident assurance of having met the prayerful goal?
- Serving is an act of generosity and unselfishness. Discuss the evident pleasure derived from obedience to the Lord expressed in this chapter. Does this undermine the moral or spiritual value of such delight? Shouldn't having to help others be a chore and a burden?
- Express your opinion of the screening process being used to ensure worthwhile meeting

contributions. List the merits or imperfections of this management style. Is it possible that the spiritual gift of administration is being employed here? Have you ever witnessed a penguin on a tightrope?

- How do you respond to these tales of God speaking or entering into conversation? Do you have any experience of this sort of divine dialogue (for yourself, or others)? What are the risks in being apparently casual about this?
- Have you ever had to suffer being falsely accused by a hi-vis clad security force of stealing your own vehicle or of breaking and entering a building (but it was open to the public when I entered, so actually, no *de facto* breaking, people) and then having the brass neck to consume an already thrown-away egg sandwich? Are either of these acts a crime? Or even a sin? Are the security men worse than that Pulledporkgate waiter? Or HD's attitude to 'signs in foreign'. Or the 'songs from the shows' cousin? Isn't it about time for me to let these things go, at last?

Corrections to surgery posters

EMERGECY APPOINTMENTS ALLECATED IN
STRICT ORDER OF IMPORTANCE, NOT NECCCESSARILY
ACCORDING BY ORDER OF REQUESTING
emergency • allocated • strict order *no need for caps*
necessarily • according by order of requesting *replace with*
order in which they are requested *or delete all after* importance

IF YOU HAVE TO CANCELL AN APOINTMENT,
ALLOW THREE DAYS NOTCE
cancel • appointment • three days' notice
• *rewrite preferred:* please let us know at least three days ahead
(where possible) if you no longer intend to keep an appointment,
so it can be offered to someone else

WAITING TIME'S MAYBE LONGER THAN EXPECTED,
THIS IS'NT RECEPTIONISTS FAULT
waiting times • may be • expected. This isn't • receptionists'
rewrite preferred: your patience is appreciated

REPEAT PRECRIPTIONS CAN BE COLLECTED
ON THE 2ND DAY IF POSTED BEFORE 10.00 A.M.
prescriptions • *rewrite preferred:* please submit requests
for repeat prescriptions by 10am; allow two working days
before attempting to collect them

TURN YOU MOBILEPHONE OF
your • mobile phone • off

AUTOMATIC DOOR — TO OPEN, GRASP
HANDEL, TWIST ANTE-CLOCKWISE & PULL (CAN BE STIFF
DO NOT USE IN EMEGRENCYS
DO NOT WEDGE OPEN FIRE EXIT IF OTHER DOOR LOCKED
turn handle anti-clockwise • & pull door firmly *fix the door,*
don't post notices on how to live with the problem • emergencies
DO NOT WEDGE OPEN FIRE EXIT IF OTHER DOOR LOCKED *I don't know*
what this means; it might be 'do not wedge open — this should be
considered to be the fire exit if the other door is locked' *or perhaps* 'do
not wedge open the fire exit if this door is locked' *under what*
circumstances would that ever be the correct procedure?
But in what way, precisely, can a door you operate by 'turning the handle
and pulling' be correctly described with the term 'automatic'?

Contents in Bible order

Page numbers indicate start of relevant chapter

Lifeline

Key: **T** Town **C** Church **E** Education **S** Spiritual
P Personal **W** Work **s/e** self-employed (*client)
numbers indicate chapters referencing relevant facts
# indicates band name

date
1958 **T** Brighton **P** birth
1959
1960
1961 **S** Sunday School **C** Park Hill FIEC (to 69)
1962 **E** 28 Patcham Infants School (to 65)
1963
1964
1965 **E** Patcham Junior School (to 69)
1966 **S** Intro *Crusaders* Bible Class (to 76) **P** 17 student Sunday teas
1966 **P** 17 noticing the syrup
1967 **S** 17 no Sabbath cycling
1968
1969 **E** Varndean Grammar School for Boys
1970
1971 **S** saved
1972 **C** Brighton; All Saints, Patcham CofE **S** 26 baptised **P** 33 #*Tradd*
1973 **S** 9 Easter peanuts **P** 33 #*Spinaker*
1974 **S** 27 President of CU (to 76) **E** O levels
1975 **E** Varndean Sixth Form College
1976 **E** A levels **W** Clerk, Alliance Building Society
1977 **T** London **C** Kentish Town FIEC **W** 18,22 Agapé (to 84)
1978 **T** Cardiff **C** Albany Rd Bapt **S** 1st preach **W** schools worker
1979 **P** 28 BM Tony&Valerie
1980 **T** Brighton **C** Park Hill
1981 **P** 2 meet HD, Lambrayne **S** 33 #*Matt Black & the Emulsions*
1982 **P** 7 Portuguese prayer **P** 28 BM Martin&Selina
1983
1984 **C** Clarendon Church **W** Research Asst, Marc Europe
1985 **W** 21 Writer, Willard Thompson **P** 33 #*In Transit*
1986 **W** Writer, New Frontiers **S** 33 Dunamis youth group (to 04)
1987 **s/e** *advertising for various churches
1988 **P** 33 #*Frosty & the Snowmen*

1989
1990 **W** Writer, s/e **S** 33 SBW (to 2001) **S** 20 *But Now* preach
1991 **P** 1 Ben & Lynette Bar-B-Q incident
1992 **s/e** *Annual UK Teddy Bear Guide
1993 **P** 28 BM Isaac&Miriam **P** 7,28 engage/break-up **S** 33 1300@SBW
1994 **P** Tenerife holiday
1995 **P** Director, *Second Impression Theatre Company*
1996
1997 **P** 2 met Sean & Kate **P** Spain holiday
1998 **W** Project Manager Jubilee Publishing
1999 **W** Editorial Team, Kingsway (to 05) **P** 28 BM Jeff&Nancy
2000
2001 **P** 2 Slimboy Phat incident; met Olly
2002 **S** 33 Newday *baton* **P** 21 Sean & Kate go to Birmingham
2003 **P** 14 Portugal trip *Coach C* **P** 11 Welsh water
2004
2005 **s/e** writer **S** multiple training seminars (to 08)
2006 **s/e** 25 *mystery shopping **W** *CCK website development
2007
2008 **S** 22 vision trip **P** 22 buy house **T** Birmingham **C** Churchcentral
2009
2010 **s/e** *Activities Co-ordinator, Oakview Care Home
2011 **S** 33 *emerge youth group* (to 20)
2012 **S** 2 Discipleship group
2013 **s/e** scriptwriting for tv **s/e** 25 *HRU admin
2014 **s/e** Fundraising, *Karis Neighbour Scheme*
2015 **P** 28 trip to Dubai **P** stroke, requiring lengthy recovery (to 17)
2016 **P** 28 BM Jacob&Gabrielle
2017 **P** 17 Churchcentral Sunday brunch begin, ends
2018 **P** 32 published *substitute*
2019 **S** 23 communion experiments **P** 19 published *The Lost Son*
2020 **P** published *They Didn't Meet Jesus* **P** 18 national lockdown
2021 **P** 18 bubble
2022 **P** established andybackauthor.co.uk **P** published *BackChat*
…to be continued…

Index

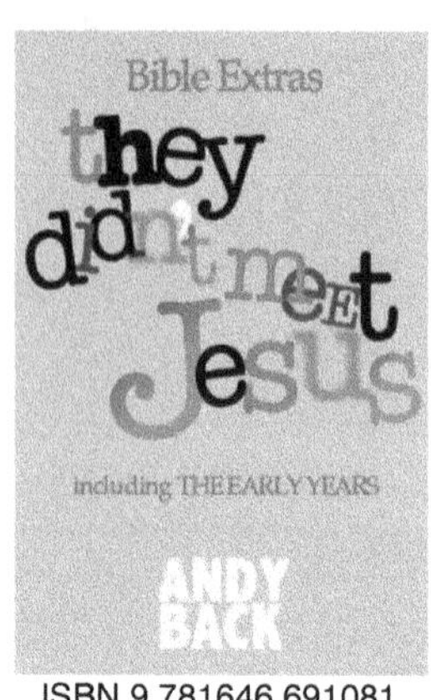

ISBN 9 781646 691081

Lightning Source UK Ltd.
Milton Keynes UK
UKHW012354250522
403550UK00002B/51